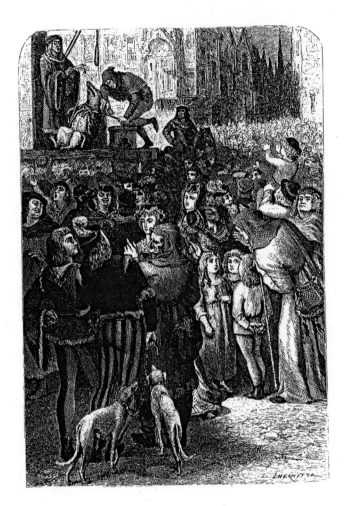

Execution of a Sow.

THE CRIMINAL PROSECUTION AND CAPITAL PUNISHMENT OF ANIMALS

By E. P. EVANS

AUTHOR OF

" ANIMAL SYMBOLISM IN ECCLESIASTICAL ARCHITECTURE,"
" EVOLUTIONAL ETHICS AND ANIMAL PSYCHOLOGY," ETC., ETC.

THE LAWBOOK EXCHANGE, LTD.
Clark, New Jersey

ISBN-13: 978-1-886363-52-6 (cloth)
ISBN-10: 1-886363-52-8 (cloth)
ISBN-13: 978-1-61619-030-9 (paperback)
ISBN-10: 1-61619-030-2 (paperback)

Lawbook Exchange edition 1998, 2009

Printed in the United States of America on acid-free paper

THE LAWBOOK EXCHANGE, LTD.
33 Terminal Avenue
Clark, New Jersey 07066-1321

*Please see our website for a selection of our other publications
and fine facsimile reprints of classic works of legal history:*
www.lawbookexchange.com

Library of Congress Cataloging-in-Publication Data

Evans, E. P. (Edward Payson), 1831-1917.
    The criminal prosecution and capital punishment of animals / by
        E.P. Evans.
            p.   cm.
    Originally published: New York : E.P. Dutton, 1906.
    Includes bibliographical references and index.
    ISBN 1-886363-52-8 (cloth : alk. paper)
    1. Trials—Europe.   2. Animals, Prosecution and punishment of-
    -History.   3. Animals—Law and legislation—Europe—History.
    I. Title.
    KJC65.E94   1998
    344'049—dc21   98-12801
                                                        CIP

THE CRIMINAL PROSECUTION
AND CAPITAL PUNISHMENT
OF ANIMALS

By E. P. EVANS

AUTHOR OF

" ANIMAL SYMBOLISM IN ECCLESIASTICAL ARCHITECTURE,"
" EVOLUTIONAL ETHICS AND ANIMAL PSYCHOLOGY," ETC., ETC.

NEW YORK
E. P. DUTTON AND COMPANY
MCMVI

Printed in England

CONTENTS

INTRODUCTION

Sources—Amira's distinction between retributive and preventive processes—Addosio's incorrect designation of the latter as civil suits—Inconsistent attitude of the Church in excommunicating animals—Causal relation of crime to demoniacal possession—Squatter sovereignty of devils —*Aura corrumpens*—Diabolical infestation and lack of ventilation—" Bewitched kine "—Greek furies and Christian demons—Homicidal bees, laying cocks and crowing hens—Theory of the personification of animals —Beasts in Frankish, Welsh, and old German laws—Animal prosecutions and witchcraft—The Mosaic code in Christian courts—Pagan deities as demons—Born malefactors among beasts—The theory of punishment in modern criminology   ...   . *p.* I

CHAPTER I

BUGS AND BEASTS BEFORE THE LAW

Criminal prosecution of rats—Chassenée appointed to defend them—Report of the trial—Chassenée employed as counsel in other cases of this kind—His dissertation on the subject—Nature of his argument—Authorities and precedents—The withering of the fig-tree at Bethany justified and explained by Dr. Trench—Eels and blood-suckers in Lake Leman cursed by the Bishop of Lausanne with the approval of Heidelberg theologians —White bread turned black, and swallows, fish, and flies

destroyed by anathema—St. Pirminius expels reptiles
—Vermifugal efficacy of St. Magnus' crosier—Papal
execratories—Animals regarded by the law as lay
persons, and not entitled to benefit of clergy—Methods
of procedure—Jurisdiction of the courts—Records of
judicial proceedings against insects—Important trial of
weevils at St. Jean-de-Maurienne extending over more
than eight months—Untenableness of Ménebréa's theory
—Summary of the pleadings—Futile attempts at compromise—Final decision doubtful—St. Eldrad and the
snakes—Views of Thomas Aquinas—Distinction between excommunication and anathema—" Sweet beasts
and stenchy beasts "—Animals as incarnations of devils
—Their diabolical character assumed in papal formula
for blessing water to kill vermin—Amusing treatise by
Père Bougeant on this subject—All animals animated by
devils, and all pagans and unbaptized persons possessed
with them—Demons the real causes of diseases—
Father Lohbauer's prescription in such cases—Formula
of exorcism issued by Leo XIII.—Recent instances of
demoniacal possession—Hoppe's psychological explanation of them—Charcot on faith-cures—Why not the duty
of the Catholic Church to inculcate kindness to animals
—Zoölatry a form of demonolatry—Gnats especially
dangerous devils—Bodelschwingh's discovery of the
bacillus infernalis—Gaspard Bailly's disquisition with
specimens of plaints, pleas, etc.—Ayrault protests against
such proceedings—Hemmerlein's treatise on exorcisms
—Criminal prosecution of field-mice—Vermin excommunicated by the Bishop of Lausanne—Protocol of
judicial proceedings against caterpillars—Conjurers of
cabbage-worms—Swallows proscribed by a Protestant
parson—Custom of writing letters of advice to rats—
Writs of ejectment served on them—Rhyming rats
in Ireland—Ancient usage mentioned by Kassianos
Bassos—Capital punishment of larger quadrupeds—
Berriat-Saint-Prix's Reports and Researches—List of
culprits—Beasts burned and buried alive and put to the
rack—Swine executed for infanticide—Bailly's bill of
expenses—An ox decapitated for its demerits—Punishment of buggery—Cohabitation of a Christian with a
Jewess declared to be sodomy—Trial of a sow and six
sucklings for murder—Bull sent to the gallows for
killing a lad—A horse condemned to death for homicide

—A cock burned at the stake for the unnatural crime of laying an egg—Lapeyronie's investigation of the subject —Racine's satire on such prosecutions in *Les Plaideurs ;* *Lex talionis*—Tit for tat the law of the primitive man and the savage—The application of this iron rule in Hebrew legislation—Flesh of a culprit pig not to be eaten—Athenian laws for punishing inanimate objects— Recent execution of idols in China—Russian bell sentenced to perpetual exile in Siberia for abetting in- surrection—Pillory for dogs in Vienna—Treatment prescribed for mad dogs in the Avesta—Cruelty of laws of talion and decrees of corruption of blood—Examples in ancient and modern legislation—Cicero approves of such penalties for political offences—Survival of this conception of justice in theology—Constitutio Criminalis Carolina—Lombroso opposed to trial by jury as a relic of barbarism—Corruption of Swiss cantonal courts— Deodand in English law—Applications of it in Mary- land and in Scotland—Blackstone's theory of it untenable —Penalties inflicted for suicide—Ancient legislation on this subject—Legalization of suicide—Abolition of deodands in England   ...   . *p.* 18

CHAPTER II

MEDIÆVAL AND MODERN PENOLOGY

Recent change in the spirit of criminal jurisprudence— Mediæval tribunals cut with the executioner's sword the intricate knots which the modern criminalist essays to untie—Phlebotomy a panacea in medicine and law— Restless ghosts of criminals who died unpunished— Execution of vampires and were-wolves—Case of a were- wolf who devoured little children "even on Friday" —Pope Stephen VI. brings the corpse of his predecessor to trial—Mediæval and modern conceptions of culpa- bility—Problems of psycho-pathological jurisprudence— Degrees of mental vitiation—Italians pioneers in the scientific study of criminality—Effects of these specula- tions upon legislation—Barbarity of mediæval penal justice—Gradual abolition of judicial torture—Cruel sentence pronounced by Carlo Borromeo—" Blue Laws"

Contents

a great advance on contemporary English penal codes—
Moral and penal responsibility—Atavism and criminality
—Physical abnormities—Capacity and symmetry of the
skull—Circumvolutions of the brain—Tattooing not a
peculiarity of criminals, but simply an indication of low
æsthetic sense—Theories of the origin and nature of
crime—Intelligence not always to be measured by the
size of the encephalon—Remarkable exceptions in
Gambetta, Bichat, Bischoff and Ugo Foscolo—Advanced criminalists justly dissatisfied with the penal
codes of to-day—Measures proposed by Lombroso and
his school—Their conclusions not sustained by facts—
Crime through hypnotic suggestion—Difficulty of defining insanity—Coleridge's definition too inclusive—
Predestination and evolution—Criminality among the
lower animals—Punishment preventive or retributive—
Schopenhauer's doctrine of responsibility for character
—Remarkable trial of a Swiss toxicomaniac, Marie
Jeanneret—"Method in Madness" not uncommon—
Social safety the supreme law—Application of this
principle to "Cranks"—Spirit of imitation peculiarly
strong in such classes — Contagiousness of crime—
Criminology now in a period of transition ... *p.* 193

APPENDIX

A. De Actis Scindicorum Communitatis Sancti Julliani
agentium contra Animalia Bruta ad formam muscarum volantia coloris viridis communi voce appellata
Verpillions seu Amblevins ... ... *p.* 259

B. Traite des Monitoires avec un Plaidoyer contre les
Insectes par Spectable Gaspard Bailly ... *p.* 287

C. Allegation, Replication, and Judgment in the process
against field-mice at Stelvio in 1519 ... ... *p.* 307

D. Admonition, Denunciation, and Citation of the Inger by
the Priest Bernhard Schmid in the name and by the
authority of the Bishop of Lausanne in 1478 *p.* 309

E. Decree of Augustus, Duke of Saxony and Elector, commending the action of Parson Greysser in putting the
sparrows under ban, issued at Dresden in 1559 *p.* 311

Contents

F. Chronological List of Excommunications and Prosecutions of Animals from the ninth to the nineteenth century ... ... *p.* 313

G. Receipt, dated January 9, 1386, in which the hangman of Falaise acknowledges to have been paid by the Viscount of Falaise ten sous and ten deniers tournois for the execution of an infanticidal sow, and also ten sous tournois for a new glove ... ... *p.* 335

H. Receipt, dated September 24, 1394, in which Jehan Micton acknowledges that he received the sum of fifty sous tournois from Thomas de Juvigney, Viscount of Mortaing, for having hanged a pig, which had killed and murdered a child in the parish of Roumaygne *p.* 336

I. Attestation of Symon de Baudemont, Lieutenant of the Bailiff of Nantes and Meullant, made by order of the said bailiff and the king's proctor, on March 15, 1403, and certifying to the expenses incurred in executing a sow that had devoured a small child ... ... *p.* 338

J. Receipt, dated October 16, 1408, and signed by Toustain Pincheon, jailer of the royal prisons in the town of Pont de Larche, acknowledging the payment of nineteen sous and six deniers tournois for food furnished to sundry men and to one pig kept in the said prisons on charge of crime ... ... *p.* 340

K. Letters Patent, by which Philip the Bold, Duke of Burgundy, on September 12, 1379, granted the petition of the Friar Humbert de Poutiers, Prior of the town of Saint-Marcel-lez-Jussey, and pardoned two herds of swine, which had been condemned to suffer the extreme penalty of the law as accomplices in an infanticide committed by three sows ... ... *p.* 342

L. Sentence pronounced by the Mayor of Loens de Chartres on the 12th of September, 1606, condemning Guillaume Guyart to be hanged and burned together with a bitch ... ... *p.* 344

M. Sentence pronounced by the Judge of Savigny in January, 1457, condemning to death an infanticidal sow. Also the sentence of confiscation pronounced nearly a month later on the six pigs of the said sow for complicity in her crime ... ... *p.* 346

N. Sentence pronounced, April 18, 1499, in a criminal prosecution instituted before the Bailiff of the Abbey of Josaphat, in the Commune of Sèves, near Chartres, against a pig condemned to be hanged for having killed an infant. In this case the owners of the pig were fined eighteen francs for negligence, because the child was their fosterling   ...   . *p.* 352

O. Sentence pronounced, June 14, 1494, by the Grand Mayor of the church and monastery of St. Martin de Laon, condemning a pig to be hanged and strangled for infanticide committed on the fee-farm of Clermont-lez-Montcornet   ...   . *p.* 354

P. Sentence pronounced, March 27, 1567, by the Royal Notary and Proctor of the Bailiwick and Bench of the Court of Judicatory of Senlis, condemning a sow with a black snout to be hanged for her cruelty and ferocity in murdering a girl of four months, and forbidding the inhabitants of the said seignioralty to let such beasts run at large on penalty of an arbitrary fine ... *p.* 356

Q. Sentence of death pronounced upon a bull, May 16, 1499, by the Bailiff of the Abbey of Beaupré, for furiously killing Lucas Dupont, a young man of fourteen or fifteen years of age   ...   . *p.* 358

R. Scene from Racine's comedy *Les Plaideurs*, in which a dog is tried and condemned to the galleys for stealing a capon   ...   . *p.* 360

S. Record of the decision of the Law Faculty of the University of Leipsic condemning a cow to death for having killed a woman at Machern near Leipsic, July 20, 1621   ...   . *p.* 361

BIBLIOGRAPHY ...   . *p.* 362

INDEX   ...   . *p.* 373

THE CRIMINAL PROSECUTION AND CAPITAL PUNISHMENT OF ANIMALS

INTRODUCTION

THE present volume is the result of the revision and expansion of two essays entitled " Bugs and Beasts before the Law," and " Modern and Mediæval Punishment," which appeared in *The Atlantic Monthly,* in August and September 1884. Since that date the author has collected a vast amount of additional material on the subject, which has also been discussed by other writers in several publications, the most noteworthy of which are Professor Karl von Amira's *Thierstrafen und Thierprocesse* (Innsbruck, 1891), Carlo d'Addosio's *Bestie Delinquenti* (Napoli, 1892), and G. Tobler's *Thierprocesse in der Schweiz* (Bern, 1893), but in none of these works, except the first-mentioned, are there any important statements of facts or citations of cases in addition to those adduced in the essays already mentioned, for which the writer was indebted chiefly to the

I

extensive and exceedingly valuable researches of Berriat-Saint-Prix and M. L. Ménebréa, and the *Consilium Primum* of Bartholomew Chassenée, cited in the appended bibliography. Professor Von Amira is a very distinguished and remarkably keen-sighted jurisprudent and treats the matter exclusively from a jurisprudential point of view, his main object being to discover some general principle on which to explain these strange phenomena, and thus to assign to them their proper place and true significance in the historical evolution of the idea of justice and the methods of attaining it by legal procedure.

Von Amira draws a sharp line of technical distinction between Thierstrafen and Thierprocesse; the former were capital punishments inflicted by secular tribunals upon pigs, cows, horses, and other domestic animals as a penalty for homicide; the latter were judicial proceedings instituted by ecclesiastical courts against rats, mice, locusts, weevils, and other vermin in order to prevent them from devouring the crops, and to expel them from orchards, vineyards, and cultivated fields by means of exorcism and excommunication. Animals, which were in the service of man, could be arrested, tried, convicted and executed, like any other members of his household; it was, therefore, not necessary to summon them to appear in court at a specified time to answer for their conduct, and thus make them, in the strict sense of the term, a party to the prosecution, for the sheriff had already taken them in charge and consigned them to the custody of the jailer. Insects and rodents, on the other hand, which were not subject to human control and could not be seized and imprisoned by the civil authorities, demanded the intervention of the Church and the exercise of its supernatural functions for the purpose of compelling them to desist from their devastations and to retire from all places devoted to the production of human sustenance. The only feasible method of staying the ravages of these swarms of noxious creatures was to resort to " metaphysical aid " and to expel or exterminate them by sacerdotal conjuring and cursing. The fact that it was customary to catch several specimens of the culprits and bring them before the seat of justice, and there solemnly put them to death while the anathema was being pronounced, proves that this summary manner of dealing would have been applied to the whole of them, had it been possible to do so. Indeed, the attempt was sometimes made to get rid of them by setting a price on their heads, as was the case with the plague of locusts at Rome in 880, when a reward was offered for their extermination, but all efforts in this direction proving futile, on account of the rapidity with which they propagated, recourse was had to exorcisms and besprinklings with holy water.

D'Addosio speaks of the actions brought against domestic animals for homicide as penal prosecutions, and those instituted against insects and vermin for injury done to the fruits of the field as civil suits (*processi civili*); but the latter designation is not correct in any proper sense of the term, since these actions were not suits to recover for damages to property, but had solely a preventive or prohibitive character. The judicial process was preliminary to the utterance of the malediction and essential to its efficacy. Before fulminating an excommunication the whole machinery of justice was put in motion in order to establish the guilt of the accused, who were then warned, admonished, and threatened, and, in cases of obduracy, smitten with the *anathema maranatha* and devoted to utter destruction. As with all bans, charms, exorcisms, incantations, and other magical hocus-pocus, the omission of any formality would vitiate the whole procedure, and, by breaking the spell, deprive the imprecation or interdiction of its occult virtue. Ecclesiastical thunder would thus be robbed of its fatal bolt and reduced to mere empty noise, the harmless explosion of a blank cartridge.

The Church was not wholly consistent in its explanations of these phenomena. In general the swarms of devouring insects and other noxious vermin are assumed to have been sent at the instigation of Satan (*instigante sathana, per maleficium diabolicum*), and are denounced and deprecated as snares of the devil and his satellites (*diaboli et ministrorum insidias*); again they are treated as creatures of God and agents of the Almighty for the punishment of sinful man; from this latter point of view every effort to exterminate them by natural means would be regarded as a sort of sacrilege, an impious attempt to war upon the Supreme Being and to withstand His designs. In either case, whether they were the emissaries of a wicked demon or of a wrathful Deity, the only proper and permissible way of relief was through the offices of the Church, whose bishops and other clergy were empowered to perform the adjurations and maledictions or to prescribe the penances and propitiations necessary to produce this result. If the insects were instruments of the devil, they might be driven into the sea or banished to some arid region, where they would all miserably perish; if, on the other hand, they were recognized as the ministers of God, divinely delegated to scourge mankind for the promotion of piety, it would be suitable, after they had fulfilled their mission, to cause them to withdraw from the cultivated fields and to assign them a spot, where they might live in comfort without injury to the inhabitants. The records contain instances of both kinds of treatment.

It was also as a protection against evil spirits that the penalty of death was inflicted upon domestic animals. A homicidal pig or bull was not necessarily assumed to be the incarnation of a demon, although it was maintained by eminent authorities, as we have shown in the present work, that all beasts and birds, as well as creeping things, were devils in disguise; but the homicide, if it were permitted to go unpunished, was supposed to furnish occasion for the intervention of devils, who were thereby enabled to take possession of both persons and places. This belief was prevalent in the Middle Ages, and is still taught by the Catholic Church. In a little volume entitled *Die Verwaltung des Exorcistats nach Massgabe der römischen Benediktionale*, of which a revised and enlarged edition was published at Stuttgart in 1893 for the use of priests as a manual of instruction in performing exorcisms, it is expressly stated by the reverend author, Dr. Theobald Bischofberger, that a spot, where a murder or other heinous crime has been committed, if the said crime remains undetected or unexpiated, is sure to be infested by demons, and that the inmates of a house or other building erected upon such a site will be peculiarly liable to diabolical possession, however innocent they may be personally. Indeed, the more pure and pious they are, the greater will be the efforts of the demons to enter into and annoy them. Not only human beings, but also all cattle after their kind, and even the fowls of the barnyard are subject to infernal

vexations of this sort. The infestation thus produced may continue for centuries, and, although
the property may pass by purchase or inheritance
into other hands and be held successively by any
number of rightful owners, the demons remain
in possession unaffected by legal conveyances.
If each proprietor imagines he has an exclusive
title to the estate, he reckons without the host
of devils, who exercise there the right of squatter
sovereignty and can be expelled only by sacerdotal authority. Dr. Bischofberger goes so far
as to affirm that it behoves the purchaser of a
piece of land to make sure that it is unencumbered by devils as well as by debts, otherwise he may have to suffer more from a demoniac
lien than from a dead pledge or any other form
of obligation in law. Information concerning
the latter can be obtained at the registry of
deeds, but it is far more difficult to ascertain
whether the infernal powers have any claims
upon it, since this knowledge can be derived only
inferentially and indirectly from inquiries into
the character of the proprietors for many generations and must always rest upon presumptive
evidence rather than positive proof. Our author
does not hesitate to assert that houses which
have been the abodes of pious people from time
immemorial ought to have a higher market value
than the habitations of notoriously wicked
families. It is thus shown that " godliness is
profitable " not only " unto all things," but also,

as mediæval writers were wont to say, unto some things besides, which the apostle Paul in his admonitions to his "son Timothy" never dreamed of. We are also told that the *aura corrumpens* resulting from diabolical infestation imparts to the dwelling a peculiar taint, which it often retains for a long time after the demons have been cast out, so that sensitive persons cannot enter such a domicile without getting nervously excited, slightly dizzy and all in a tremble. The carnal mind, which is at enmity with all supernatural explanations of natural phenomena, would seek the source of such sensations in an *aura corrumpens* arising from the lack of proper ventilation, and find relief by simply opening the windows instead of calling in a priest with aspergills, and censers, and *benedictiones locorum*.

We have a striking illustration of this truth in the frequent cases of "bewitched kine." European peasants often confine their cattle in stalls so small and low that the beasts have not sufficient air to breathe. The result is that a short time after the stalls are closed for the night the cattle get excited and begin to fret and fume and stamp, and are found in the morning weak and exhausted and covered with sweat. The peasant attributes these phenomena to witchcraft, and calls in an exorcist, who proceeds to expel the evil spirits. Before performing the ceremony of conjuration, he opens the doors and windows and the admission of fresh air makes it quite easy to cast out the demons. A German veterinarian, who reports several instances of this kind, tried in vain to convince the peasants that the trouble was due, not to sorcery, but to the absence of proper sanatory conditions, and finally, in despair of accomplishing his purpose in any other way, told them that if the windows were left open so that the witches could go in and out freely, the demons would not enter into the cattle. This advice was followed and the malign influence ceased.

The ancient Greeks held that a murder, whether committed by a man, a beast, or an inanimate object, unless properly expiated, would arouse the furies and bring pestilence upon the land; the mediæval Church taught the same doctrine, and only substituted the demons of Christian theology for the furies of classical mythology. As early as 864, the Council of Worms decreed that bees, which had caused the death of a human being by stinging him, should be forthwith suffocated in the hive before they could make any more honey, otherwise the entire contents of the hive would become demoniacally tainted and thus rendered unfit for use as food; it was declared to be unclean, and this declaration of impurity implied a liability to diabolical possession on the part of those who, like Achan, "transgressed in the thing accursed." It was the same horror of aiding and abetting demons and enabling them to extend their power over mankind that caused a cock, which was suspected of having laid the so-called " basilisk-egg," or a hen, addicted to the ominous habit of crowing, to be summarily put to death, since it was only by such expiation that the evil could be averted.

A Swiss jurist, Eduard Osenbrüggen (*Studien zur deutschen und schweizerischen Rechtsgeschichte*. Schaffhausen, 1868, p. 139–149), endeavours to explain these judicial proceedings on the theory of the personification of animals. As only a human being can commit crime and thus render himself liable to punishment, he concludes that it is only by an act of personification that the brute can be placed in the same category as man and become subject to the same penalties. In support of this view he refers to the fact that in ancient and mediæval times domestic animals were regarded as members of the household and entitled to the same legal protection as human vassals. In the Frankish capitularies all beasts of burden or so-called juments were included in the king's ban and enjoyed the peace guaranteed by royal authority : *Ut jumenta pacem habent similiter per bannum regis.* The weregild extended to them as it did to women and serfs under cover of the man as master of the house and lord of the manor. The beste covert, to use the old legal phraseology, was thus invested with human rights and inferentially endowed with human responsibilities. According to old Welsh law atonement was made for killing a cat or dog belonging to another person by suspending the animal by the tail so that its nozzle touched the ground, and then pouring wheat over it until its body was entirely covered. Old Germanic law also recognized the competency of these animals as witnesses in certain cases, as, for example, when burglary had been committed by night, in the absence of human testimony, the house-holder was permitted to appear before the court and make complaint, carrying on his arm a dog, cat or cock, and holding in his hand three straws taken from the roof as symbols of the house. Symbolism and personification, as applied to animals and inanimate objects, unquestionably played an important part in primitive legislation, but this principle does not account for the excom-munication and anathematization of noxious vermin or for the criminal prosecution and capital punishment of homicidal beasts, nor does it throw the faintest light upon the origin and purpose of such proceedings. Osenbrüggen's statement that the cock condemned to be burned at Bâle was personified as a heretic (Ketzer) and therefore sentenced to the stake, is a far-fetched and wholly fanciful explanation. As we have already seen, the unfortunate fowl, suspected of laying an egg in violation of its nature, was feared as an abnormal, inauspicious, and therefore diabolic creature; the fatal cockatrice, which was supposed to issue from this egg when hatched, and the use which might be made of its contents for promoting intercourse with evil spirits, caused such a cock to be dreaded as a dangerous purveyor to His Satanic Majesty, but no member of the Kohlenberg Court ever thought of consigning Chanticleer to the flames as the peer of Wycliffe or of Huss in heresy.

The judicial prosecution of animals, resulting in their excommunication by the Church or their execution by the hangman, had its origin in the common superstition of the age, which has left such a tragical record of itself in the incredibly absurd and atrocious annals of witchcraft. The same ancient code that condemned a homicidal ox to be stoned, declared that a witch should not be suffered to live, and although the Jewish lawgiver may have regarded the former enactment chiefly as a police regulation designed to protect persons against unruly cattle, it was, like the decree of death against witches, genetically connected with the Hebrew cult and had therefore an essentially religious character. It was these two paragraphs of the Mosaic law that Christian tribunals in the Middle Ages were wont to adduce as their authority for prosecuting and punishing both classes of delinquents, although in the application of them they were undoubtedly incited by motives and influenced by fears wholly foreign to the mind of the

Levitical legislator. The extension of Christianity beyond the boundaries of Judaism and the conversion of Gentile nations led to its gradual but radical transformation. The propagation of the new and aggressive faith among the Greeks and Romans, and especially among the Indo-Germanic tribes of Northern Europe, necessarily deposed, degraded and demonized the ancestral deities of the proselytes, who were taught henceforth to abjure the gods of their fathers and to denounce them as devils. Thus missionary zeal and success, while saving human souls from endless perdition, served also to enlarge the realm of the Prince of Darkness and to increase the number of his subjects and satellites. The new convert saw them with his mind's eye skulking about in obscure places, haunting forest dells and mountain streams by day, approaching human habitations by night and waiting for opportunities to lure him back to the old worship or to take vengeance upon him for his recreancy. Every untoward event furnished an occasion for their intervention, which could be averted or repelled only by the benedictions, exorcisms or anathemas of the Church. The ecclesiastical authorities were therefore directly interested in encouraging this superstitious belief as one of the chief sources of their power, and it was for this reason that diabolical agencies were assumed to be at work in every maleficent force of nature and to be incarnate in every noxious creature. That this docrine is still held and this policy still pursued by the bishops and other clergy of the Roman Catholic Church, no one familiar with the literature of the subject can deny.

Besides the manuals and rituals already cited, consult, for example, *Die deutschen Bischöfe und der Aberglaube:* Eine Denkschrift von Dr. Fr. Heinrich Reusch, Professor of Theology in the University of Bonn, who vigorously protests against the countenance given by the bishops to the crassest superstitions. For specimens of the literature condemned by the German professor, but approved by the prelates and the pope, see such periodicals as *Monat-Rosen zu Ehren der Unbefleckten Gottes-Mutter Maria* and *Der Sendbote des göttlichen Herzens Jesu,* published by Jesuits at Innsbruck in the Tyrol.

It is a curious fact that the most recent and most radical theories of juridical punishment, based upon anthropological, sociological and psychiaterical investigations, would seem to obscure and even to obliterate the line of distinction between man and beast, so far as their capacity for committing crime and their moral responsibility for their misdeeds are concerned. According to Lombroso there are *i delinquenti nati fra gli animali,* beasts which are born criminals and wilfully and wantonly injure others of their kind, violating with perversity and premeditation the laws of the society in which they live. Thus the modern criminologist recognizes the existence of the kind of malefactor characterized by Jocodus Damhouder, a Belgian jurist of the sixteenth century, as *bestia laedens ex interna malitia;* but although he might admit that the beast perpetrated the deed with malice aforethought and with the clear consciousness of wrong-doing, he would never think of bringing such a creature to trial or of applying to it the principle of retributive justice. This example illustrates the radical change which the theory of punishment has undergone in recent times and the far-reaching influence which it is beginning to exert upon penal legislation. In the second part of the present work the writer calls attention to this important revolution in the province of criminology, discussing as concisely as possible its essential features and indicating its general scope and practical tendencies, so far as they have been determined. It must be remembered, however, that, although the savage spirit of revenge, that eagerly demands blood for blood without the slightest consideration of the ana- tomical, physiological or psychological con- ditions upon which the commission of the specific act depends, has ceased to be the controlling factor in the enactment and execution of penal codes, the new system of jurisprudence, based upon more enlightened conceptions of human responsibility, is still in an inchoate state and very far from having worked out a satisfactory solution of the intricate problem of the origin and nature of crime and its proper penalty.

In 1386, an infanticidal sow was executed in the old Norman city of Falaise, and the scene was represented in fresco on the west wall of the Church of the Holy Trinity in that city. This curious painting no longer exists, and, so far as can be ascertained, has never been engraved. It has been frequently and quite fully described by different writers, and the frontispiece of the present volume is not a reproduction of the original picture, but a reconstruction of it according to these descriptions. It is taken from Arthur Mangin's *L'Homme et la Bête* (Paris, 1872), of which all the illustrations are more or less fancy sketches. A full account of the trial and execution is given in the present volume.

The iconographic edition of Jocodus Damhouder's *Praxis Rerum Criminalium* (Antverpiæ, 1562) contains at the beginning of each section an engraving representing the perpetration of the crimes about to be discussed. That at the head of the chapter entitled " De Damno Pecuario " is a lively picture of the injuries done by animals and rendering them liable to criminal process; it is reproduced facing page 161 of the present work.

The most important documents, from which our knowledge of these judicial proceedings is derived, are given in the Appendix, together with a complete list of prosecutions and excommunications during the past ten centuries, so far as we have been able to discover any record of them.

The bibliography, although making no claim to be exhaustive, comprises the principal works on the subject. Articles and essays, which are merely a rehash of other publications, it has not been deemed necessary to mention. Such, for example, are "Criminalprocesse gegen Thiere," in *Miscellen aus der neuesten ausländischen Literatur* (Jena, 1830, LXV. pp. 152–55), Jörgensen's *Nogle Frugter af mit Otium* (Kopenhagen, 1834, pp. 216–23); Cretella's "Gli Animali sotto Processo," in *Fanfulla della Domenica* (Florence, 1891, No. 65), all three based upon the archival researches of Berriat-Saint-Prix and Ménabréa, and Soldan's "La Personification des Animaux in Helvetia," in *Monatsschrift der Studentenverbindung Helvetia* (VII. pp. 4–17), which is a mere restatement of Osenbrüggen's theory.

In conclusion the author desires to express his sincere thanks to Dr. Laubmann, Director of the Munich Hof- und Staatsbibliothek, as well as to the other custodians of that library, for their uniform kindness and courtesy in placing at his disposal the printed and manuscript treasures committed to their keeping.

2

CHAPTER I

BUGS AND BEASTS BEFORE THE LAW

IT is said that Bartholomew Chassenée,[1] a distinguished French jurist of the sixteenth century (born at Issy-l'Evêque in 1480), made his reputation at the bar as counsel for some rats, which had been put on trial before the ecclesiastical court of Autun on the charge of having feloniously eaten up and wantonly destroyed the barley-crop of that province. On complaint formally presented by the magistracy, the official or bishop's vicar, who exercised jurisdiction in such cases, cited the culprits to appear on a certain day and appointed Chassenée to defend them.

In view of the bad repute and notorious guilt of his clients, Chassenée was forced to employ all sorts of legal shifts and chicane, dilatory pleas and other technical objections, hoping thereby to find some loophole in the meshes of the law through which the accused might escape,

[1] The name is also spelled Chassanée and Chasseneux. In the Middle Ages, and even as late as the end of the eighteenth century, the orthography of proper names was very uncertain.

or at least to defer and mitigate the sentence of the judge. He urged, in the first place, that inasmuch as the defendants were dispersed over a large tract of country and dwelt in numerous villages, a single summons was insufficient to notify them all; he succeeded, therefore, in obtaining a second citation, to be published from the pulpits of all the parishes inhabited by the said rats. At the expiration of the considerable time which elapsed before this order could be carried into effect and the proclamation be duly made, he excused the default or non-appearance of his clients on the ground of the length and difficulty of the journey and the serious perils which attended it, owing to the unwearied vigilance of their mortal enemies, the cats, who watched all their movements, and, with fell intent, lay in wait for them at every corner and passage. On this point Chassenée addressed the court at some length, in order to show that if a person be cited to appear at a place, to which he cannot come with safety, he may exercise the right of appeal and refuse to obey the writ, even though such appeal be expressly precluded in the summons. The point was argued as seriously as though it were a question of family feud between Capulet and Montague in Verona or Colonna and Orsini in Rome.

At a later period of his life Chassenée was reminded of the legal principle thus laid down and urged to apply it in favour of clients more

worthy of its protection than a horde of vagrant
rodents. In 1540 he was president of the judicial
assembly known as the Parliament of Provence
on a memorable occasion when the iniquitous
measure for the extirpation of heresy by exterminating the Waldenses in the villages of
Cabrières and Merindol was under discussion.
One of the members of the tribunal, a gentleman
from Arles, Renaud d'Alleins, ventured to
suggest to the presiding officer that it would be
extremely unjust to condemn these unfortunate
heretics without granting them a hearing and
permitting an advocate to speak in their defence,
so that they might be surrounded by all the safeguards of justice, adding that the eminent jurist
had formerly insisted upon this right before the
court of Autun and maintained that even animals
should not be adjudged and sentenced without
having a proper person appointed to plead their
cause. Chassenée thereupon obtained a decree
from the king commanding that the accused
Waldenses should be heard; but his death,
which occurred very soon afterwards, changed
the state of affairs and prevented whatever good
effects might have been produced by this simple
act of justice. [Cf. Desnoyers : *Recherches*, etc.
(*vide* Bibliography), p. 18.]

In the report of the trial published in the *Thémis
Jurisconsulte* for 1820 (Tome I. pp. 194 sqq.)
by Berriat Saint-Prix, on the authority of the
celebrated Jacques Auguste De Thou, President

of the Parliament of Paris, the sentence pronounced by the official is not recorded. But
whatever the judicial decision may have been,
the ingenuity and acumen with which Chassenée
conducted the defence, the legal learning which
he brought to bear upon the case, and the eloquence of his plea enlisted the public interest
and established his fame as a criminal lawyer and
forensic orator.

Chassenée is said to have been employed in
several cases of this kind, but no records of
them seem to have been preserved, although it is
possible that they may lie buried in the dusty
archives of some obscure provincial town in
France, once the seat of an ecclesiastical tribunal.
The whole subject, however, has been treated
by him exhaustively in a book entitled *Consilium
primum, quod tractatus jure dici potest, propter
multiplicem et reconditam doctrinam, ubi luculenter et accurate tractatur quaestio illa: De
excommunicatione animalium insectorum.* This
treatise, which is the first of sixty-nine consilia,
embodying opinions on various legal questions
touching the holding and transmission of property, entail, loans, contracts, dowries, wills, and
kindred topics, and which holds a peculiar place
in the history of jurisprudence, was originally
published in 1531, and reprinted in 1581, and
again in 1588. The edition referred to in the
present work is the first reprint of 1581, a copy
of which is in the Royal Court and State Library
of Munich.

This curious dissertation originated, as it appears, in an application of the inhabitants of Beaune to the ecclesiastical tribunal of Autun for a decree of excommunication against certain noxious insects called huberes or hurebers, probably a kind of locust or harvest-fly. The request was granted, and the pernicious creatures were duly accursed. Chassenée now raises the query whether such a thing may be rightfully and lawfully done (*sed an recte et de jure fieri possit*), and how it should be effected. "The principal question," he says, "is whether one can by injunction cause such insects to withdraw from a place in which they are doing damage, or to abstain from doing damage there, under penalty of anathema and perpetual malediction. And although in times past there has never been any doubt on this point, yet I have thought that the subject should be thoroughly examined anew, lest I should seem to fall into the vice censured by Cicero (*De Off.* I. 6), of regarding things which we do not know as if they were well understood by us, and therefore rashly giving them our assent." He divides his treatise into five parts, or rather discusses the subject under five heads : " First, lest I may seem to discourse to the populace, how are these our animals called in the Latin language; secondly, whether these our animals can be summoned; thirdly, whether they can be summoned by procurators, and, if they are cited to appear personally, whether they can appear by proxy, *i. e.* through procurators appointed by the judge who summons them; fourthly, what judge, whether layman or ecclesiastic, is competent to try them, and how he is to proceed against them and to pass and execute sentence upon them; fifthly, what constitutes an anathema and how does it differ from an excommunication.'' Chassenée's method of investigation is not that of the philosophic thinker, who marshals facts under general laws and traces them to rational causes, but combines that of the lawyer, who quotes precedents and examines witnesses, with that of the theologian, who balances authorities and serves us with texts instead of arguments. He scrupulously avoids all psychological speculation or metaphysical reasoning, and simply aims to show that animals have been tried, convicted, and sentenced by civil and ecclesiastical courts, and that the competence of these tribunals has been generally recognized.

The documentary evidence adduced is drawn from a great variety of sources: the scriptures of the Old and New Testament, pagan poets and philosophers, patristic theologians and homilists, mediæval hagiologists, Virgil, Ovid, Pliny, Cicero, Cato, Aristotle, Seneca, Silius Italicus, Boethius, Gregory the Great, Pico della Mirandola, the laws of Moses, the prophecies of Daniel, and the Institutes of Justinian are alike laid under contribution and quoted as of equal authority. All is fish that comes to his net out

of his erudition, be it salmon or sea-urchin. If
twelve witnesses can be produced in favour of
a statement, and only two against it, his reason
bows to the will of the majority, and accepts
the proposition as proved. It must be added,
however, to his credit, that he proceeds in this
matter with strict impartiality and perfect rectitude, takes whatever evidence is at hand, and
never tries to pack the witness-box.

His knowledge of obscure and now utterly for-
gotten authors, secular and ecclesiastic, is
immense. Like so many scholars of his day he
was prodigiously learned, without being remarkable for clearness or originality of thought.
Indeed, the vastness of his erudition seems rather
to have hampered than helped the vigorous
growth of his intellectual faculties. He often
indulges in logical subtilties so shallow in their
speciousness, that they ought not to deceive the
veriest smatterer in dialectics; and the reader is
constantly tempted to answer his laboured argu-
mentations, as Tristram Shandy's Uncle Toby
did the lucubrations of Corporal Trim, by
" whistling half-a-dozen bars of Lillibullero."
The examples he adduces afford striking illustrations of the gross credulity to which the strongly
conservative, precedent-mongering mind of the
jurisconsult is apt to fall an easy prey. The
habit of seeking knowledge and guidance exclusively in the records and traditions of the past, in
the so-called " wisdom of ages," renders him

peculiarly liable to regard every act and utterance of antiquity as necessarily wise and authoritative.

In proof of the power of anathemas, Chassenée refers to the cursing of the serpent in the Garden of Eden, causing it to go upon its belly for all time; David's malediction of the mountains of Gilboa, so that they had neither rain nor dew; God's curse upon the city of Jericho, making its strong walls fall before the blasts of trumpets; and in the New Testament the withered fig-tree of Bethany. The words of Jesus, " Every tree that bringeth not forth good fruit is hewn down and cast into the fire," he interprets, not merely as the best means of getting rid of a cumberer of the orchard, but as a condemnation and punishment of the tree for its delinquencies, and adds : " If, therefore, it is permitted to destroy an irrational thing, because it does not produce fruit, much more is it permitted to curse it, since the greater penalty includes the less (*cum si liceat quid est plus, debet licere quid est minus*).

An English professor of divinity, Richard Chevenix Trench, justifies the withering of the fruitless fig-tree on the same ground or, at least, by a similar process of reasoning : " It was punished, not for being without fruit, but for proclaiming by the voice of those leaves that it had such; not for being barren, but for being false." According to this exegesis, it was the telling of a wilful lie that " drew on it the curse." The guilty fig is thus endowed with a moral character and made clearly conscious of the crime for which it suffered the penalty of death: " Almost as soon as the word of the Lord was spoken, a shuddering fear may have run through all the leaves of the tree, which was thus stricken at the heart." As regards the culpability and punishableness of the object, the modern divine and the mediæval jurist occupy the same standpoint; only the latter, with a stricter judicial sense, insists that there shall be no infliction of punishment until the malefactor has been convicted by due process of law, and that he shall enjoy all the safeguards which legal forms and technicalities have thrown around him and under whose covert even the vilest criminal has the right to take refuge. The Anglican hermeneutist, on the contrary, would justify the curse and admit the validity of the anathema, although it was only the angry expression of an unreasonable impatience disappointed in not finding fruit at the wrong season, " for the time of figs was not yet."

A curious and characteristic specimen of the absurd and illogical inferences, which Chassenée is constantly deducing from his texts, is the use he makes of the passage in Virgil's first Georgic, in which the poet remarks that " no religion has forbidden us to draw off water-courses for irrigating purposes, to enclose crops with fences, or to lay snares for birds," all these things being essential to successful husbandry. But from the right to snare birds, our jurisprudent infers the right to excommunicate them, since "no snares are stronger than the meshes of an anathema." Far-fetched deductions and wretched twaddle of this sort fill many pages of the famous lawyer's dissertation.

Coming down to more recent times, Chassenée mentions several instances of the effectiveness of anathemas, accepting as convincing testimony the ecstacies of saints and the extravagant statements of hagiologists without the slightest expression of doubt as to the truth of these legends. Thus he relates how a priest anathematized an orchard, because its fruits tempted the children of his parish and kept them away from mass. The orchard remained barren until, at the solicitation of the Duchess of Burgundy, the ban was removed. In like manner the Bishop of Lausanne freed Lake Leman from eels, which had become so numerous as seriously to interfere with boating and bathing; on another occasion in the year 1451 the same ecclesiastic expelled from the waters of this lake an immense number of enormous blood-suckers, which threatened to destroy all the large fish and were especially fatal to salmon, the favourite article of food on fast-days. This method of procedure was both cheap and effective and, as Felix Malleolus informs us in his *Tractatus de Exorcismis* (I), received the approbation of all the learned doctors of the University of Heidelberg: *omnes studii Heydelber-*

*gensis Doctores hujusmodi ritus videntes et
legentes consenserunt.*   By the same agency an
abbot changed the sweet white bread of a Count
of Toulouse, who abetted and protected heresy,
into black, mouldy bread, so that he, who would
fain feed souls with corrupt spiritual food, was
forced to satisfy his bodily hunger with coarse
and unsavoury provender.   No sooner was the
excommunication removed than the bread resumed its original purity and colour.   Egbert,
Bishop of Trier, anathematized the swallows,
which disturbed the devotions of the faithful by
their chirping and chattering, and sacrilegiously
defiled his head and vestments with their drop-
pings, when he was officiating at the altar.   He
forbade them to enter the sacred edifice on pain
of death; and it is still a popular superstition at
Trier, that if a swallow flies into the cathedral,
it immediately falls to the ground and gives up
the ghost.   Another holy man, known as John
the Lamb, cursed the fishes, which had incurred
his anger, with results equally fatal to the finny
tribe.   It is also related of the honey-tongued St.
Bernard, that he excommunicated a countless
swarm of flies, which annoyed the worshippers
and officiating priests in the abbey church of
Foigny, and lo, on the morrow they were, like
Sennacherib's host, "all dead corpses." William,
Abbot of St. Theodore in Rheims, who records
this miraculous event, states that as soon as the
execration was uttered, the flies fell to the floor

in such quantities that they had to be thrown out with shovels (*palis ejicientes*). This incident, he adds, was so well known that the cursing of the flies of Foigny became proverbial and formed the subject of a parable. [*Vita S. Bernardi,* auctore Wilhelmo abbate S. Thod. Rhem. I. 11.] According to the usual account, the malediction was not so drastic in its operation and did not cause the flies to disappear until the next day. The rationalist, whose chill and blighting breath is ever nipping the tender buds of faith, would doubtless suggest that a sharp and sudden frost may have added to the force and efficacy of the excommunication. The saint resorted to this severe and summary measure, says the monkish chronicler, because the case was urgent and " no other remedy was at hand." Perhaps this lack of other means of relief may refer to the absence of " deacons with fly-flaps," who, according to a contemporary writer, were appointed " to drive away the flies when the Pope celebrateth."

The island Reichenau in Lake Constance, which derives its name from its fertility and is especially famous for the products of its vineyards and its orchards, was once so infested by venomous reptiles as to be uninhabitable by human beings. Early in the eighth century, as the legend goes, it was visited by St. Pirminius, and no sooner had he set foot upon it than these creatures all crawled and wriggled into the water, so that the surface of the lake was covered for three days and three nights with serpents, scorpions and hideous worms. Peculiar vermifugal efficacy was ascribed to the crosier of St. Magnus, the apostle of Algau, which was preserved in the cloister of St. Mang at Füssen in Bavaria, and from 1685 to 1770 was repeatedly borne in solemn procession to Lucerne, Zug, Schwyz and other portions of Switzerland for the expulsion and extermination of rats, mice, cockchafers and other insects. Sometimes formulas of malediction were procured directly from the pope, which, like saints' curses, could be applied without legal formalities. Thus in 1660 the inhabitants of Lucerne paid four pistoles and one Roman thaler for a document of this kind; on Nov. 15, 1731, the municipal council of Thonou in Savoy resolved to join with other parishes of that province to obtain from Rome an excommunication against insects, the expenses for which are to be assessed *pro rata*;[1] in 1740 the commune of Piuro purchased from His Holiness a similar anathema; in the same year the common council of Chiavenna discussed the propriety of applying to Rome for an execratory against beetles and bears; and in December 1752 it was proposed by the same body to take like summary measures

---

1 "Item : a été délibéré que la ville se joindra aux paroisses de cette province qui voudront obtenir de Rome une excommunication contre les insects et que l'on contribuera aux frais au pro rata."

in order to get rid of a pest of rodents. In 1729, 1730 and 1749 the municipal council of Lucerne ordered processions to be made on St. Magnus' Day from the Church of St. Francis to Peter's Chapel for the purpose of expelling weevils. This custom was observed annually from 1749 to 1798. The pompous ceremony has been superseded in Protestant countries by an officially appointed day of fasting and prayer.

In his " First Counsel " Chassenée not only treats of methods of procedure, and gives forms of plaints to be drawn up and tendered to the tribunal by the injured party, as well as useful hints to the pettifogger in the exercise of his tortuous and tricky profession, but he also discusses many legal principles touching the jurisdiction of courts, the functions of judges, and other characteristic questions of civil, criminal, and canonical law. Animals, he says, should be tried by ecclesiastical tribunals, except in cases where the penalty involves the shedding of blood. An ecclesiastical judge is not competent *in causa sanguinis,* and can impose only canonical punishments, although he may have jurisdiction in temporal matters and punish crimes not involving a capital sentence. [*Nam judex ecclesiasticus in causa sanguinis non est competens judex, licet habeat jurisdictionem in temporalibus et possit crimina poenam sanguinis non existentia (exigentia* is obviously the correct reading) *castigare.* Cons. prim. IV. § 5.] For

this reason the Church never condemned
heretics to death, but, having decided that they
should die, gave them over to the secular power
for formal condemnation, usually under the
hollow and hypocritical pretence of recommending them to mercy. In the prosecution of
animals the summons was commonly published
from the parish pulpit and the whole judicial
process bore a distinctively ecclesiastical
character. In most cases the presiding judge or
official was the vicar of the parish acting as the
deputy of the bishop of the diocese. Occasionally the curate officiated in this capacity. Sometimes the trial was conducted before a civil
magistrate under the authority of the Church,
or the matter was submitted to the adjudication
of a conjurer, who, however, appointed two
proctors to plead respectively for the plaintiff
and the defendant and who rendered his
verdict in due legal form. Indeed, the word
" conjurer " seems to have been used as a
popular designation of the person, whether
priest or layman, who exercised judicatory
functions in such trials, probably because, as a
rule, the sentence could be executed only by
conjuration or the invocation of supernatural
aid.

Another point, which strikes us very comic-
ally, but which had to be decided before the trial
could proceed, was whether the accused were to
be regarded as clergy or laity. Chassenée

thinks that there is no necessity of testing each individual case, but that animals should be looked upon as lay persons. This, he declares, should be the general presumption; but if any one wishes to affirm that they have *ordinem clericatus* and are entitled to benefit of clergy, the burden of proof rests upon him and he is bound to show it (*deberet estud probare*). Probably our jurist would have made an exception in favour of the beetle, which entomologists call *clerus*; it is certain, at any rate, that if a bug bearing this name had been brought to trial, the learning and acuteness displayed in arguing the point in dispute would have been astounding. We laugh at the subtilties and quiddities of mediæval theologians, who seriously discussed such silly questions as the digestibility of the consecrated elements in the eucharist; but the importance attached to these trivialities was not so much the peculiarity of a single profession as the mental habit of the age, the result of scholastic training and scholastic methods of investigation, which tainted law no less than divinity. Nevertheless the ancillary relations of all other sciences and disciplines to theology render the latter chiefly responsible for this fatal tendency.

Chassenée also makes a distinction between punitive and preventive purposes in the prosecution of animals, between inflicting penalties upon them for crimes committed and taking precautionary measures to keep them from doing

3

damage. By this means he seeks to evade the objection, that animals are incapable of committing crimes, because they are not endowed with rational faculties. He then proceeds to show that " things not allowable in respect to crimes already committed are allowable in respect to crimes about to be committed in order to prevent them." Thus a layman may not arrest an ecclesiastic for a delict fully consummated, but may seize and detain him in order to hinder the consummation of a delict. In such cases, an inferior may coerce and correct a superior; even an irrational creature may put restraint upon a human being and hold him back from wrongdoing. In illustration of this legal point he cites an example from Holy Writ, where " Balaam, the prophet and servant of the Most High, was rebuked by a she-ass."

Chassenée endeavours to clinch his argument as usual by quoting biblical texts and adducing incidents from legendary literature. The province of zoö-psychology, which would have furnished him with better material for the elucidation of his subject, he leaves untouched, simply because it was unknown to him. If crime consists in the commission of deeds hurtful to other sentient beings, knowing such actions to be wrong, then the lower animals are certainly guilty of criminal offences. It is a well-established fact, that birds, beasts and insects, living together in communities, have certain laws, which are designed to promote the general welfare of the herd, the flock or the swarm, and the violation of which by individual members they punish corporally or capitally as the case may require. It is likewise undeniable, that domestic animals often commit crimes against man and betray a consciousness of the nature of their acts by showing fear of detection or by trying to conceal what they have done. Man, too, recognizes their moral responsibility by inflicting chastisement upon them, and sometimes feels justified in putting incorrigible offenders, a vicious bull, a thievish cat or a sheep-killing dog, summarily to death. Of course this kind of punishment is chiefly preventive, nevertheless it is provoked by acts already perpetrated and is not wholly free from the element of retributive justice. Such a proceeding, however, is arbitrary and autocratic, and if systematically applied to human beings would be denounced as intolerable tyranny. Chassenée insists that under no circumstances is a penalty to be imposed except by judicial decision—*nam poena nunquam imponitur, nisi lex expresse dicat*— and in support of this principle refers to the apostle Paul, who declares that "sin is not imputed when there is no law." He appears to think that any technical error would vitiate the whole procedure and reduce the ban of the Church to mere *brutum fulmen*. If he lays so great stress upon the observance of legal forms, which in the criminal prosecution of brute beasts strike us as the caricature and farce of justice, it is because he deems them essential to the effectiveness of an excommunication. The slightest mispronunciation of a word, an incorrect accentuation or false intonation in uttering a spell suffices to dissolve the charm and nullify the occult workings of the magic. The lack of a single link breaks the connection and destroys the binding force of the chain; everything must be " well-thought, well-said and well-done," not ethically, but ritually, as prescribed in the old Avestan formula: *humata hûkhta huvarshta.* All the mutterings and posturings, which accompany the performance of a Brahmanical sacrifice, or a Catholic mass, or any other kind of incantation have their significance, and none of them can be omitted without marring the perfection of the ceremonial and impairing its power. An anathema of animals pronounced in accordance with the sentence passed upon them by a tribunal, belongs to the same category of conjurations and is rendered nugatory by any formal defect or judicial irregularity.

Sometimes the obnoxious vermin were generously forewarned. Thus the grand-vicars of Jean Rohin, Cardinal Bishop of Autun, having been informed that slugs were devastating several estates in different parts of his diocese, on the 17th of August, 1487, ordered public processions to be made for three days in every parish, and enjoined upon the said slugs to quit the territory within this period under penalty of being accursed. On the 8th of September, 1488, a similar order was issued at Beaujeu. The curates were charged to make processions during the offices, and the slugs were warned three times to cease from vexing the people by corroding and consuming the herbs of the fields and the vines, and to depart; " and if they do not heed this our command, we excommunicate them and smite them with our anathema." In 1516, the official of Troyes pronounced sentence on certain insects (*adversus brucos seu eurucas vel alia non dissimilia animalia, Gallicè urebecs,* probably a species of *curculio*), which laid waste the vines, and threatened them with anathema, unless they should disappear within six days. Here it is expressly stated that a counsellor was assigned to the accused, and a prosecutor heard in behalf of the aggrieved inhabitants. As a means of rendering the anathema more effective, the people are also urged to be prompt and honest in the payment of tithes. Chassenée, too, endorses this view, and in proof of its correctness refers to Malachi, where God promises to rebuke the devourer for man's sake, provided all the tithes are brought into the storehouse.

The archives of the old episcopal city of St. Jean-de-Maurienne contain the original records of legal proceedings instituted against some insects, which had ravaged the vineyards of St. Julien, a hamlet situated on the route over Mt. Cenis and famous for the excellence of its vintage. The defendants in this case were a species of greenish weevil (charançon) known to entomologists as *rychites auratus,* and called by different names, amblevin, bèche, verpillion, in different provinces of France.

Complaint was first made by the wine-growers of St. Julien in 1545 before François Bonnivard, doctor of laws. The procurator Pierre Falcon and the advocate Claude Morel defended the insects, and Pierre Ducol appeared for the plaintiffs. After the presentation and discussion of the case by both parties, the official, instead of passing sentence, issued a proclamation, dated the 8th of May, 1546, recommending public prayers and beginning with the following characteristic preamble: " Inasmuch as God, the supreme author of all that exists, hath ordained that the earth should bring forth fruits and herbs (*animas vegetativas*), not solely for the sustenance of rational human beings, but likewise for the preservation and support of insects, which fly about on the surface of the soil, therefore it would be unbecoming to proceed with rashness and precipitance against the animals now actually accused and indicted; on the contrary, it would be more fitting for us to have recourse to the mercy of heaven and to implore pardon for our

sins." Then follow instructions as to the manner
in which the public prayers are to be conducted
in order to propitiate the divine wrath.   The
people are admonished to turn to the Lord with
pure and undivided hearts (*ex toto et puro corde*),
to repent of their sins with unfeigned contrition,
and to resolve to live henceforth justly and
charitably, and above all to pay tithes.   High
mass is to be celebrated on three consecutive
days, namely on May 20th, 21st, and 22nd, and
the host to be borne in solemn procession with
songs and supplications round the vineyards.
The first mass is to be said in honour of the Holy
Spirit, the second in honour of the Blessed
Virgin, and the third in honour of the tutelar
saint of the parish.   At least two persons of each
household are required to take part in these
religious exercises.   A *procès-verbal,* signed by
the curate Romanet, attests that this programme
was fully carried out and that the insects soon
afterwards disappeared.

About thirty years later, however, the scourge
was renewed and the destructive insects were
actually brought to trial.   The proceedings are
recorded on twenty-nine folia and entitled :
De actis scindicorum communitatis Sancti Julli-
ani agentium contra animalia bruta ad formam
muscarum volantia coloris viridis communi voce
appellata verpillions seu amblevins.   The documents, which are still preserved in the archives
of St. Julien, were communicated by M. Victor

Dalbane, secretary of the commune, to M. Léon Ménebréa, who printed them in the appendix to his volume: *De l'origine de la forme et de l'esprit des jugements rendus au moyen-âge contre les animaux*. Chambery, 1846. This treatise appeared originally in the twelfth tome of the *Mémoires de la Société Royale Académique de Savoie*.

It may be proper to add that Ménebréa's theory of " the spirit, in which these judgments against animals were given," is wholly untenable. He maintains that "these procedures formed originally only a kind of symbol intended to revive the sentiment of justice among the masses of the people, who knew of no right except might and of no law except that of intimidation and violence. In the Middle Ages, when disorder reigned supreme, when the weak remained without support and without redress against the strong, and property was exposed to all sorts of attacks and all forms of ravage and rapine, there was something indescribably beautiful in the thought of assimilating the insect of the field to the masterpiece of creation and putting them on an equality before the law. If man should be taught to respect the home of the worm, how much more ought he to regard that of his fellow-man and learn to rule in equity."

This explanation is very fine in sentiment, but expresses a modern, and not a mediæval way of thinking. The penal prosecution of animals, which prevailed during the Middle Ages, was by no means peculiar to that period, but has been frequently practised by primitive peoples and savage tribes; neither was it designed to inculcate any such moral lesson as is here suggested, nor did it produce any such desirable result. So far from originating in a delicate and sensitive sense of justice, it was, as will be more fully shown hereafter, the outcome of an extremely crude, obtuse, and barbaric sense of justice. It was the product of a social state, in which dense ignorance was governed by brute force, and is not to be considered as a reaction and protest against club-law, which it really tended to foster by making a travesty of the administration of justice and thus turning it into ridicule. It was also in the interest of ecclesiastical dignities to keep up this parody and perversion of a sacred and fundamental institute of civil society, since it strengthened their influence and extended their authority by subjecting even the caterpillar and the canker-worm to their dominion and control.

But to return to the records of the trial. On the 13th of April, 1587, the case was laid before " his most reverend lordship, the prince-bishop of Maurienne, or the reverend lord his vicar-general and official " by the syndics and procurators, François Amenet and Petremand Bertrand, who, in the name of the inhabitants of St. Julien, presented the following statement and petition : " Formerly by virtue of divine services

and earnest supplications the scourge and in-
ordinate fury of the aforesaid animals did cease;
now they have resumed their depredations and
are doing incalculable injury. If the sins of men
are the cause of this evil, it behoveth the representatives of Christ on earth to prescribe such
measures as may be appropriate to appease the
divine wrath. Wherefore we the afore-mentioned syndics, François Amenet and Petremand
Bertrand, do appear anew (*ex integro*) and
beseech the official, first, to appoint another
procurator and advocate for the insects in place
of the deceased Pierre Falcon and Claude
Morel, and secondly, to visit the grounds and
observe the damage, and then to proceed with
the excommunication."

In compliance with this request, the distinguished Antoine Filliol was appointed procurator for the insects, with a moderate fee
(*salario moderato*), and Pierre Rembaud their
advocate. The parties appeared before the
official on the 30th day of May and the case
was adjourned to the 6th of June, when the
advocate, Pierre Rembaud, presented his answer
to the declaration of the plaintiffs, showing that
their action is not maintainable and that they
should be nonsuited. After approving of the
course pursued by his predecessor in office, he
affirms that his clients have kept within their
right and not rendered themselves liable to
excommunication, since, as we read in the sacred

book of Genesis, the lower animals were created before man, and God said to them: Let the earth bring forth the living creature after his kind, cattle and creeping thing, and beast of the earth after his kind; and he blessed them saying, Be fruitful and multiply and fill the waters of the seas, and let fowl multiply in the earth. Now the Creator would not have given this command, had he not intended that these creatures should have suitable and sufficient means of support; indeed, he has expressly stated that to every thing that creepeth upon the earth every green herb has been given for meat. It is therefore evident that the accused, in taking up their abode in the vines of the plaintiffs, are only exercising a legitimate right conferred upon them at the time of their creation. Furthermore, it is absurd and unreasonable to invoke the power of civil and canonical law against brute beasts, which are subject only to natural law and the impulses of instinct. The argument urged by the counsel for the plaintiffs, that the lower animals are made subject to man, he dismisses as neither true in fact nor pertinent to the present case. He suggests that the complainants, instead of instituting judicial proceedings, would do better to entreat the mercy of heaven and to imitate the Ninevites, who, when they heard the warning voice of the prophet Jonah, proclaimed a fast and put on sackcloth. In conclusion, he demands that the petition of the plaintiffs be dismissed, the monitorium revoked and annulled, and all further proceedings stayed, to which end the gracious office of the judge is humbly implored (*humiliter implorato benigno officio judicis*).

The case was adjourned to the 12th and finally to the 19th of June, when Petremand Bertrand, the prosecuting attorney, presented a lengthy replication, of which the defendants' advocate demanded a copy with due time for deliberation. This request led to a further adjournment till the 26th of June, but as this day turned out to be a *dies feriatus* or holiday, no business could be transacted until the 27th, when the advocate of the commune, François Fay (who seems to have taken the place of Amenet, if he be not the same person), in reply to the defendants' plea, argued that, although the animals were created before man, they were intended to be subordinate to him and subservient to his use, and that this was, indeed, the reason of their prior creation. They have no *raison d'être* except as they minister to man, who was made to have dominion over them, inasmuch as all things have been put under his feet, as the Psalmist asserts and the apostle Paul reiterates. On this point, he concludes, our opponent has added nothing refutatory of the views, which have been held from time immemorial by our ancestors; we need only refer to the opinions formerly expressed by the honourable Hippolyte Ducol as satisfactory. The advocate for the defence merely remarked that he had not yet received the document ordered on the 19th of June, and the further consideration of the case was postponed till the 4th of July. Antoine Filliol then made a rejoinder to the plaintiffs' replication, denying that the subordination of the lower animals to man involves the right of excommunicating them, and insisting upon his former position, which the opposing counsel had not even attempted to disprove, namely, that the lower animals are subject solely to natural law, "a law originating in the eternal reason and resting upon a basis as immutable as that of the divine law of revelation, since they are derived from the same source, namely, the will and power of God." It is evident, he adds, that the action brought by the plaintiffs is not maintainable and that judgment should be given accordingly.

On the 18th of July, the same parties appear before the official of St. Jean-de-Maurienne. The procurator of the insects demands that the case be closed and the plaintiffs debarred from drawing up any additional statements or creating any further delay by the introduction of irrelevant matter, and requests that a decision be rendered on the documents and declarations already adduced. The prosecuting attorney, whose policy seems to have been to keep the suit pending as long as possible, applies for a new term (*alium terminum*), which was granted.

Meanwhile, in view of the law's long delay, other measures were taken for the speedier adjustment of the affair by compromise. On the 29th of June, 1587, a public meeting was called at noon immediately after mass on the great square of St. Julien, known as Parloir d'Amont, to which all hinds and habitants (*manantz et habitantz*) were summoned by the ringing of the church bell to consider the propriety and necessity of providing for the said animals a place outside of the vineyards of St. Julien, where they might obtain sufficient sustenance without devouring and devastating the vines of the said commune. This meeting appears to have been held by the advice of the plaintiffs' advocate, François Fay, and at the suggestion of the official. A piece of ground in the vicinity was selected and set apart as a sort of insect enclosure, the inhabitants of St. Julien, however, reserving for themselves the right to pass through the said tract of land, " without prejudice to the pasture of the said animals," and to make use of the springs of water contained therein, which are also to be at the service of the said animals; they reserve furthermore the right of working the mines of ochre and other mineral colours found there, without doing detriment to the means of subsistence of said animals, and finally the right of taking refuge in this spot in time of war or in case of like distress. The place chosen is called La Grand Feisse and described with the exactness of a topographical survey, not only as to its location and dimensions, but also as to the character of its foliage and herbage. The assembled people vote to make this appropriation of land and agree to draw up a conveyance of it "in good form and of perpetual validity," provided the procurator and advocate of the insects may, on visitation and inspection of the ground, express themselves satisfied with such an arrangement; in witness whereof the protocol is signed " L. Prunier, curial," and stamped with the seal of the commune.

But this attempt of the inhabitants to conciliate the insects and to settle their differences by mutual concessions did not put an end to the litigation. On the 24th of July, an " Extract from the Register of the Curiality of St. Julien," containing the proceedings of the public meeting, was submitted to the court by Petremand Bertrand, procurator of the plaintiffs, who called attention to the very generous offer made by the commune and prayed the official to order the grant to be accepted on the conditions specified, and to cause the defendants to vacate the vineyards and to forbid them to return to the same on pain of excommunication. Antoine Filliol, procurator of the insects, requested a copy of the *procès-verbal* and time for deliberation. The court complied with this request and adjourned the case till " the first juridical day after the harvest vacation," which fell on the

11th of August, and again by common consent till the 20th of the same month.

At this time, Charles Emanuel I., Duke of Savoy, was preparing to invade the Marquisate of Saluzzo, and the confusion caused by the expedition of troops over Mt. Cenis interfered with the progress of the trial, which was postponed till the 27th of August, and again, since the passage of armed men was still going on (*actento transitu armigerorum*), till the 3rd of September, when Antoine Filliol declared that he could not accept for his clients the offer made by the plaintiffs, because the place was sterile and neither sufficiently nor suitably supplied with food for the support of the said animals; he demanded, therefore, that the proposal be rejected and the action dismissed with costs to the complainants (*petit agentes repelli cum expensis*). The " egregious Petremand Bertrand," in behalf of the plaintiffs, denies the correctness of this statement and avers that the spot selected and set apart as an abode for the insects is admirably adapted to this purpose, being full of trees and shrubs of divers kinds, as stated in the conveyance prepared by his clients, all of which he is ready to verify. He insists, therefore, upon an adjudication in his favour. The official took the papers of both parties and reserved his decision, appointing experts, who should in the meantime examine the place, which the plaintiffs had proffered as an asylum for the insects, and submit a written report upon the fitness of the same.

The final decision of the case, after such careful deliberation and so long delay, is rendered doubtful by the unfortunate circumstance that the last page of the records has been destroyed by rats or bugs of some sort. Perhaps the prosecuted weevils, not being satisfied with the results of the trial, sent a sharp-toothed delegation into the archives to obliterate and annul the judgment of the court. At least nothing should be thought incredible or impossible in the conduct of creatures, which were deemed worthy of being summoned before ecclesiastical tribunals and which succeeded as criminals in claiming the attention and calling forth the legal learning and acumen of the greatest jurists of their day.

In the margin of the last page are some interesting items of expenses incurred : " *pro visitatione III flor.,*" by which we are to understand three florins to the experts, who were appointed to visit the place assigned to the insects; then " *solverunt scindici Sancti Julliani incluso processu Animalium sigillo ordinationum et pro copia que competat in processu dictorum Animalium omnibus inclusis XVI flor.,*" which may be summed up as sixteen florins for clerical work including seals; finally, " *item pro sportulis domini vicarii III flor.,*" three florins to the vicar, who acted as the bishop's official and did not receive a regular fee, but was not permitted to go

4

away empty-handed. The date, which follows, Dec. 20, 1587, may be assumed to indicate the time at which the trial came to an end, after a pendency of more than eight months. (*Vide* Appendix A.)

In the legal proceedings just described, two points are presented with great clearness and seem to be accepted as incontestable : first, the right of the insects to adequate means of subsistence suited to their nature. This right was recognized by both parties ; even the prosecution did not deny it, but only maintained that they must not trespass cultivated fields and destroy the fruits of man's labour. The complainants were perfectly willing to assign to the weevils an uncultivated tract of ground, where they could feed upon such natural products of the soil as were not due to human toil and tillage. Secondly, no one appears to have doubted for a moment that the Church could, by virtue of its anathema, compel these creatures to stop their ravages and cause them to go from one place to another. Indeed, a firm faith in the existence of this power was the pivot on which the whole procedure turned, and without it, the trial would have been a dismal farce in the eyes of all who took part in it.

It is related in the chronicles of an ancient abbey (*Le Père Rochex: Gloire de l'Abbaye et Vallée de la Novalaise*), that St. Eldrad commanded the snakes, which infested the environs of a priory in the valley of Briançon, to depart, and, taking a staff in his hand, conducted them to a desert place and shut them up in a cave, where they all miserably perished. Perhaps the serpent, which suffered Satan to take possession of its seductive form and thus played such a fatal part in effecting the fall of man and in introducing sin into the world, may have been regarded as completely out of the pale and protection of law, and as having no rights which an ecclesiastical excommunicator or a wonder-working saint would be bound to respect. As a rule, however, such an arbitrary abuse of miraculous power to the injury or destruction of God's creatures was considered illegal and unjustifiable, although irascible anchorites and other holy men under strong provocation often gave way to it. Mediæval jurists frowned upon summary measures of this sort, just as modern lawyers condemn the practice of lynch-law as mobbish and essentially seditious, and only to be excused as a sudden outburst of public indignation at some exceptionally brutal outrage.

Properly speaking, animals cannot be excommunicated, but only anathematized; just as women, according to old English law, having no legal status of their own and not being bound in frankpledge as members of the decennary or tithable community, could not be outlawed, but only " waived " or abandoned. This form of ban, while differing theoretically from actual

outlawry, was practically the same in its effects
upon the individual subjected to it. Excommunication is, as the etymology of the word
implies, the exclusion from the communion of the
Church and from whatever spiritual or temporal
advantages may accrue to a person from this
relation. It is one of the consequences of an
anathema, but is limited in its operation to
members of the ecclesiastical body, to which the
lower animals do not belong. This was the
generally accepted view, and is the opinion maintained by Gaspard Bailly, advocate and coun-
cillor of the Sovereign Senate of Savoy, in his
*Traité des Monitoires, avec un Plaidoyer contre
les Insects,* printed at Lyons in 1668, but it has
not always been held by writers on this subject,
some of whom do not recognize this distinction
between anathema and excommunication on the
authority of many passages of Holy Writ,
affirming that, as the whole creation was corrupted by the fall, so the atonement extends
to all living creatures, which are represented
as longing for the day of their redemption and
regeneration.

One of the strong points made by the counsel
for the defence in prosecutions of this kind was
that these insects were sent to punish man for his
sins, and should therefore be regarded as agents
and emissaries of the Almighty, and that to
attempt to destroy them or to drive them away
would be to fight against God (*s'en prendre à*

Dieu). Under such circumstances, the proper
thing to do would be, not to seek legal redress
and to treat the noxious creatures as criminals,
but to repent and humbly to entreat an angry
Deity to remove the scourge. This is still the
standpoint of Christian orthodoxy, Protestant as
well as Catholic, and the argument applies with
equal force to the impious and atheistic substitu-
tion of Paris green and the chlorate of lime for
prayer and fasting as exterminators of potato-
bugs. The modern, like the mediæval horti-
culturist may ward off devouring vermin from his
garden by the use of ashes, but he strews them
on his plants instead of sprinkling them on his
own head, and thus indicates to what extent
scientific have superseded theological methods in
the practical affairs of life.

Thomas Aquinas, the "angelic doctor," in
his *Summa Theologiæ* raises the query, whether
it is permissible to curse irrational creatures
(*utrum liceat irrationabiles creaturas adjurare*).
He states, in the first place, that curses and bless-
ings can be pronounced only upon such things as
are susceptible of receiving evil or good impres-
sions from them, or in other words, upon sentient
and rational beings, or upon irrational creatures
and insentient things in their relation to rational
beings, so that the latter are the objects ultimately aimed at and favourably or unfavourably
affected. Thus God cursed the earth, because it
is essential to a man's subsistence; Jesus cursed

the barren fig-tree symbolizing the Jews, who
made a great show of leafage in the form of rites
and ceremonies, but bore no fruits of righteousness; Job cursed the day on which he was born,
because he took from his mother's womb the
taint of original sin; David cursed the rocks and
mountains of Gilboa, because they were stained
with the blood of " the beauty of Israel "; in like
manner the Lord sends locusts and blight and
mildew to destroy the harvests, because these are
intimately connected with the happiness of mankind, whose sins he wishes to punish.

It is laid down as a legal maxim by mediæval
jurisprudents that no animal devoid of understanding can commit a fault (*nec enim potest
animal injuriam fecisse quod sensu caret*).   This
doctrine is endorsed by the great theologian and
scholastic Thomas of Aquino.   If we regard the
lower animals, he says, as creatures coming from
the hand of God and employed by him as
agents for the execution of his judgments, then
to curse them would be blasphemous; if, on the
other hand, we curse them *secundem se*, i. e.
merely as brute beasts, then the malediction is
odious and vain and therefore unlawful (*est
odiosum et vanum et per consequens illicitum*).
There is, however, another ground, on which the
right of excommunication or anathematization
may be asserted and fully vindicated, namely,
that the lower animals are satellites of Satan
" instigated by the powers of hell and therefore

proper to be cursed," as the Doctor angelicus puts it. Chassenée refers to this opinion in the treatise already cited (I. § 75), and adds " the anathema then is not to be pronounced against the animals as such, but should be hurled inferentially (*per modum conclusionis*) at the devil, who makes use of irrational creatures to our detriment." This notion seems to have been generally accepted in the Middle Ages, and the fact that evil spirits are often mentioned in the Bible metaphorically or symbolically as animals and assumed to be incarnate in the adder, the asp, the basilisk, the dragon, the lion, the leviathan, the serpent, the scorpion, etc., was considered confirmatory of this view.

But not all animals were regarded as diabolical incarnations; on the contrary, many were revered as embodiments and emblems of divine perfections. In a work entitled *Le Liure du Roy Modus et de la Reyne Racio* (The Book of King Mode and Queen Reason), which, as the colophon records, was " printed at Chambery by Anthony Neyret in the year of grace one thousand four hundred and eighty-six on the thirtieth day of October," King Mode discourses on falconry and venery in general. Queen Reason brings forward, in reply to these rather conventional commonplaces, " several fine moralities," and dilates on the natural and mystic qualities of animals, which she divides into two classes, sweet beasts (*bestes doulces*) and stenchy beasts (*bestes puantes*). Foremost among the sweet beasts stands that which Milton characterizes as

"Goodliest of all the forest, hart and hind."

According to the Psalmist, the hart panting after the water-brooks represents the soul thirsting for the living God and is the type of religious ardour and aspiration. It plays an important part in the legends of saints, acts as their guide, shows them where holy relics are concealed, and causes St. Eustace and St. Hubert to abandon the chase and to lead lives of pious devotion by appearing to them with a luminous cross between its antlers. The ten branches of its horns symbolize the ten commandments of the Old Testament and signify in the Roman ritual the ten fingers of the outstretched hand of the priest as he works the perpetual miracle of transubstantiation of the eucharist.

Chief of the stenchy beasts is the pig. In paganism, which to the Christians was merely devil-worship, the boar was an object of peculiar adoration; for this reason the farrow of the sow is supposed to number seven shotes, corresponding to the seven deadly sins. To the same class of offensive beasts belong the wolf, typical of bad spiritual shepherds, and the fox, which is described as follows : " Reynard is a beast of small size, with red hair, a long bushy tail and an evil physiognomy, for his visage is thin and sharp, his eyes deep-set and piercing, his ears small, straight and pointed; moreover he is deceitful and tricky above all other beasts and exceedingly malicious." " We are all," adds Queen Reason in a moralizing strain, " more or less of the brotherhood of Saint Fausset, whose influence is now-a-days quite extended." Among birds the raven is pre-eminently a malodorous creature and imp of Satan, whereas the dove is a sweet beast and the chosen vessel for the outpouring of the Holy Spirit, the form in which the third person of the Trinity became incarnate.

This division of beasts corresponds in principle to that which is given in the Avesta, and according to which all animals are regarded as belonging either to the good creation of Ahuramazda or to the evil creation of Angrô-mainyush. The world is the scene of perpetual conflict between these hostile forces summed up in the religion and ethics of Zarathushtra as the trinity of the good thought, the good word, and the good deed (*humata, hûkhta, huvarshta*), which are to be fostered in opposition to the evil thought, the evil word, and the evil deed (*dushmata, duzhûkhta, duzhvarshta*), which are to be constantly combated and finally suppressed. Every man is called upon by the Iranian prophet to choose between these contraries; and not only the present and future state of his own soul, the complexion of his individual character, but also the welfare of the whole world, the ultimate destiny of the universe, depend, to no inconsiderable extent, upon his choice. His thoughts, words, and deeds do not cease with the immediate effect which they are intended to produce, but, like force in the physical world, are persistent and indestructible. As the very slightest impulse given to an atom of matter communicates itself to every other atom, and thus disturbs the equilibrium of the globe—the footfall of a child shaking the earth to its centre—so the influence of every human life, however small, contributes to the general increase and ascendency of either good or evil, and helps to determine which of these principles shall ultimately triumph. In the universal strife of these " mighty opposites," the vicious are the allies of the devil; while the virtuous are not merely engaged in working out their own salvation, but have also the ennobling consciousness of being fellow-combatants with the Deity, who needs and appreciates their services in overcoming the adversary. This sense of solidarity with the Best and the Highest imparts additional elevation and peculiar dignity to human aims and actions, and lends to devotion a warmth of sympathy and fervour of enthusiasm springing from personal attachment and loyalty, which it is difficult for the Religion of Humanity to inspire. The fact, too, that evil exists in the world, not by the will and design of the Good Being, but in spite of him, and that all his powers are put forth to eradicate it, while detracting from his omnipotence, frees him from all moral obliquity and exalts his character for benevolence, thus rendering him far more worthy of love and worship and a much better model for human imitation than that " dreadful idealization of wickedness " which is called God in the Calvinistic creed. The idea that the humblest person may, by the purity and rectitude of his life, not only strengthen himself in virtue, but also increase the actual aggregate of goodness in the universe and even endue the Deity with greater power and aggressive energy in subduing and extirpating evil, is surely a sublime thought and a source of lofty inspiration and encouragement in well-doing, although it has been degraded by Parsi Dasturs—as all grand conceptions and ideals are apt to be under priestly influences—into a ridiculous and childish hatred of snakes, scorpions, frogs, lizards, water-rats, and other animals supposed to have been produced by Angrô-mainyush.

Plato held a similar theory of creation, regarding it not as the manifestation of pure benevolence endowed with almighty power, but rather as the expression of perfect goodness working at disadvantage in an intractable material, which by its inherent stubbornness prevented the full embodiment and realization of the original purpose and desire of the Creator or Cosmourgos, who was therefore obliged to content himself with what was, under the circumstances, the only possible, but by no means the best imaginable, world. The Manicheans attributed the same unsatisfactory result to the activity of an evil principle, which thwarted the complete actualization of the designs of the Deity. So conspicuous, indeed, is the defectiveness of nature as a means of promoting the highest conceivable human happiness, so marked and manifold are the causes of suffering in all spheres of sentient existence, and so often do the elements seem to conspire for the destruction of mankind, raging relentlessly like a wild beast

> "Red in tooth and claw
> With ravin,"

that every cosmogony has been compelled to assume the persistent intervention of some malignant spirit or perverse agency as the only rational explanation of such a condition of things. The orthodox Christianity of to-day gives over the earth entirely to the sovereignty of Satan, the successful usurper of Eden, and instead of bidding the righteous to look forward to the final re-enthronement and absolute supremacy of truth and goodness in this world as the

> "One far-off divine event,
> To which the whole creation moves,"

consoles them with the vague promise of compensation in a future state of being. Even this remote prospect of redemption is confined to a select few; not only is the earth destined to be burned with fire on account of its utter corruption, but the great majority of its inhabitants are doomed to eternal torments in the abode of evil spirits.

Scientific research also leads to the same conclusions in respect to the incompleteness of Nature's handiwork, which it is the function of art and culture to amend and improve. Everywhere the correcting hand and contriving brain of man are needed to eliminate the worthless and noxious productions, in which Nature is so fatally prolific, and to foster and develop those that are useful and salutary, thus beautifying and ennobling all forms of vegetable and animal life. By a like process man himself has attained his present pre-eminence. Through long ages of strife and struggle he has emerged from brutishness and barbarism, and rising by a slow, spiral ascent, scarcely perceptible for generations, has been able gradually to

> "Move upward, working out the beast,
> And let the ape and tiger die."

The more man increases in wisdom and intellectual capacity, the more efficient he becomes as a co-worker with the good principle. At the same time, every advance which he makes in civilization brings with it some new evil for him to overcome; or, as the Parsi would express it mythologically, every conquest achieved by Ahuramazda and his allies stimulates Angrô-mainyush and his satellites to renewed exertions, who convert the most useful discoveries, like dynamite, into instruments of diabolical devastation. The opening of the Far West in the United States to agriculture and commerce, and the completion of the Pacific Railroad, not only served to multiply and diffuse the gifts of the beneficent and bountiful spirit (*speñtô mainyush*), but also facilitated the propagation and spread of the plagues of the grasshopper and the Colorado beetle. The power of destruction insidiously concealed in the minutest insect organism often exceeds that of the tornado and the earthquake, and baffles the most persistent efforts of human ingenuity to resist it. The genius and energy of Pasteur were devoted for years to the task of detecting and destroying a microscopic parasite, which threatened to ruin for ever the silk industry of France; and the Phylloxera and Doryphora still continue to ravage with comparative impunity the vineyards of Europe and the potato-fields of America, defying at once all the appliances of science for their extermination and all the attempts of casuistic theology to reconcile such scourges with a perfectly benevolent and omnipotent Creator and Ruler of the Universe. It is the observation of phenomena like these that confirms the modern Parsi in the faith of his fathers, and reveals to him, in the operations of nature and the conflicts of life, unquestionable evidences of a contest between warring elements personified as Hormazd and Ahriman, the ultimate issue of which is to be the complete triumph of the former and the consequent purification and redemption of the world from the curse of evil. The Parsi, however, recognizes no Saviour, and repudiates as absurd and immoral any scheme of atonement whereby the burden of sin can be shifted from the shoulders of the guilty to those of an innocent, vicarious victim. Every person must be redeemed by his own good thoughts, words, and deeds, as creation must be redeemed by the good thoughts, words, and deeds of the race. After death, the character of each individual thus formed appears to him, either in the form of a beautiful and brilliant maiden, who leads him over the Chinvad (or gatherer's) bridge, into the realms of everlasting light, or in the form of a foul harlot, who thrusts him down into regions of eternal gloom.

But to return from this digression; it is not only in the Venidad that certain classes of animals are declared to be creations of the archfiend, and therefore embodiments of devils; additional proofs of this doctrine were derived by mediæval writers from biblical and classical sources. A favourite example was the metamorphosis of Nebuchadnezzar, who, when given over to Satan, dwelt with the beasts of the field and ate grass as oxen, while his hair grew like eagles' feathers and his nails like birds' claws.

Still more numerous and striking instances of
this kind were drawn from pagan mythology,
which, being of diabolical origin, would naturally be prolific of such phenomena. Thus,
besides centaurs and satyrs, " dire chimeras "
and other " delicate monsters," there were
hybrids like the semi-dragon Cecrops and trans-
formations by which Io became a heifer,
Dædalion a sparrow-hawk, Corone a crow,
Actæon a stag, Lyncus a lynx, Mæra a dog,
Calisto a she-bear, Antigone a stork, Arachne a
spider, Iphigenia a roe, Talus a partridge, Itys
a pheasant, Tereus Ascalaphus and Nyctimene
owls, Philomela a nightingale, Progne a
swallow, Cadmus and his spouse Harmonia
snakes, Decertis a fish, Galanthis a weasel, and
the warriors of Diomedes birds, while the companions of Ulysses were changed by Circe, the
prototype of the modern witch, into swine. All
these metamorphoses are adduced as the results
of Satanic agencies and proofs of the tendency of
evil spirits to manifest themselves in bestial
forms.

Towards the end of the ninth century the
region about Rome was visited by a dire plague
of locusts. A reward was offered for their
extermination and the peasants gathered and
destroyed them by millions; but all efforts were
in vain, since they propagated faster than it was
possible to kill them. Finally Pope Stephen
VI. prepared great quantities of holy water and

had the whole country sprinkled with it, whereupon the locusts immediately disappeared. The formula used in consecrating the water and devoting it to this purpose implies the diabolical character of the vermin against which it was directed : " I adjure thee, creature water, I adjure thee by the living God, by Him, who at the beginning separated thee from the dry land, by the true God, who caused thee to fertilize the garden of Eden and parted thee into four heads, by Him, who at the marriage of Cana changed thee into wine, I adjure thee that thou mayst not suffer any imp or phantom to abide in thy substance, that thou mayst be indued with exorcising power and become a source of salvation, so that when thou art sprinkled on the fruits of the field, on vines, on trees, on human habitations in the city or in the country, on stables, or on flocks, or if any one may touch or taste thee, thou shalt become a remedy and a relief from the wiles of Satan, that through thee plagues and pestilence may be driven away, that through contact with thee weevils and caterpillars, locusts and moles may be dispersed and the maliciousness of all visible and invisible powers hostile to man may be brought to nought." In the prayers which follow, the water is entreated to " preserve the fruits of the earth from insects, mice, moles, serpents and other foul spirits."

This subject was treated in a lively and enter-

5

taining manner by a Jesuit priest, Père
Bougeant, in a book entitled *Amusement Philosophique sur le Langage des Bestes,* which was
written in the form of a letter addressed to a
lady and published at Paris in 1739. In the
first place, the author refers to the intelligence
shown by animals and refutes the Cartesian
theory that they are mere machines or animated
automata. This tenet, we may add, was not
original with Descartes, but was set forth at
length by a Spanish physician, Gomez Pereira,
in a bulky Latin volume bearing the queer
dedicatory title : " *Antoniana Margarita opus
nempe physicis, medicis ac theologis non minus
utile quam necessarium,*" and printed in 1554,
nearly a century before the publication of
Descartes' *Meditationes de prima philosophia*
and *Principia philosophiae,* which began a new
epoch in the history of philosophy.

If animals are nothing but ingenious pieces
of mechanism, argues the Jesuit father, then the
feelings of a man towards his dog would not
differ from those which he entertains towards
his watch, and they would both inspire him
with the same kind of affection. But such is
not the case. Even the strictest Cartesian would
never think of petting his chronometer as he
pets his poodle, or would expect the former to
respond to his caresses as the latter does. Practically he subverts his own metaphysical system by
the distinction which he makes between them,

treating one as a machine and the other as a
sentient being, endowed with mental powers
and passions corresponding, in some degree, to
those which he himself possesses. We infer
from our own individual consciousness that
other persons, who act as we do, are free and
intelligent agents, as we claim to be. The
same reasoning applies to the lower animals,
whose manifestations of joy, sorrow, hope, fear,
desire, love, hatred and other emotions, akin
to those passing in our own minds, prove that
there is within them a spiritual principle, which
does not differ essentially from the human soul.

But this conclusion, he adds, is contrary to
the teachings of the Christian religion, since it
involves the immortality of animal souls and
necessitates some provision for their reward or
punishment in a future life. If they are capable
of merits and demerits and can incur praise and
blame, then they are worthy of retribution hereafter and there must be a heaven and a hell
prepared for them, so that the pre-eminence
of a man over a beast as an object of God's
mercy or wrath is lost. " Beasts, in that case,
would be a species of man or men a species
of beast, both of which propositions are incom-
patible with the teachings of religion." The
only means of reconciling these views, endowing
animals with intellectual sense and immortal
souls without running counter to Christian
dogmas, is to assume that they are incarnations
of evil spirits.

Origen held that the scheme of redemption embraced also Satan and his satellites, who would be ultimately converted and restored to their primitive estate. Several patristic theologians endorsed this notion, but the Church rejected it as heretical. The devils are, therefore, from the standpoint of Catholic orthodoxy, irrevocably damned and the blood of Christ has made no atonement for them. But, although their fate is sealed their torments have not yet begun. If a man dies in his sins, his soul, as soon as it departs from his body, receives its sentence and goes straight to hell. The highest ecclesiastical authorities have decided that this is not true of devils, who, although condemned to everlasting fire, do not enter upon their punishment until after the judgment-day. This view is supported by many passages and incidents of Holy Writ. Thus Christ declares that, when the Son of man shall come in his glory, he shall say unto them on his left hand, " Depart from me, ye cursed, into everlasting fire prepared for the devil and his angels." Here it is not stated that the devils are already burning, but that the fire has been " prepared " for them, a form of expression which leads us to infer that they were not yet in it. Again the devils, which Christ drove out of the two " exceeding fierce " demoniacs, protested against such interference, saying, " Art thou come hither to torment us before the time ?" This question has no significance,

unless we suppose that they had a right to
inhabit such living beings as had been assigned
to them, until the time of their torment should
come on the last day. Père Bougeant is
furthermore of the opinion that, when these
devils were sent miraculously and therefore
abnormally into the swine, they came into conflict with the devils already in possession of the
pigs, and thus caused the whole herd to run
violently down a steep place into the sea. Even
a hog, he thinks, could not stand it to harbour
more than one devil at a time, and would be
driven to suicide by having an intrinsic and
superfluous demon conjured into it. A still more
explicit and decisive declaration on this point
is found in the Epistle of Jude and the Second
Epistle of Peter, where it is stated that the angels
which kept not their first estate the Lord hath
reserved in everlasting chains under darkness
unto the judgment of the great day. These
words are to be understood figuratively as
referring to the irrevocableness of their doom
and the durance vile to which they are meanwhile subjected. That they are held in some
sort of temporary custody and are not actually
undergoing, but still awaiting the punishment,
which divine justice has imposed upon them, the
sacred scriptures and the teachings of the Church
leave no manner of doubt.

Now the question arises as to what these
legions of devils are doing in the meantime.

Some of them are engaged in "going to and fro in the earth and walking up and down in it," in order to spy out and take advantage of human infirmities. God himself makes use of them to test the fealty of men and their power of holding fast to their integrity under severe temptations, just as the Creator made fossils and concealed them in the different strata of the earth, in order to see whether Christian faith in the truth of revelation would be strong enough to resist the seductions of "science falsely so called." Other devils enter into living human bodies and give themselves up to evil enchantments as wizards and witches; others still reanimate corpses or assume the form and features of the dead and wander about as ghosts and hobgoblins. Not only were pagans regarded by the Christian Church as devil-worshippers and exorcised before being baptized, but it is also a logical deduction from the doctrine of original sin, that a devil takes possession of every child as soon as it is born and remains there until expelled by an ecclesiastical functionary, who combines the office of priest with that of conjurer and is especially appointed for this purpose. Hence arose the necessity of abrenunciation, as it was called, which preceded baptism in the Catholic Church and which Luther and the Anglican reformers retained. Before the candidate was christened he was exorcised and adjured personally, if an adult, or through a sponsor, if an infant, to " forsake the devil and all his works." These words, which still hold a place in the ritual, but are now repeated in a perfunctory manner by persons, who have no conception of the magic potency formerly ascribed to them, are a survival of the old formula of exorcism. In the seventeenth century there was a keen competition between the Roman Catholic and the Lutheran clergy in casting out devils, the former claiming that to them alone had been transmitted the exorcising power conferred by Christ upon his apostles. The Protestant churches finally gave up the hocus-pocus and during the eighteenth century it fell into general discredit and disuse among them, although some of the stiffest and most conservative Lutherans never really abandoned it in principle and have recently endeavoured to revive it in practice.

The Catholic Church, on the contrary, still holds that men, women and cattle may be possessed by devils and prescribes the means of their expulsion. In a work entitled *Rituale ecclesiasticum ad usum clericorum S. Fransisci* by Pater Franz Xaver Lohbauer (Munich, 1851), there is a chapter on the mode of helping those who are afflicted by demons (*Modus juvandi afflictos a daemone*). The author maintains that nearly all so-called nervous diseases, hysteria, epilepsy, insanity, and milder forms of mental alienation, are either the direct result of diabolical agencies or attended and greatly aggravated by them. A sound mind in a sound body may make a man devil-proof, but Satan is quick to take advantage of his infirmities in order to get possession of his person. The adversary is constantly lying in wait watching for and trying to produce physical derangements as breaches in the wall, through which he may rush in and capture the citadel of the soul. In all cases of this sort the priest is to be called in with the physician, and the medicines are to be blessed and sprinkled with holy water before being administered. Exorcisms and conjurations are not only to be spoken over the patient, but also to be written on slips of consecrated paper and applied, like a plaster, to the parts especially affected. The physician should keep himself supplied with these written exorcisms, to be used when it is impossible for a priest to be present. As with patent medicines, the public is warned against counterfeits, and no exorcism is genuine unless it is stamped with the seal and bears the signature of the bishop of the diocese. According to Father Lohbauer, the demon is the efficient cause of the malady, and there can be no cure until the evil one is cast out. This is the office of the priest; the physician then heals the physical disorder, repairing the damage done to the body, and, as it were, stopping the gaps with his drugs so as to prevent the demon from getting in again. Thus science and religion are reconciled and work together harmoniously for the healing of mankind.

The Catholic Church has a general form of *Benedictio a daemone vexatorum*, for the relief of those vexed by demons; and Pope Leo XIII., who was justly esteemed as a man of more than ordinary intelligence and more thoroughly imbued with the modern spirit than any of his predecessors, composed and issued, November 19, 1890, a formula of *Exorcismus in Satanam et Angelos Apostatas* worthy of a place in any mediæval collection of conjurations. His Holiness never failed to repeat this exorcism in his daily prayers, and commended it to the bishops and other clergy as a potent means of warding off the assaults of Satan and of casting out devils. In 1849 the Bishop of Passau published a *Manuale Benedictionum,* and as late as 1893 Dr. Theobald Bischofberger described and defended the practice of the papal see, in this respect, in a brochure printed in Stuttgart and entitled *Die Verwaltung des Exorcistats nach Massgabe der römischen Benediktionale.*

That these formulas are still deemed highly efficacious is evident from the many recent cases in which they have been employed. Thus in 1842 a devil named Ro-ro-ro-ro took possession of " a maiden of angelic beauty " in Luxemburg and was cast out by Bishop Laurentius. This demon claimed to be one of the archangels expelled from heaven, and appears to have rivalled Parson Stöcker and Rector Ahlwardt in Anti-semitic animosity; when the name of Jesus was mentioned, he cried out derisively: "O, that Jew! Didn't he have to drink gall?" When commanded to depart, he begged that he might go into some Jew. The bishop, however, refused to give him leave and bade him "go to hell," which he forthwith did, "moaning as he went, in melancholy tones, that seemed to issue from the bowels of the earth, 'Burning, burning, everlastingly burning in hell!' The voice was so sad," adds the bishop, "that we should have wept for sheer compassion, had we not known that it was the devil."

Again, a lay brother connected with an educational institute in Rome became diabolically possessed on January 3, 1887, and was exorcised by Father Jordan. In this instance the leading spirit was Lucifer himself, attended by a host of satellites, of whom Lignifex, Latibor, Monitor, Ritu, Sefilie, Shulium, Haijunikel, Exaltor, and Reromfex were the most important. It took about an hour and a half to cast out these demons the first time, but they renewed their assaults on February 10th, 11th, and 17th, and were not completely discomfited and driven back into the infernal regions until February 23rd, and then only by using the water of Lourdes, which, as Father Jordan states, acted upon them like poison, causing them to writhe to and fro. Lucifer was especially rude and saucy in his remarks. Thus, for example, when Father Jordan said, "Every knee in heaven and on the

earth shall bow to the name of Jesus," the fallen
" Son of the Morning " retorted, " Not Luci,
not Luci—never !''

It would be easy to multiply authentic reports
of things of this sort that have happened within
the memory of the present generation, such as
the exorcism of a woman of twenty-seven at Laas
in the Tyrol in the spring of 1892, and the expulsion of an evil spirit from a boy ten years of age
at Wemding in Bavaria by a capuchin, Father
Aurelian, July 13th and 14th, 1891, with the
sanction of the bishops of Augsburg and Eich-
stätt. In the latter case we have a circumstantial
account of the affair by the exorcist himself, who,
in conclusion, uses the following strong language : " Whosoever denies demoniacal possession in our days confesses thereby that he has
gone astray from the teaching of the Catholic
Church ; but he will believe in it when he himself
is in the possession of the devil in hell. As for
myself I have the authority of two bishops." In
a pamphlet on this subject printed at Munich in
1892, and entitled *Die Teufelsaustreibung in
Wemding,* the author, Richard Treufels, takes
the same view, declaring that diabolical possession " is an incontestable fact, confirmed by the
traditions of all nations of ancient and modern
times, by the unequivocal testimony of the Old
and New Testaments, and by the teaching and
practice of the Catholic Church." Christ, he
says, gave his disciples power and authority

over all devils to cast them out, and the same power is divinely conferred upon every priest by his consecration, although it is never to be exercised without the permission of his bishop.

Doubtless modern science by investigating the laws and forces of nature is gradually diminishing the realm of superstition; but there are vast low-lying plains of humanity that have not yet felt its enlightening and elevating influence. It has been estimated that nine-tenths of the rural population of Europe and ninety-nine hundredths of the peasantry, living in the vicinity of a cloister and darkened by its shadow, believe in the reality of diabolical possession and attribute most maladies of men and murrain in cattle to the direct agency of Satan, putting their faith in the " metaphysical aid " of the conjurer rather than in medical advice and veterinary skill.

Unfortunately this belief is not confined to Catholics and boors, but is held by Protestants, who are considered persons of education and superior culture. Dr. Lyman Abbott asserted in a sermon preached in Plymouth Church, that " what we call the impulses of our lower nature are the whispered suggestions of fiend-like natures, watching for our fall and exultant if they can accomplish it." But while affirming that " evil spirits exercise an influence over mankind," and that cranks like Guiteau, the assassin of President Garfield, are diabolically possessed, the reverend divine would hardly risk his reputation for sanity by attempting to exorcise the supposed demon. The Catholic priest holds the same view, but has the courage of his convictions and goes solemnly to work with bell, book and candle to effect the expulsion of the indwelling fiend.

The fact that such methods of healing are sometimes successful is adduced as conclusive proof of their miraculous character; but this inference is wholly incorrect. Professor Dr. Hoppe, in an essay on *Der Teufels- und Geisterglaube und die psychologische Erklärung des Besessenseins* (*Allgemeine Zeitschrift für Psychiatrie*, Bd. LV. p. 290), gives a psychological explanation of these puzzling phenomena. "The priest," he says, "exerts a salutary influence upon the brain through the respect and dignity which he inspires, just as Christ in his day wrought upon those who were sick and possessed with devils." Indeed, it is expressly stated by the evangelist that Jesus did not attempt to do wonderful works among people who did not believe. According to this theory the exorcism effects a cure by its powerful action on the imagination, just as there are frequent ailments, for which a wise physician administers bread pills and a weak solution of powdered sugar as the safest and best medicaments. Professor Hoppe, therefore, approves of "priestly conjurations for the expulsion of devils as a psychical means of healing," and thinks that the more ceremoniously the rite can be performed in the presence of grave and venerable witnesses, the more effective it will be. This opinion is endorsed by a Catholic priest, Friedrich Jaskowski, in a pamphlet entitled *Der Trierer Rock und seine Patienten vom Jahre* 1891 (Saarbrücken : Carl Schmidtke, 1894). The author belongs to the diocese of Trier and is therefore under the jurisdiction of the bishop, Dr. Felix Korum, whose statements concerning the miracles wrought and the evidences of divine mercy manifested during the exhibition of the " holy coat " in 1891 he courageously reviews and conclusively refutes. The bishop had printed what he called " documentary proofs," consisting of certificates issued by obscure curates and country doctors, that certain persons suffering chiefly from diseases of the nervous system had been healed, and sought to discover in these cures the working of divine agencies. Jaskowski shows that in several instances the persons said to have found relief died shortly afterwards, and maintains that where cures actually occurred they " were not due to a miracle or any direct interference of God with the established order of things, but happened in a purely natural manner." He quotes the late Professor Charcot, Dr. Forel, and other neuropathologists to establish the fact that hetero-suggestion emanating from a physician or priest, or auto-suggestion originating in the person's own mind, may often be the most effective remedy for neurotic disorders of every kind. In auto-suggestion the patient is possessed with the fixed idea that the doing of a certain thing, which may be in itself absolutely indifferent, will afford relief. As an example of this faith-cure Jaskowski refers to the woman who was diseased with an issue of blood, and approaching Jesus said within herself: "If I may but touch his garment, I shall be whole." This is precisely the position taken by Jesus himself, who turned to the woman and said: "Daughter, be of good comfort; thy faith hath made thee whole." Jaskowski also quotes the declaration of the evangelist referred to above, that in a certain place the people's lack of faith prevented Jesus from doing many wondrous works, and does not deny that on this principle, which is now recognized by the most eminent physicians, some few of the hundreds of pilgrims may have been restored to health by touching the holy coat of Trier; and there is no doubt that the popular belief in Bishop Korum's assertion that it is the same garment which Jesus wore and the woman touched, would greatly increase its healing efficacy through the force of auto-suggestion (see my article on "Recent Recrudescence of Superstition" in Appleton's *Popular Science Monthly* for Oct. 1895, pp. 762–66).

The Bishop of Bamberg in Bavaria has been stigmatized as a hypocrite because he sends the

infirm of his flock on a pilgrimage to Lourdes or
Laas or some other holy shrine, while he prefers
for himself the profane waters of Karlsbad or
Kissingen. But in so doing he is not guilty of
any inconsistency, since a journey to sacred
places and contact with sacred relics would not
act upon him with the same force as upon the
ignorant and superstitious masses of his diocese.
His conduct only evinces his disbelief in the
supernatural character of the remedies he
prescribes. The distinguished French physician,
Professor Charcot, as already mentioned, recognized the curative power of faith under certain
circumstances, and occasionally found it eminently successful in hysterical and other purely
nervous affections. In some cases he did not
hesitate to prescribe a pilgrimage to the shrine
of any saint for whom the patient may have had
a peculiar reverence; but in no instance in his
experience did faith or exorcism or hagiolatry
heal an organic disease, set a dislocated joint or
restore an amputated limb. What Falstaff says
of honour is equally true of faith, it " hath no
skill in surgery."

But to return from this digression, Père
Bougeant's theory of the diabolical possession of
pagans and unbaptized persons would provide
for comparatively few devils, and the gradual
diffusion of Christianity would constantly
diminish the supply of human beings available
as their proper habitations. The ultimate con-

version of the whole world and the custom of baptizing infants as soon as they are born would, therefore, produce serious domiciliary destitution and distress among the evil spirits and set immense numbers of them hopelessly adrift as vagabonds, and thus create an extremely undesirable diabolical proletariat. This difficulty is avoided by assuming that the vast majority of devils are incarnate in the billions of beasts of all kinds, which dwell upon the earth or fly in the air or fill the waters of the rivers and the seas. This hypothesis, he adds, "enables me to ascribe to the lower animals thought, knowledge, feeling, and a spiritual principle or soul without running counter to the truths of religion. Indeed, so far from being astonished at their manifestations of intelligence, foresight, memory and reason, I am rather surprised that they do not display these qualities in a higher degree, since their soul is probably far more perfect than ours. Their defects are, as I have discovered, owing to the fact that in brute as in us, the mind works through material organs, and inasmuch as these organs are grosser and less perfect in the lower animals than in man, it follows that their exhibitions of intelligence, their thoughts and all their mental operations must be less perfect; and, if these proud spirits are conscious of their condition, how humiliating it must be for them to see themselves thus embruted! Whether they are conscious of it or not, this deep degradation is

6

the first act of God's vengeance executed on his
foes. It is a foretaste of hell.''

Only by such an assumption, as our author
proceeds to show, is it possible to justify the
ways of man to the lower animals and to reconcile his cruel treatment of them with the goodness
of an all-wise and all-powerful maker and ruler
of the universe. For this reason, he goes on to
explain, the Christian Church has never deemed
it a duty to take the lower animals under its protection or to inculcate ordinary natural kindness
towards them. Hence in countries, like Italy and
Spain, where the influence of Catholicism has
been supreme for centuries, not only are wild
birds and beasts of chase relentlessly slaughtered
and exterminated, but even useful domestic
animals, asses, sumpter-mules and pack-horses,
are subjected to a supererogation of suffering at
the hands of ruthless man. As the pious Parsi
conscientiously comes up to the help of Ahuramazda against the malevolent Angrô-mainyush by
killing as many as possible of the creatures
which the latter has made, so the good Catholic
becomes an efficient co-worker with God by mal-
treating brutes and thus aiding the Almighty in
punishing the devils, of which they are the
visible and bruisable forms. Whatever pain is
inflicted is felt, not by the physical organism,
but by the animated spirit. It is the embodied
demon that really suffers, howling in the beaten
dog and squealing in the butchered pig.

There are doubtless many persons of tender
susceptibilities, who cannot bear to think that the
animals, whose daily companionship we enjoy,
the parrot we feed with sugar, the pretty pug we
caress and the noble horse, which ministers to
our comfort and convenience, are nothing but
devils predestined to everlasting torture. But
these purely sentimental considerations are of no
weight in the scale of reason. " What matters
it," replies the Jesuit Father, " whether it is a
devil or another kind of creature that is in our
service or contributes to our amusement? For
my part, this idea pleases rather than repels me;
and I recognize with gratitude the beneficence of
the Creator in having provided me with so many
little devils for my use and entertainment. If it
be said that these poor creatures, which we have
learned to love and so fondly cherish, are fore-
ordained to eternal torments, I can only adore
the decrees of God, but do not hold myself
responsible for the terrible sentence; I leave the
execution of the dread decision to the sovereign
judge and continue to live with my little devils,
as I live pleasantly with a multitude of persons,
of whom, according to the teachings of our holy
religion, the great majority will be damned."
The crafty disciple of Loyola, elusive of dis-
agreeable deductions, is content to accept the
poodle in its phenomenal form and to make the
most of it, without troubling himself about " des
Pudels Kern."

This doctrine, he thinks, is amply illustrated and confirmed by an appeal to the consentient opinion of mankind or the argument from universal belief, which has been so often and so effectively urged in proof of the existence of God. If the maxim *universitas non delinquit* has the same validity in the province of philosophy as in that of law, then we are justified in assuming that the whole human race cannot go wrong even in purely metaphysical speculation and that unanimity in error is a psychological impossibility. The criterion of truth, *quod semper, quod ubique, quod ab omnibus,* by which the Roman hierarchy is willing to have its claims to ecclesiastical catholicity and doctrinal orthodoxy tested, is confined to Christendom in its application and does not consider the views of persons outside of the body of believers. In the question under discussion the argument is not subject to such limitations, but gathers testimony from all races and religions, showing that there is not a civilized nation or savage tribe on the face of the earth, which does not regard or has not regarded the lower animals as embodiments of evil spirits and sought to propitiate them. That " the devil is an ass " is a truth so palpable that it has passed into a proverb. Baal-zebub means fly-god; and the Christian Satan betrays his presence by the cloven foot of the goat or the solid hoof of the horse. In folk-lore, which is the *débris* of exploded mythologies adrift on the stream of popular tradition, cats, dogs, otters, apes, ravens, blackcocks, capercailzies, rabbits, hedgehogs, wolves, were-wolves, foxes, pole-cats, swine, serpents, toads, and countless varieties of insects, reptiles and vermin figure as incarnations and instruments of the devil; and Mephistopheles reveals himself to Faust as

> "Der Herr der Ratten und der Mäuse,
> Der Fliegen, Frösche, Wanzen, Läuse."

> "The Lord of rats and of the mice,
> Of flies and frogs, bed-bugs and lice."

The worship of animals originates in the belief that they are embodiments of devils, so that zoölatry, which holds such a prominent place in primitive religions, is only a specific form of demonolatry. The objection that a flea or a fly, a mite or a mosquito is too small a creature to furnish fit lodgment for a demon, Father Bougeant dismisses with an indulgent smile and disparaging shrug as implying a gross misconception of the nature and properties of spirit, which is without extension or dimension and therefore capable of animating the most diminutive particle of organized matter. Large and little are purely relative terms. God, he says, could have made man as small as the tiniest puceron without any decrease of his spiritual powers. "It is, therefore, no more difficult to believe that a devil may be incorporated in the delicate body of a gnat than in the huge bulk of

an elephant.'' The size of the physical habitation, in which spirits take up their temporary
abode, is a thing of no consequence. In fact,
devils in the forms of gnats and tiny insects were
thought to be especially dangerous, since one
might swallow them unawares and thus become
diabolically possessed. The demon, liberated by
the death and dissolution of the insect, was supposed to make a tenement of the unfortunate
person's stomach, producing gripes and playing
ventriloquous tricks. Thus it is recorded in the
Dies Caniculuares of Majolus (Meyer : *Der
Aberglaube des Mittelalters,* p. 296–7) that a
young maiden in the Erzgebirge near Joachims-
thal, in 1559, swallowed a fly, while drinking
beer. The evil spirit, incarnate in the fly, took
possession of the maiden and began to speak out
of her, thus attracting crowds of people, who put
questions to the devil and tried to drive him out
by prayers, in which the unhappy girl sometimes
joined, greatly to her discomfort, since the devil
waxed exceeding wroth and unruly and caused
her much suffering, whenever she uttered the
name of Christ. Finally the parish priest had
her brought into the church, where he succeeded
with considerable difficulty in exorcising her.
The stubborn demon resisted for two years all
efforts to cast him out; he even tried to compromise with the girl, promising to be content
with a finger nail or a single hair of her head,
but she declined all overtures, and he was at last

expelled by means of a potent conjuration, which lasted from midnight till midday.

As the human soul is released by death, so the extinction of life in any animal sets its devil free, who, instead of entering upon a spiritual state of existence, goes into the egg or embryo of another animal and resumes his penal bondage to the flesh. " Thus a devil, after having been a cat or a goat, may pass, not by choice, but by constraint, into the embryo of a bird, a fish or a butterfly. Happy are those who make a lucky hit and become household pets, instead of beasts of burden or of slaughter. The lottery of destiny bars them the right of voluntary choosing." The doctrine of transmigration, continues our author, " which Pythagoras taught of yore and some Indian sages hold to-day, is untenable in its application to men and contrary to religion, but it fits admirably into the system already set forth concerning the nature of beasts, and shocks neither our faith nor our reason." Furthermore, it explains why " all species of animals produce many more eggs or embryos than are necessary to propagate their kind and to provide for a normal increase." Of the millions of germs, of which " great creating nature " is so prolific, comparatively few ever develop into living creatures; only those which are vivified by a devil are evolved into complete organisms; the others perish. This seeming superfluity and waste can be most easily reconciled with the careful economy and wise frugality of nature by viewing it as a manifestation of the bountiful and beneficent providence of God in preventing " any lack of occupation or abode on the part of the devils," which are being constantly dis-embodied and re-embodied. "This accounts for the prodigious clouds of locusts and countless hosts of caterpillars, which suddenly desolate our fields and gardens. The cause of these astonishing multiplications has been sought in cold, heat, rain and wind, but the real reason is that, at the time of their appearance, extraordinary quantities of animals have died or their embryos been destroyed, so that the devils that animated them were compelled to avail themselves at once of whatever species they found most ready to receive them, which would naturally be the superabundant eggs of insects." The more profoundly this subject is investigated, he concludes, and the more light our observations and researches throw upon it from all sides, the more probable does the hypothesis here suggested in explanation of the puzzling phenomena of animal life and intelligence appear.

Father Bougeant calls his lucubration " a new system of philosophy "; but this is not strictly true. He has only given a fuller and more facetious exposition of a doctrine taught by many of the greatest lights of the Catholic Church, among others by Thomas Aquinas, whose authority as a thinker Pope Leo XIII.

distinctly recognized and earnestly sought to
restore to its former prestige. Bougeant's ingenious dissertation has a vein of irony or at
least a strain of jocundity in it, approaching at
times so perilously near the fatal brink of persi-
flage, that one cannot help surmising an intention to render the whole thing ridiculous in a
witty and underhand way eminently compatible
with Jesuitical habits of mind; but whether serious or satirical, his treatise is an excellent
example and illustration of the kind of dialectic
hair-splitting and syllogistic rubbish, which
passed for reasoning in the early and middle
ages of the Christian era, and which the greatest
scholars and acutest intellects of those days
fondly indulged in and seem to have been fully
satisfied with. Here, too, we come upon the
metaphysical and theological groundwork, upon
which was reared by a strictly logical process a
vast superstructure of ecclesiastical excommunication and criminal prosecution against bugs and
beasts. He protests with never-tiring and need-
less iteration his absolute devotion to the pre-
cepts of religion; indeed, like the lady in the
play, he " protests too much, methinks." In all
humbleness and submission he bows to the
authority of the Church, and would not touch the
ark of the covenant even with the tip of his
finger, but his easy acquiescence has an air of
perfunctoriness, and in his assenting lips there
lurks a secret, semi-sarcastic leer, which casts

suspicion on his words and looks like poking fun at the principles he professes and turning them into raillery.

Indeed, such covert derision would have been a suitable way of ridiculing the gross popular superstition of his time, which saw a diabolical incarnation in every unfamiliar form of animal life. During the latter half of the sixteenth century a Swiss naturalist named Thurneysser, who held the position of physician in ordinary to the Elector Johann Georg von Brandenburg, kept some scorpions bottled in olive oil, which were feared by the common people as terrible devils endowed with magic power (*fürchterliche Zauberteufel*). Thurneysser presented also to Basel, his native city, a large elk, which had been given to him by Prince Radziwil; but the good Baselers looked upon the strange animal as a most dangerous demon, and a pious old woman finally rid the town of the dreaded beast by feeding it with an apple stuck full of broken needles.

A distinguished Spanish theologian of the sixteenth century, Martin Azpilcueta, commonly known as Dr. Navarre, refers, in his work on excommunication, to a case in which anathemas were fulminated against certain large sea-creatures called terones, which infested the waters of Sorrento and destroyed the nets of the fishermen. He speaks of them as "fish or cacodemons" (*pisces seu cacodemones*), and maintains that they are subject to anathematization, not as fish, but only as devils. In his Five Counsels and other tractates on this subject (Opera, Lyons, 1589; reprinted at Venice, 1601–2, and at Cologne, 1616) he often takes issue with Chassenée on minor points, but the French jurist and the Spanish divine agree on the main question.

In this connection it may be a matter of interest to add, that a German neuropathologist of our own day, Herr von Bodelschwingh, ascribes epilepsy to what he calls " demonic infection " due to the presence of the *bacillus infernalis* in the blood of those who are subject to this disease. The microbe, to which the jocose scientist has been pleased to give this name, differs from all other bacilli hitherto discovered in having two horns and a tail, although the most powerful lenses have not yet revealed any traces of a cloven foot. An additional indication of its infernal qualities is the fact that it liquefies the gelatine, with which it comes in contact, and turns it black, emitting at the same time a pestilential stench. Doubtless this discovery will be hailed by theologians as a striking confirmation of divine revelation by modern science, proving that our forefathers were right in attributing the falling-sickness to diabolical agencies. We know now that it was a legion of *bacilli infernales* which went out of the tomb-haunting man into the Gadarene swine and drove them tumultuously over a precipice into the sea. In fact, who can tell what microbes really are! Père Bougeant would certainly have regarded them as nothing less than microscopic devils.

The Savoyan jurist, Gaspard Bailly, in the second part of the disquisition entitled *Traité des Monitoires,* already mentioned, treats " Of the Excellence of Monitories " and discusses the main points touching the criminal prosecution and punishment of insects. He begins by saying that " one should not contemn monitories (a general term for anathemas, bans and excommunications), seeing that they are matters of great importance, inasmuch as they bear with them the deadliest sword, wielded by our holy mother, the Church, to wit, the power of excommunication, which cutteth the dry wood and the green, sparing neither the quick nor the dead, and smiting not only rational beings, but turning its edge also against irrational creatures; since it hath been shown at sundry times and in divers places, that worms and insects, which were devouring the fruits of the earth, have been excommunicated and, in obedience to the commands of the Church, have withdrawn from the cultivated fields to the places prescribed by the bishop who had been appointed to adjudge and to adjure them."

M. Bailly then cites numerous instances of this kind, in which a writer on logic would find ample illustrations of the fallacy known as *post hoc,*

ergo propter hoc. Thus in the latter half of the
fifteenth century, during the reign of Charles the
Bold, Duke of Burgundy, a plague of locusts
threatened the province of Mantua in Northern
Italy with famine, but were dispersed by excommunication. He quotes some florid lines from
the poet Altiat descriptive of these devastating
swarms, which " came, after so many other woes,
under the leadership of Eurus (*i. e.* brought by
the east wind), more destructive than the hordes
of Attila or the camps of Corsicans, devouring
the hay, the millet and the corn, and leaving only
vain wishes, where the hopes of August stood."
Again in 1541, a cloud of locusts fell upon
Lombardy, and by destroying the crops, caused
many persons to perish with hunger. These
insects " were as long as a man's finger, with
large heads and bellies filled with vileness; and
when dead they infected the air and gave forth
a stench, which even carrion kites and carnivor-
ous beasts could not endure." Another instance
is given, in which swarms of four-winged insects
came from Tartary, identified in the popular
mind with Tartarus, obscuring the sun in their
flight and covering the plains of Poland a cubit
deep. In the year 1338, on St. Bartholomew's
Day, these creatures began to devastate the
region round Botzen in the Tyrol, consuming
the crops and laying eggs and leaving a numerous progeny, which seemed destined to continue
the work of destruction indefinitely. A prosecu-

tion was therefore instituted against them before the ecclesiastical court at Kaltern, a large market-town about ten miles south of Botzen, then as now famous for its wines, and the parish priest instructed to proceed against them with the sentence of excommunication in accordance with the verdict of the tribunal.   This he did by the solemn ceremony of " inch of candle," and anathematized them " in the name of the Blessed Trinity, Father, Son and Holy Ghost." Owing to the sins of the people and their remissness in the matter of tithes the devouring insects resisted for a time the power of the Church, but finally disappeared. Under the reign of Lotharius II., early in the twelfth century, enormous quantities of locusts, " having six wings with two teeth harder than flint " and " darkening the sky and whitening the air like a snowstorm," laid waste the most fertile provinces of France.   Many of them perished in the rivers and the sea, and being washed ashore sent forth a putrescent smell and produced a fearful pestilence. Precisely the same phenomenon, with like disastrous results, is described by St. Augustine in the last book of *De Civitate Dei* as having occurred in Africa and caused the death of 800,000 persons.

In the majority of cases adduced there is no evidence that the Church intervened at all with its fulminations, and, even when the anathema was pronounced, the insects appear to have departed of their own free-will after having eaten up every green thing and reduced the inhabitants to the verge of starvation; and yet M. Bailly, supposed to be a man of judicial mind, disciplined by study, accustomed to reason and to know what sound reasoning is, goes on giving accounts of such scourges, as though they proved in some mysterious way the effectiveness of ecclesiastical excommunications and formed a cumulative argument in support of such claims.

The most important portion of M. Bailly's work is that in which he shows how actions of this kind should be brought and conducted, with specimens of plaints, pleas, replications, rejoinders, and decisions. First in order comes the petition of the inhabitants seeking redress (*requeste des habitans*), which is followed in regular succession by the declaration or plea of the inhabitants (*plaidoyer des habitans*), the defensive allegation or plea for the insects (*plaidoyer pour les insectes*), the replication of the inhabitants (*réplique des habitans*), the rejoinder of the defendant (*réplique du defendeur*), the conclusions of the bishop's proctor (*conclusions du procureur episcopal*), and the sentence of the ecclesiastical judge (*sentence du juge d'église*), which is solemnly pronounced in Latin. The pleadings on both sides are delivered in French and richly interlarded with classical allusions and Latin quotations, being even more heavily weighted with the spoils of erudition than the set speech of a member of the British Parliament.

The following abridgment of the plea, in which the prosecuting attorney sets forth the cause of complaint, is a fair specimen of the forensic eloquence displayed on such occasions :

" Gentlemen, these poor people on their knees and with tearful eyes, appeal to your sense of justice, as the inhabitants of the islands Majorica and Minorica formerly sent an embassy to Augustus Cæsar, praying him for a cohort of soldiers to exterminate the rabbits, which were burrowing in their fields and consuming their crops. In the power of excommunication you have a weapon more effective than any wielded by that emperor to save these poor suppliants from impending famine produced by the ravages of little beasts, which spare neither the corn nor the vines, ravages like those of the boar that laid waste the environs of Calydon, as related by Homer in the first book of the *Iliad,* or those of the foxes sent by Themis to Thebes, which destroyed the fruits of the earth and the cattle and assailed even the husbandmen themselves. You know how great are the evils which famine brings with it, and you have too much kindness and compassion to permit my clients to be involved in such distress, thus constraining them to perpetrate cruel and unlawful deeds; *nec enim rationem patitur, nec ulla aequitate mitigatur, nec prece ulla flectitur esuriens populus:* for a starving people is not amenable to reason, nor tempered by equity, nor moved by any prayer. Witness the mothers,

of whom it is recorded in the Fourth Book of
the Kings, that they ate their own children, the
one saying to the other : ' Give thy son that we
may eat him to-day, and we will eat my son to-
morrow.' '' The advocate then discourses at
length of the horrors of hunger and its disastrous effects upon the individual and the community, lugging in what Milton calls a '' horse-
load of citations '' from Arianus Marcellinus,
Ovid and other Latin prosaists and poets, intro-
duces an utterly irrelevant allusion to Joshua
and the crafty Gibeonites, and concludes as
follows : '' The full reports received as the result
of an examination of the fields, made at your
command, suffice for your information concerning the damage done by these animals. It
remains, therefore, after complying with the
usual forms, only to adjudicate upon the case in
accordance with the facts stated in the Petition
of the Plaintiffs, which is right and reasonable,
and, to this effect, to enjoin these animals from
continuing their devastations, ordering them to
quit the aforesaid fields and to withdraw to the
place assigned them, pronouncing the necessary
anathemas and execrations prescribed by our
Holy Mother, the Church, for which your peti-
tioners do ever pray.''

It is doubtful whether any speaking for Bun-
combe in the halls of Congress or any spouting
of an ignorant bumpkin in the moot-court of an
American law-school ever produced such a

7

rhetorical hotchpotch of "matter and impertinency mixed" as the earnest plea, of which the above is a brief abstract.

Rather more to the point, but equally overburdened with legal lore and literary pedantry, is the rejoinder of the counsel for the insects:

"Gentlemen, inasmuch as you have chosen me to defend these little beasts (*bestioles*), I shall, an it please you, endeavour to right them and to show that the manner of proceeding against them is invalid and void. I confess that I am greatly astonished at the treatment they have been subjected to and at the charges brought against them, as though they had committed some crime. Thus information has been procured touching the damage said to have been done by them; they have been summoned to appear before this court to answer for their conduct, and, since they are notoriously dumb, the judge, wishing that they should not suffer wrong on account of this defect, has appointed an advocate to speak in their behalf and to set forth in conformity with right and justice the reasons, which they themselves are unable to allege.

"Since you have permitted me to appear in defence of these poor animals, I will state, in the first place, that the summons served on them is null and void, having been issued against beasts, which cannot and ought not to be cited before this judgment seat, inasmuch as such a procedure implies that the parties summoned are endowed with reason and volition and are therefore capable of committing crime. That this is not the case with these creatures is clear from the paragraph *Si quadrupes,* etc., in the first book of the Pandects, where we find these words : *Nec enim potest animal injuriam fecisse, quod sensu caret.*

" The second ground, on which I base the defence of my clients, is that no one can be judicially summoned without cause, and whoever has had such a summons served renders himself liable to the penalty prescribed by the statute *De poen. tem. litig.* As regards these animals there is no *causa justa litigandi;* they are not bound in any manner, *non tenentur ex contractu,* being incompetent to make contracts or to enter into any compact or covenant whatsoever, *neque ex quasi contractu, neque ex stipulatione, neque ex pacto,* and still less *ex delicto seu quasi,* can there be any question of a delict or any semblance thereof, since, as has just been shown, the rational faculties essential to the capability of committing criminal actions are wanting.

" Furthermore, it is illicit to do that which is nugatory and of non-effect (*qui ne porte coup*); in this respect justice is like nature, which, as the philosopher affirms, does nothing *mal à propos* or in vain : *Deus enim et Natura nihil operantur frustra.* Now I leave it to you to decide whether anything could be more futile than to summon these irrational creatures, which can neither speak for themselves, nor appoint proxies to defend their cause; still less are they able to present memorials stating grounds of their justification. If then, as I have shown, the summons, which is the basis of all judicial action, is null and void, the proceedings dependent upon it will not be able to stand : *cum enim principalis causa non consistat, neque ea quae consequuntur locum habent."*

The counsel for the defence rests his argument, of which the extract just given may suffice as a sample, upon the irrationality and consequent irresponsibility of his clients. For this reason he maintains that the judge cannot appoint a procurator to represent them, and cites legal authorities to show that the incompetency of the principal implies the incompetency of the proxy, in conformity with the maxim : *quod directe fieri prohibetur, per indirectum concedi non debet.* In like manner the invalidity of the summons bars any charge of contempt of court and condemnation for contumacy. Furthermore, the very nature of excommunication is such that it cannot be pronounced against them, since it is defined as *extra ecclesiam positio, vel è qualibet communione, vel quolibet legitimo actu separatio.* But these animals cannot be expelled from the Church, because they are not members of it and do not fall under its jurisdiction, as the apostle Paul says : " Ye judge them that are within and not them also that are without." *Excommunicatio afficit animam, non corpus, nisi per quandam consequentiam, cujus medicina est.* The animal soul, not being immortal, cannot be affected by such sentence, which involves the loss of eternal salvation (*quae vergit in dispendium aeternae salutis*).

A still more important consideration is that these insects are only exercising an innate right conferred upon them at their creation, when God expressly gave them "every green herb for meat," a right which cannot be curtailed or abrogated, simply because it may be offensive to man. In support of this view he quotes passages from Cicero's treatise *De Officiis*, the Epistle of Jude and the works of Thomas Aquinas. Finally, he maintains that his clients are agents of the Almighty sent to punish us for our sins, and to hurl anathemas against them would be to fight against God (*s'en prendre à Dieu*), who has said : " I will send wild beasts among you, which shall destroy you and your cattle and make you few in number." That all flesh has corrupted its way upon the earth, he thinks is as true now as before the deluge, and cites about a dozen lines from the *Metamorphoses* of Ovid in confirmation of this fact. In conclusion he demands the acquittal of the defendants and their exemption from all further prosecution.

The prosecuting attorney in his replication answers these objections in regular order, showing, in the first place, that, while the law may not punish an irrational creature for a crime already committed, it may intervene, as in the case of an insane person, to prevent the commission of a crime by putting the madman in a strait-jacket or throwing him into prison. He elucidates this principle by a rather far-fetched illustration from the legal enactments concerning betrothal and breach of promise of marriage. " It follows then inferentially that the aforesaid animals can be properly summoned to appear and that the summons is valid, inasmuch as this is done in order to prevent them from causing damage henceforth (*d'ores en avant*) and only incidentally to punish them for injuries already inflicted."

" To affirm that such animals cannot be anathematized and excommunicated is to doubt the authority conferred by God upon his dear spouse, the Church, whom he has made the sovereign of the whole world, having, in the words of the Psalmist, put all things under her feet, all sheep and oxen, the beasts of the field, the fowl of the air, the fish of the sea and whatsoever passeth through the paths of the seas. Guided by the Holy Spirit she does nothing unwisely; and if there is anything in which she should show forth her power it is in protecting and preserving the most perfect work of her

heavenly husband, to wit, man, who was made
in the divine image and likeness." The orator
then dilates on the grandeur and glory of man
and interlards his harangue with quotations
from sacred and profane writers, Moses, Paul,
Pliny, Ovid, Silius Italicus and Pico di Mirandola, and declares that nothing could be more
absurd than to deprive such a being of the fruits
of the earth for the sake of "vile and paltry
vermin." In reply to the statement of Thomas
Aquinas, quoted by the counsel for the defence,
that it is futile to curse animals as such, the
plaintiffs' advocate says that they are not viewed
merely as animals, but as creatures doing harm
to man by eating and wasting the products of
the soil designed for human sustenance; in other
words he ascribes to them a certain diabolical
character. "But why dwell upon this point,
since besides the instances recorded in Holy
Writ, in which God curses inanimate things and
irrational creatures, we have an infinite number
of examples of holy men, who have excommunicated noxious animals. It will suffice to mention
one familiar to us all and constantly before our
eyes in the town of Aix, where St. Hugon,
Bishop of Grenoble, excommunicated the serpents, which infested the warm baths and killed
many of the inhabitants by biting them. Now
it is well known, that if the serpents in that place
or in the immediate vicinity bite any one, the
bite is no longer fatal. The venom of the reptile
was stayed and annulled by virtue of the excom-

munication, so that no hurt ensues from the bite, although the bite of the same kind of serpent outside of the region affected by the ban, is followed by death."

That serpents and other poisonous reptiles could be deprived of their venom by enchantment and thus rendered harmless is in accord with the teachings of the Bible. Thus we read in Ecclesiastes (x. 11): "Surely the serpent will bite without enchantment," *i. e.* unless it be enchanted and its bite disenvenomed. A curious superstition concerning the adder is referred to in the Psalms (lviii. 4, 5), where the wicked are said to be "like the deaf adder that stoppeth her ear; which will not hearken to the voice of charmers, charming never so wisely." The Lord is also represented by Jeremiah (viii. 17) as threatening to "send serpents, cockatrices, among you, which will not be charmed, and they shall bite you." It does not seem to have occurred to the prosecutor that the defendants might be locusts, which would not be excommunicated.

The objection that God has sent these insects as a scourge, and that to anathematize them would be to fight against him, is met by saying that to have recourse to the offices of the Church is an act of religion, which does not resist, but humbly recognizes the divine will and makes use of the means appointed for averting the divine wrath and securing the divine favour.

After the advocates had finished their pleadings, the case was summed up by the episcopal
procurator substantially as follows :

" The arguments offered by the counsel for
the defence against the proceedings instICUtued by
the inhabitants as complainants are worthy of
careful consideration and deserve to be examined
soberly and maturely, because the bolt of excommunication should not be hurled recklessly and
at random (à la volée), being a weapon of such
peculiar energy and activity that, if it fails to
strike the object against which it is hurled, it
returns to smite him, who hurled it." [This
notion that an anathema is a dangerous missile
to him who hurls it unlawfully or for an
unjust purpose, retroacting like an Australian
boomerang, survives in the homely proverb :
" Curses, like chickens, come home to roost."]
The bishop's proctor reviews the speeches of the
lawyers, but seems to have his brains somewhat
muddled by them.   " It is truly a deep sea," he
says, " in which it is impossible to touch bottom.
We cannot tell why God has sent these animals
to devour the fruits of the earth ; this is for us
a sealed book (lettres closes)."   He suggests it
may be " because the people turn a deaf ear to
the poor begging at their doors," and goes off
into a long eulogy on the beauty of charity, with
an anthology of extracts from various writers in
praise of alms-giving, among which is one from
Eusebius descriptive of hell as a cold region,

where the wailing and gnashing of teeth are attributed to the torments of eternal frost instead of everlasting fire (*liberaberis ab illo frigore, in quo erit fletus et stridor dentium*). Again, the plague of insects may be due to irreverence shown in the churches, which, he declares, have been changed from the house of God into houses of assignation. On this point he quotes from Tertullian, Augustine, and Numa Pompilius, and concludes by recommending that sentence of excommunication be pronounced upon the insects, and that the prayers and penances, customary in such cases, be imposed upon the inhabitants.

After this discourse, which reads more like a homily from the pulpit than a plea at the bar and in the mouth of the bishop's proctor is simply an *oratio pro domo,* the official gave judgment in favour of the plaintiffs. The sentence, which was pronounced in Latin befitting the dignity and solemnity of the occasion, condemned the defendants to vacate the premises within six days on pain of anathema.

The official begins by stating the case as that of " The People *versus* Locusts," declaring that the guilt of the accused has been clearly proved " by the testimony of worthy witnesses and, as it were, by public rumour," and inasmuch as the people have humbled themselves before God and supplicated the Church to succour them in their distress, it is not fitting to refuse them help and solace. " Walking in the footsteps of the fathers, sitting on the judgment-seat, having the fear of God before our eyes and confiding in his mercy, relying on the counsel of experts, we pronounce and publish our sentence as follows :

" In the name and by virtue of God, the omnipotent, Father, Son and Holy Spirit, and of Mary, the most blessed Mother of our Lord Jesus Christ, and by the authority of the holy apostles Peter and Paul, as well as by that which has made us a functionary in this case, we admonish by these presents the aforesaid locusts and grasshoppers and other animals by whatsoever name they may be called, under pain of malediction and anathema to depart from the vineyards and fields of this district within six days from the publication of this sentence and to do no further damage there or elsewhere." If, on the expiration of this period, the animals have refused to obey this injunction, then they are to be anathematized and accursed, and the inhabitants of all classes are to beseech " Almighty God, the dispenser of all good gifts and the dispeller of all evils," to deliver them from so great a calamity, not forgetting to join with devout supplications the performance of all good works and especially " the payment of tithes without fraud according to the approved custom of the parish, and to abstain from blasphemies and such other sins as are of a public and particularly offensive character." (*Vide* Appendix B.)

It is doubtful whether one could find in the ponderous tomes of scholastic divinity anything surpassing in comical *non sequiturs* and sheer nonsense the forensic eloquence of eminent lawyers as transmitted to us in the records of legal proceedings of this kind. Although the counsel for the defendants, as we have seen, ventured to question the propriety and validity of such prosecutions, his scepticism does not seem to have been taken seriously, but was evidently smiled at as the trick of a pettifogger bound to use every artifice to clear his clients. In the writings of mediæval jurisprudents the right and fitness of inflicting judicial punishment upon animals appear to have been generally admitted. Thus Guy Pape, in his *Decisions of the Parliament of Grenoble* (Qu. 238), raises the query, whether a brute beast, if it commit a crime, as pigs sometimes do in devouring children, ought to suffer death, and answers the question unhesitatingly in the affirmative: *si animal brutum delinquat, sicut quandoque faciunt porci qui comedunt pueros, an debeat mori? Dico quod sic*." Jean Duret, in his elaborate Treatise on Pains and Penalties (*Traicté des Peines et des Amendes*, p. 250; cf. *Thémis Jurisconsulte*, VIII. p. 57), takes the same view, declaring that " if beasts not only wound, but kill and eat any person, as experi-

ence has shown to happen frequently in cases
of little children being eaten by pigs, they
should pay the forfeit of their lives and be condemned to be hanged and strangled, in order to
efface the memory of the enormity of the deed."
The distinguished Belgian jurist, Jodocus
Damhouder, discusses this question in his
Rerum Criminalium Praxis (cap. CXLII.), and
holds that the beast is punishable, if it
commits the crime through natural malice, and
not through the instigation of others, but
that the owner can redeem it by paying for
the damage done; nevertheless he is not
permitted to keep ferocious or malicious beasts
and let them run at large, so as to be a constant peril to the community. Occasionally
a more enlightened jurist had the common-sense
and courage to protest against such perversions
and travesties of justice. Thus Pierre Ayrault,
lieutenant-criminel au siége présidial d'Angers,
published at Angers, in 1591, a small quarto
entitled : *Des Procez faicts au Cadaver, aux
Cendres, à la Mémoire, aux Bestes brutes, aux
Choses inanimées et aux Contumax,* in which
he argued that corpses, the ashes and the
memory of the dead, brute beasts and inanimate
things are not legal persons (*legales homines*)
and therefore do not come within the jurisdiction
of a court. Curiously enough a case somewhat
analogous to those discussed by Pierre Ayrault
was adjudicated upon only a few years ago. A

Frenchman bequeathed his property to his own corpse, in behalf of which his entire estate was to be administered, the income to be expended for the preservation of his mortal remains and the adornment of the magnificent mausoleum in which they were sepulchred. His heirs-at-law contested the will, which was declared null and void by the court on the ground that "a subject deprived of individuality or of civil personality" could not inherit. The same principle would apply to the infliction of penalties upon such subjects. The only kind of legacy that will cause a man's memory to be cherished is the form of bequest which makes the public weal his legatee. The Chinese still hold to the barbarous custom of bringing corpses to trial and passing sentence upon them. On the 6th of August, 1888, the cadaver of a salt-smuggler, who was wounded in the capture and died in prison, was brought before the criminal court in Shanghai and condemned to be beheaded. This sentence was carried out by the proper officers on the place of execution outside of the west gate of the city.

Felix Hemmerlein, better known as Malleolus, a distinguished doctor of canon law and protomartyr of religious reform in Switzerland, states in his *Tractatus de Exorcismis,* that in the fourteenth century the peasants of the Electorate of Mayence brought a complaint against some Spanish flies, which were accordingly cited to

appear at a specified time and answer for their
conduct; but "in consideration of their small
size and the fact that they had not yet reached
their majority," the judge appointed for them a
curator, who "defended them with great
dignity"; and, although he was unable to prevent the banishment of his wards, he obtained
for them the use of a piece of land, to which they
were permitted peaceably to retire. How they
were induced to go into this insect reservation
and to remain there we are not informed. The
Church, as already stated, claimed to possess the
power of effecting the desired migration by
means of her ban. If the insects disappeared,
she received full credit for accomplishing it; if
not, the failure was due to the sins of the people;
in either case the prestige of the Church was
preserved and her authority left unimpaired.

In 1519, the commune of Stelvio, in Western
Tyrol, instituted criminal proceedings against
the moles or field-mice,[1] which damaged the

---

[1] These animals are spoken of as *unvernünftige Thierlein
genannt Lutmäuse*. *Lut* might be derived from the Old
German *lût* (*Laut*, Schrei), in which case *Lutmaus* would
mean shrew-mouse; but it is more probably from *lutum*
(loam, mould), and signifies mole or field-mouse. Field-mice
are exceedingly prolific rodents, and in modern as well as in
mediæval times have often done grievous harm to husbandry
and arboriculture by consuming roots and fruits and gnawing
the bark of young trees. The recklessness of hunters in
exterminating foxes, hedgehogs, polecats, weasels, buzzards,
crows, kites, owls and similar beasts and birds, which are
destructive of field-mice, has frequently caused the latter to
multiply so as to become a terrible plague. This was the

crops "by burrowing and throwing up the earth, so that neither grass nor green thing could grow." But "in order that the said mice may be able to show cause for their conduct by pleading their exigencies and distress," a procurator, Hans Grinebner by name, was charged with their defence, "to the end that they may have nothing to complain of in these proceedings." Schwarz Mining was the prosecuting attorney, and a long list of witnesses is given, who testified that the serious injury done by these creatures rendered it quite impossible for tenants to pay their rents. The counsel for the defendants urged in favour of his clients the many benefits which they conferred upon the community, and especially upon the agricultural class by destroying noxious insects and larvæ and by stirring up and enriching the soil, and concluded by expressing the hope that, if they should be sentenced to depart, some other suitable place of abode might be assigned to them. He demanded, furthermore, that they should be provided with a safe conduct securing them against harm or annoyance from dog, cat or other foe. The judge recognized the reasonableness of the latter request, in its application to the weaker and more defenceless of the culprits, and mitigated the sentence of perpetual banishment by ordering that "a free safe-con-

case in England in 1813-14, and in Germany in 1822, and again in 1856.

duct and an additional respite of fourteen days be granted to all those which are with young and to such as are yet in their infancy; but on the expiration of this reprieve each and every must be gone, irrespective of age or previous condition of pregnancy." (*Vide* Appendix C.)

An old Swiss chronicler named Schilling gives a full account of the prosecution and anathematization of a species of vermin called inger, which seems to have been a coleopterous insect of the genus Brychus and very destructive to the crops. The case occurred in 1478 and the trial was conducted before the Bishop of Lausanne by the authority and under the jurisdiction of Berne. The first document recorded is a long and earnest declaration and admonition delivered from the pulpit by a Bernese parish-priest, Bernhard Schmid, who begins by stating that his " dearly beloved " are doubtless aware of the serious injury done by the inger and of the suffering which they have caused. The Leutpriester, as he is termed, gives a brief history of the matter and of the measures taken to procure relief. The mayor and common council of Berne were besought in their wisdom to devise some means of staying the plague, and after much earnest deliberation they held counsel with the Bishop of Lausanne, who " with fatherly feeling took to heart so great affliction and harm " and by an episcopal mandate enjoined the inger from committing further

8

depredations. After exhorting the people to
entreat God by " a common prayer from house
to house " to remove the scourge, he proceeds to
warn and threaten the vermin in the following
manner : " Thou irrational and imperfect creature, the inger, called imperfect because there
was none of thy species in Noah's ark at the time
of the great bane and ruin of the deluge, thou
art now come in numerous bands and hast done
immense damage in the ground and above the
ground to the perceptible diminution of food for
men and animals; and to the end that such
things may cease, my gracious Lord and
Bishop of Lausanne has commanded me in his
name to admonish you to withdraw and to
abstain; therefore by his command and in his
name and also by virtue of the high and holy
trinity and through the merits of the Redeemer
of mankind, our Saviour Jesus Christ, and in
virtue of and obedience to the Holy Church, I
do command and admonish you, each and all, to
depart within the next six days from all places
where you have secretly or openly done or might
still do damage, also to depart from all fields,
meadows, gardens, pastures, trees, herbs, and
spots, where things nutritious to men and to
beasts spring up and grow, and to betake yourselves to the spots and places, where you and
your bands shall not be able to do any harm
secretly or openly to the fruits and aliments
nourishing to men and beasts. In case, how-

ever, you do not heed this admonition or obey this command, and think you have some reason for not complying with them, I admonish, notify and summon you in virtue of and obedience to the Holy Church to appear on the sixth day after this execution at precisely one o'clock after midday at Wifflisburg, there to justify yourselves or to answer for your conduct through your advocate before His Grace the Bishop of Lausanne or his vicar and deputy. Thereupon my Lord of Lausanne or his deputy will proceed against you according to the rules of justice with curses and other exorcisms, as is proper in such cases in accordance with legal form and established practice." The priest then exhorts his " dear children " devoutly to beg and to pray on their knees with Paternosters and Ave Marias to the praise and honour of the high and holy trinity, and to invoke and crave the divine mercy and help in order that the inger may be driven away. (*Vide* Appendix D.)

There is no further record of proceedings at this time, and it is highly probable that the detection of some technical error rendered it necessary to postpone the case, since this pettifogger's trick was almost always resorted to and proved generally successful in procuring an adjournment. At any rate either this or a precisely similar trial occurred in the following year. Early in May 1479, the mayor and common council of Berne sent copies of the monitorium

and citation issued by the Bishop of Lausanne
to their representative for distribution among the
priests of the afflicted parishes, in order that it
might be promulgated from their respective
pulpits and thus brought to the knowledge of
the delinquents. About a week later, on May 15,
the same authorities sent also a letter to the
Bishop of Lausanne asking for new instructions
in the matter, as they were not certain how they
should proceed, urging that immediate steps
should be taken, as the further delay would be
" utterly intolerable." This impatience would
seem to imply that the anathema had been
hanging fire for some time and that the prosecution was identical with that of the preceding
year.

The appointed term having elapsed and the
inger still persisting in their obduracy, the
mayor and common council of Berne issued the
following document conferring plenipotentiary
power of attorney on Thüring Fricker to prosecute the case : " We, the mayor, council and
commune of the city of Berne, to all those of the
bishopric of Lausanne, who see, read, or hear
this letter. We make known that after mature
deliberation we have appointed, chosen and
deputed and by virtue of the present letter do
appoint, choose and depute the excellent Thüring
Fricker, doctor of the liberal arts and of laws,
our now chancellor, to be our legal delegate
and agent and that of our commune, as well as

of all the lands and places of the bishopric of
Lausanne, which are directly or indirectly subject and appurtenant to us and of which a complete list is herein contained. And indeed he has
assumed this general and special attorneyship,
whereof the one shall not be prejudicial to the
other, in the case which we have undertaken and
prosecute and have determined to prosecute before
the court of the right reverend in Christ Benedict
de Montferrand, Bishop of Lausanne, Count and
our most worthy Superior, against the noxious
host of the inger (*brucorum*), which creeping
secretly in the earth devastate the fields,
meadows and all kinds of grain, whereby with
grievous wrong they do detriment to the ever-
living God, to whom the tithes belong, and to
men, who are nourished therewith and owe
obedience to him. In this cause he shall act
in our stead, and in the name of all of us collect-
ively and severally shall plead, demur, reply,
prove by witnesses, hear judgment or judgments, appoint other defenders and in general
and specially do each and every thing which the
importance of the cause may demand and which
we ourselves in case of our presence would be
able to do. We solemnly promise in good faith
that all and the whole of what may be transacted, performed, provided, pledged, and ordained in this cause by our aforesaid attorney
or by the proxy appointed by him shall be firmly
and gratefully observed by us, with the express

renunciation of each and every thing that might either by right or actually, in any wise, either wholly or partially impair, weaken or assail our ordainment, conclusion and determination, also over against any reservation of right, which permits a general renunciation, even if no special reservation has preceded, with the exclusion of every fraud and every deceit. In corroboration and confirmation of the aforesaid we ratify this letter with the warranty of our seal. Given on the twenty-second of May 1479.''

The trial began a couple of days later and was conducted with less '' of the law's delay '' than usual, inasmuch as it ended on the twenty-ninth day of the same month. The defender of the insects was a certain Jean Perrodet of Freiburg, who according to all accounts was a very inefficient advocate and does not appear to have contested the case with the ability and energy which the interests of his clients required. The sentence of the court with the appended anathema of the bishop was as follows: '' Ye accursed uncleanness of the inger, which shall not be called animals nor mentioned as such, ye have been heretofore by virtue of the appeal and admonition of our Lord of Lausanne enjoined to withdraw from all fields, grounds and estates of the bishopric of Lausanne, or within the next six days to appear at Lausanne, through your proctor, to set forth and to hear the cause of your procedure, and to act with just judgment either for or against you, pursuant to the said citation. Thereupon our gracious Lords of Berne solicited by their mandate such a day in court at Lausanne, and there before the tribunal renewed their plaint in their name and in that of all the provinces of the said bishopric, and your reply thereto through your proctor has been fully heard, and the legal terms have been justly observed by both parties, and a lawful decision pronounced word for word in this wise:

"We, Benedict of Montferrand, Bishop of Lausanne, etc., having heard the entreaty of the high and mighty lords of Berne against the inger and the ineffectual and rejectable answer of the latter, and having thereupon fortified ourselves with the Holy Cross, and having before our eyes the fear of God, from whom alone all just judgments proceed, and being advised in this cause by a council of men learned in the law, do therefore acknowledge and avow in this our writing that the appeal against the detestable vermin and inger, which are harmful to herbs, vines, meadows, grain and other fruits, is valid, and that they be exorcised in the person of Jean Perrodet, their defender. In conformity therewith we charge and burden them with our curse, and command them to be obedient and anathematize them in the name of the Father, the Son and the Holy Ghost, that they turn away from all fields, grounds, enclosures, seeds, fruits and produce, and depart. By virtue of

the same sentence I declare and affirm that you
are banned and exorcised, and through the
power of Almighty God shall be called accursed
and shall daily decrease whithersoever you may
go, to the end that of you nothing shall remain
save for the use and profit of man. *Adiungendo
aliquid in devotionem populi.*" The phrase *das
si beswärt werden in die person Johannis Perro-
deti irs beschirmers* does not imply that the
vermin or the devils, of which they were supposed to be incarnations, were to be conjured
into him, but refer to him merely as their proctor
and legal representative. The results of the
prosecution, which had been awaited with
intense and anxious interest by the people, were
received with great joy, and the Bernese government ordered a full report of the proceedings to
be made. The ecclesiastical anathema, however, proved to be *brutum fulmen;* nothing more
came of it, says Schilling, " owing to our sins."
Another chronicler adds that God permitted the
inger to remain as a plague and a punishment
until the people repented of their wickedness and
gave evidence of their love and gratitude to
Him, namely, by giving to the Church tithes of
what the insects had not destroyed.

The Swiss priest in his malediction declares
that the inger were not in Noah's ark and even
denies that they are animals properly speaking,
stigmatizing them as living corruption, products
of spontaneous generation perhaps, or more

probably creations of the devil. This position
was assumed in order to escape the gross im-
propriety and glaring incongruity of having the
Church of God curse the creatures which God
had made and pronounced very good, and afterwards took pains to preserve from destruction
by the deluge. This difficulty, always a serious
one, was, as we have seen, one of the chief
points urged by the counsel for the defence in
favour of his clients.

Malleolus gives the following formula for
banning serpents and expelling them from
human habitations, inculcating incidentally the
iniquity of perjury and judicial injustice : " By
virtue of this ban and conjuration I command
you to depart from this house and cause it to be
as hateful and intolerable to you, as the man,
who knowingly bears false witness or pronounces
an unjust sentence, is to God." Sometimes the
exorcism was in the form of a prayer, as, for
example, in that used for the purgation and
disinfection of springs and water-courses : " O
Lord Jesus, thou who didst bless the river
Jordan and wast baptized in it and hast purified
and cleansed it to the end that it might be a
healing element for the redemption from sin,
bless, sanctify and purify this water, so that there
may be left in it nothing noxious, nothing
pestiferous or contagious, nothing pernicious,
but that everything in it may be pure and im-
maculate, in order that we may use whatever

is created in it for our welfare and to thy glory, through our Lord Jesus Christ. Amen."

In a Latin protocol of legal proceedings in Crollolanza's *Storia del Contado di Chiavenna* it is recorded that on June 26, 1659, Capt. J. B. Pestalozzi came, in behalf of the communes of Chiavenna, Mese, Gordona, Prada and Samolico, before the commissioner Hartmann Planta and brought complaint against certain caterpillars on account of the devastations committed by them, demanding that these hurtful creatures should be summoned by the proper sheriff to appear in court on June 28 at a specified hour in order to have a curator and defender appointed, who should answer for them to the plaintiffs. A second document, dated June 28, 1659, and signed by the notary Battista Visconti, certifies that the said summons had been duly issued and five copies of the same been posted each on a tree in the five forests in the territory of the aforesaid five communes. A third document of the same date required the advocate of the accused, Cesare de Peverello, to appear before the court on the following Tuesday, July 1, in behalf of his recusant clients, who were charged with trespassing upon the fields, gardens and orchards and doing great damage therein, instead of remaining in their habitat, the forest. The prosecutors required that they should seek their food in wild and wooded places and cease from ravaging cultivated grounds. A fourth docu-

ment contains an account of the trial; the pleadings of the respective parties, so far as they are
preserved, do not differ essentially from those
already quoted. In the fifth and final document
the court recognizes the right of the caterpillars
to life, liberty, and the pursuit of happiness, provided the exercise of this right " does not destroy
or impair the happiness of man, to whom all
lower animals are subject." Accordingly a
definite place of abode is to be assigned to them
and various places are proposed. The protocol
is incomplete, so that we are left in ignorance
of the ultimate decision. The whole is written
in execrable Latin quite worthy of the subject.

More than half-a-century later the Franciscan
friars of the cloister of St. Anthony in the
province of Piedade no Maranhão, Brazil, were
greatly annoyed by termites, which devoured
their food, destroyed their furniture, and even
threatened to undermine the walls of the
monastery. Application was made to the bishop
for an act of interdiction and excommunication,
and the accused were summoned to appear before
an ecclesiastical tribunal to give account of their
conduct. The lawyer appointed to defend them
urged the usual plea about their being God's
creatures and therefore entitled to sustenance,
and made a good point in the form of an *argumentum ad monachum* by praising the industry
of his clients, the white ants, and declaring them
to be in this respect far superior to their pro-

secutors, the Gray Friars. He also maintained that the termites were not guilty of criminal aggression, but were justified in appropriating the fruits of the fields by the right derived from priority of possession, inasmuch as they had occupied the land long before the monks came and encroached upon their domain. The trial lasted for some time and called forth remarkable displays of legal learning and forensic eloquence, with numerous citations of sacred and profane authorities on both sides, and ended in a compromise, by the terms of which the plaintiffs were obliged to provide a suitable reservation for the defendants, who were commanded to go thither and to remain henceforth within the prescribed limits. In the chronicles of the cloister it is recorded, under date of Jan. 1713, that no sooner was the order of the prelatic judge promulgated by being read officially before the hills of the termites than they all came out and marched in columns to the place assigned. The monkish annalist regards this prompt obedience as conclusive proof that the Almighty endorsed the decision of the court. [Cited by Emile Angel on the authority of Manoel Bernardes' *Nova Floresta, ou Sylva de varios apophthegmas e ditos sentencios espirituaes e moraes*, etc. Vol. V., Lisboá, 1747.]

About the middle of the sixteenth century the inhabitants of several villages in Aargau were greatly annoyed by swarms of gadflies and petitioned the Bishop of Constance for relief. In the episcopal rescript, written and signed by the vidame Georg Winterstetter, the people are enjoined to abstain from dancing on Sundays and feast days, from all forms of libidinousness, gambling with cards or dice and other frivolities. These injunctions are followed by prayer and the usual formulas of conjuration and exorcism. The original document was written in Latin and preserved in the archives of Baden in Switzerland, but is now lost. In 1566 the Landamman of Unterwalden, Johannes Wirz, took a German translation of it home with him to be used in case of need against the " vergifteten Würmer," and deposited it in the archives of Obwalden, where it still remains. It was published in 1898 by Dr. Merz.

In Protestant communities, the priest as exorcist has been superseded, to a considerable extent, by the professional conjurer, who in some portions of Europe is still employed to save crops from devouring insects and similar plagues. A curious instance of this kind is recorded in Görres' *Historisch-Politische Blätter* for 1845 (Heft VII. p. 516). A Protestant gentleman in Westphalia, whose garden was devastated by worms, after having tried divers vermicidal remedies in vain, resolved to have recourse to a conjurer. The wizard came and walked about among the vegetables, touching them with a wand and muttering enchantments. Some workmen, who were repairing the roof of a stable near by, made fun of this hocus-pocus and began to throw bits of lime at the conjurer. He requested them to desist, and finally said : " If you don't leave me in peace, I shall send all the worms up on the roof." This threat only excited the hilarity of the scoffers, who continued to ridicule and disturb him in his incantations. Thereupon he went to the nearest hedge, cut a number of twigs, each about a finger in length, and placed them against the wall of the stable. Soon the vermin began to abandon the plants and, crawling in countless numbers over the twigs and up the wall, took complete possession of the roof. In less than an hour the men were obliged to stop working and stood in the court below covered with confusion and cabbage-worms.

The writer, who relates this strange incident, fully believes that it actually occurred, and ascribes it to " the force of human faith and the magnetic power of a firm will over nature." This, too, is the theory held by Paracelsus, who maintained that the effectiveness of a curse lay in the energy of the will, by which the wish, so to speak, concretes into a deed, just as anger directs the arm and actualizes itself in a blow. By " fervent desire " merely, without any physical effort or aggressive act, he deemed it possible to wound a man's body or to pierce it through as with a sword. He also held that

brutes are more easily exorcised or accursed than
men, "for the spirit of man resists more than
that of the brute." Similar notions were entertained nearly a century later by Jacob Boehme,
who defines magic as " doing in the spirit of the
will," an idea which finds more recent and more
scientific expression in Schopenhauer's doctrine
of "the objectivation of the will." Indeed,
Schopenhauer's postulate of the will as the sole
energy and actuality in the universe is only the
philosophic statement of an assumption, upon
which magicians and medicine-men, enchanters,
exorcists and anathematizers have acted more or
less in all ages. We have a striking illustration
of the workings of some such mysterious, quasi-
hyperphysical force in hypnotism, the reality of
which it is no longer possible to deny, however
wonderful and incomprehensible its manifestations may appear.

It is natural that a religion of individual initiative and personal responsibilty, like Protestantism, should put less confidence in theurgic
machinery and formularies of ex-cathedral
execration than a religion like Catholicism, in
which man's spiritual concerns are entrusted to
a hierarchical corporation to be managed according to traditional and infallible methods. This
tendency crops out in a decree published at
Dresden, in 1559, by "Augustus Duke and
Elector," wherein he commends the " Christian
zeal of the worthy and pious parson, Daniel

Greysser," for having " put under ban the sparrows, on account of their unceasing and extremely vexatious chatterings and scandalous
unchastity during the sermon, to the hindrance
of God's word and of Christian devotion." But
the Saxon parson, unlike the Bishop of Trier,
did not expect that his ban would cause the
offending birds to avoid the church or to fall
dead on entering it. He relied less on the
directly coercive or withering action of the curse
than on the human agencies, which he might
thereby set at work for the accomplishment of his
purpose. By his proscription he put the culprits
out of the pale of public sympathy and protection and gave them over as a prey to the spoiler,
who was persuaded that he was doing a pious
work by exterminating them. It was solemnly
enjoined upon the hunter and the fowler to lie in
wait for the anathematized sparrows with guns
and with snares (*durch mancherlei visirliche
und listige Wege*); and the Elector issued his
decree in order to enforce this duty on all good
Christians. (See Appendix E.)

A faded and somewhat droll survival of
ecclesiastical excommunication and exorcism is
the custom, still prevailing in European
countries and some portions of the United States,
of serving a writ of ejectment on rats or simply
sending them a friendly letter of advice in order
to induce them to quit any house, in which their
presence is deemed undesirable. Lest the rats

should overlook and thus fail to read the epistle, it is rubbed with grease, so as to attract their attention, rolled up and thrust into their holes. Mr. William Wells Newell, in a paper on "Conjuring Rats," printed in *The Journal of American Folk-Lore* (Jan.–March, 1892), gives a specimen of such a letter, dated, "Maine, Oct. 31, 1888," and addressed in business style to "Messrs. Rats and Co." The writer begins by expressing his deep interest in the welfare of said rats as well as his fears lest they should find their winter quarters in No. 1, Seaview Street, uncomfortable and poorly supplied with suitable food, since it is only a summer residence and is also about to undergo repairs. He then suggests that they migrate to No. 6, Incubator Street, where they "can live snug and happy" in a splendid cellar well stored with vegetables of all kinds and can pass easily through a shed leading to a barn containing much grain. He concludes by stating that he will do them no harm if they heed his advice, otherwise he shall be forced to use "Rough on Rats." This threat of resorting to rat poison in case of the refusal to accept his kind counsel is all that remains of the once formidable anathema of the Church.

In Scotland, when these domestic rodents became too troublesome, people of the lower classes are wont to post the following notice on the walls of their houses:

> "Ratton and mouse,
> Lea' the puir woman's house,

9

> Gang awa' owre by to 'e mill,
> And there ane and a' ye'll get your fill."

In order to make the conjuration effective some particular abode must be assigned to them; it is not sufficient to bid them begone, but they are to be told to go to a definite place.   The fact that they are usually sent across a river or brook may indicate a lingering tradition of their demoniacal character, since, according to a widespread popular superstition, a water-course is a barrier to hobgoblins and evil spirits :

> "A running stream they dare na cross."

In this case the rats, as imps of Satan, having reached their destination, would find it impossible to return.

It was in Ireland, the native realm of bulls and like incongruities, that conjuring or " rhyming " rats seems to have been most common, if we may judge from the manner in which it is alluded to by the Elizabethan poets.   Thus in *As you Like It* Rosalind says in reference to Orlando's verses : " I was never so be-rhymed since Pythagoras' time, that I was an Irish rat, which I can hardly remember."   Randolph declares :

> "My poets
> Shall with a satire, steep'd in gall and vinegar,
> Rhime 'em to death, as they do rats in Ireland."

Ben Jonson is still more specific :

> "Rhime 'em to death, as they do Irish rats,
> In drumming tunes."

From this reference to the mode of conjuring it appears that the repeating of the rhymes was accompanied with the beating of a drum, as is still the usage in France. From the very earliest times a peculiar magical potency has been ascribed to words woven into rhythmic form. The fascination which metrical expression, even as a mere jingle and jargon, still retains for the youth of the individual was yet far more strongly felt in the youth of the race. The simple song was intoned as a spell and the rude chant mumbled as a charm.

In France the conjuration of field-mice bears a more distinctly religious stamp. On the first Sunday in Lent, the so-called Feast of the Torches (*la Fête des Brandons ou des Bures*), the peasants wander in all directions through the fields and orchards with lighted torches of twisted straw, uttering the following incantation, which not only threatens to burn the whiskers of obdurate mice, but also hints at the wine-bibbing propensities of the curate :

> " Sortez, sortez d'ici, mulots !
> Ou je vais vous bruler les crocs !
> Quittez, quittez ces blés !
> Allez, vous trouverez
> Dans la cave du curé
> Plus à boire qu'à manger."

The form of imprecation varies in different provinces, but usually includes some threat of breaking the bones or burning the beards of the refractory rodents, in case they refuse to quit the close, as in the following summons :

> "Taupes et mulots,
> Sors de mon clos,
> Ou je te casse les os ;
> Barbassione ! Si tu viens dans non clos,
> Je te brûle la barbe jusqu'aux os."

The utterance of these words is emphasized by loud and discordant noises of cat-calls, tin horns, and similar instruments of " Callithumpian " music.

Gregory, who was Bishop of Tours in the latter half of the sixth century, states in his *History of the Franks* (VIII. 35) that bronze talismans representing dormice and serpents were used in Paris to protect the city against the ravages of these creatures; and when the town of Le Mans was rebuilt after its destruction by fire in 1145, a toad with a gold chain round its neck, was enclosed in a block of stone as a preservative against venomous reptiles. (Le Corvasier : *Hist. des Évêques du Mans*, 1648, p. 441. Cf. Desnoyers : *Recherches*, etc., p. 7.)

The use of the above-mentioned means of conjuration is unquestionably of very ancient date. Thus in a treatise on agriculture entitled τὰ γεωπονικά and consisting of twenty books, written in the tenth century by the Bithynian Byzantine, Kassianos Bassos, the following prescription is given for getting rid of field-mice :

" Take a slip of paper and write on it these

words: I adjure you, O mice, who dwell here not to injure me yourselves nor to permit any other mouse to do so; and I make over to you this field (describing it). But should I find you staying here after having been warned, with the help of the mother of the gods I will cut you in seven pieces." The author quotes this recipe, in order, as he says, that nothing may remain unrecorded, but expressly declares that he has no confidence in its efficiency and advises the husbandman to put his trust in good rat-bane. Bassos derived the materials for his popular encyclopædia chiefly from the " Geoponics " composed by Anatolios and Didymos some six centuries earlier, and even most of his citations of classical writers are taken from the same sources. That the above-mentioned exorcism is pagan in its origin is evident from the invocation of the aid of Cybele for the destruction of disobedient vermin. In a Christian conjuration the Mother of God would have been substituted for the mother of the gods, whom the Greeks revered as the personification of all-creating and all-sustaining nature. The resemblance of this formula, which the Greeks may have borrowed with the worship of Cybele from the Phrygians, to the Yankee's letter of advice is peculiarly interesting.

In the ancient conjuration the harmful or undesirable animals were commanded to go to a certain locality, set apart for them, and this injunction was accompanied with dire threats in case of disobedience; the milder epistolary form of the present day is more advisory and persuasive and offers them inducements to migrate and to take up their abode elsewhere. Sometimes this kind counsel is given verbally, as, for example, in Thuringia, where it is customary to get rid of cabbage-worms by going into the garden, requesting them to depart, and calling out: "In yonder village is church-ale (*Kirmes*)"; thus implying that they will find better entertainment at this festival. (Witzschel: *Sagen, Sitten und Gebräuche aus Thüringen.* Wien, 1878, p. 217.) The willingness of peasant communities to ward off evil from themselves at the expense of their neighbours is a survival of the primitive ethics, which recognizes only the rights of the family or tribe and treats all aliens as foes. It is the same feeling that causes the inhabitants of the Alps to erect so-called weather-crosses (*Wetterkreuze*) for the purpose of averting thunder-storms and hailstones from themselves by diverting them into an adjacent valley. This method of protection is based upon the theory that tempests, hurricanes, and all violent commotions of nature are the work of demons or witches, who avoid the symbol of Christ's death and the world's redemption and direct their fury elsewhere. A like egotism is expressed in the inscription on many houses of peasants entreating St. Florian to preserve their habitation from flames and to set fire to others, as though the

holy man must indulge his incendiary passion by
pouring out upon some human abode the blazing
vessel, which he is represented as bearing in his
hand. The inscription is the same as that with
which Reynard the Fox adorned his castle Male-
partus, and which might be translated :

> " Saint Florian, thou martyr blessed,
> Protect this house and burn the rest."

Not only were insects, reptiles and small
mammals, such as rats and mice, legally prosecuted and formally excommunicated, but
judicial penalties, including capital punishment,
were also inflicted upon larger quadrupeds. In
the Report and Researches on this subject, published by Berriat-Saint-Prix in the *Memoirs of
the Royal Society of Antiquaries of France*
(Paris, 1829, Tome VIII. pp. 403-50), numerous
extracts from the original records of such proceedings are given, and also a list of the kinds
of animals thus tried and condemned, extending
from the beginning of the twelfth to the middle
of the eighteenth century, and comprising in all
ninety-three cases. This list has been enlarged
by D'Addosio so as to cover the period from
824 to 1845, and to include one hundred and
forty-four prosecutions resulting in the execution or excommunication of the accused, but
even this record is by no means complete. (*Vide*
Appendix F for a still fuller list.)

The culprits are a miscellaneous crew, consisting chiefly of caterpillars, flies, locusts, leeches,

snails, slugs, worms, weevils, rats, mice, moles, turtle-doves, pigs, bulls, cows, cocks, dogs, asses, mules, mares and goats. Only those cases are reported in which the accused were found guilty; of these prosecutions, according to the above-mentioned registers, two belong to the ninth century, one to the eleventh, three to the twelfth, two to the thirteenth, six to the four-teenth, thirty-four to the fifteenth, forty-five to the sixteenth, forty-three to the seventeenth, seven to the eighteenth and one to the nineteenth century. To this list might be added other cases, such as the prosecution and malediction of noxious insects at Glurns in the Tyrol in 1519, at Als in Jutland in 1711, at Bouranton in 1733, at Lyö in Denmark in 1805-6, and at Pozega in Slavonia in 1866. In the latter case one of the largest of the locusts was seized and tried and then put to death by being thrown into the water with anathemas on the whole species. A few years ago swarms of locusts devastated the region near Kallipolis in Turkey, and a petition was sent by the Christian population to the monks of Mount Athos begging them to bear in solemn procession through the fields the girdle of St. Basilius, in order to expel the insects. This request was granted, and as the locusts gradually disappeared, because there was little or nothing left for them to eat, the orthodox of the Greek Church from the bishop to the humblest laymen firmly believed or at least maintained that a

miracle had been wrought. Pious Mohammedans exorcise and ostracize locusts and other
harmful insects by reading the Koran aloud in
the ravaged fields, as was recently done at
Denislue in Asia Minor with satisfactory results.
Also as late as 1864 at Pleternica in Slavonia, a
pig was tried and executed for having malici-
ously bitten off the ears of a female infant aged
one year. The flesh of the condemned animal
was cut in pieces and thrown to the dogs, and
the head of the family, in which the pig lived, as
is the custom of pigs among the peasants of that
country, was put under bonds to provide a dowry
for the mutilated child, so that the loss of her
ears might not prove to be an insuperable
obstacle to her marriage. (*Amira*, p. 578.) It
would be incorrect to infer from the tables just
referred to that no judicial punishment of animals
occurred in the tenth century or that the fifteenth,
sixteenth, and seventeenth centuries were peculiarly addicted to such practices. It is well known
that during some of the darkest periods of the
Middle Ages and even in later times the registers of the courts were very imperfectly kept, and
in many instances the archives have been entirely
destroyed. It is highly probable, therefore, that
the cases of capital prosecution and conviction of
animals, which have been collected and printed
by Berriat-Saint-Prix and others, however
thorough their investigations may have been,
constitute only a very small percentage of those
which actually took place.

Beasts were often condemned to be burned alive; and strangely enough, it was in the latter half of the seventeenth century, an age of comparative enlightenment, that this cruel penalty seems to have been most frequently inflicted. Occasionally a merciful judge adhered to the letter of the law and curbed its barbarous spirit by sentencing the culprit to be slightly singed and then to be strangled before being committed to the flames. Sometimes brutes were doomed to be buried alive. Thus we have the receipt of " Phélippart, sergeant of high justice of the city of Amiens," for the sum of sixteen soldi, in payment for services rendered in March 1463, in " having buried in the earth two pigs, which had torn and eaten with their teeth a little child in the faubourg of Amiens, who for this cause passed from life to death (*étoit allé de vie a trépas*)." In 1557, on the 6th of December, a pig in the Commune of Saint-Quentin was condemned to be "buried all alive" (*enfoui tout vif*), "for having devoured a little child in l'hostel de la Couronne." Again, a century earlier, in 1456, two pigs were subjected to this punishment, " on the vigil of the Holy Virgin," at Oppenheim on the Rhine, for having killed a child. More than three centuries later the same means were employed for curing murrain, which in the summer of 1796 had broken out at Beutelsbach in Würtemberg and carried off many head of cattle. By the advice of a French veterinary doctor, who was quartered there with the army of General Moreau, the town bull was buried alive at the crossroads in the presence of several hundred persons. We are not informed whether this sacrifice proved to be a sufficiently " powerful medicine " to stay the epizoötic plague; the noteworthy fact is that the superstitious rite was prescribed and performed, not by an Indian magician or an African sorcerer, but by an official of the French republic.

Animals are said to have been even put to the rack in order to extort confession. It is not to be supposed that, in such cases, the judge had the slightest expectation that any confession would be made; he wished merely to observe all forms prescribed by the law, and to set in motion the whole machinery of justice before pronouncing judgment. The statement of a French writer, Arthur Mangin (*L'Homme et la Bête*. Paris, 1872, p. 344), that " the cries which they uttered under torture were received as confessions of guilt," is absurd. No such notion was ever entertained by their tormentor. " The question," which under the circumstances would seem to be only a wanton and superfluous act of cruelty, was nevertheless an important element in determining the final decision, since the sentence of death could be commuted into banishment, whipping, incarceration or some milder form of punishment, provided the criminal had not confessed his guilt under torture. The use of the rack might be, therefore, a merciful means of escaping the gallows. Appeals were sometimes made to higher tribunals and the judgments of the lower courts annulled or modified. In one instance a sow and a she-ass were condemned to be hanged; on appeal, and after a new trial, they were sentenced to be simply knocked on the head. Occasionally an appeal led to the acquittal of the accused.

In 1266, at Fontenay-aux-Roses, near Paris, a pig convicted of having eaten a child was publicly burned by order of the monks of Sainte Geneviève. In 1386, the tribunal of Falaise sentenced a sow to be mangled and maimed in the head and forelegs, and then to be hanged, for having torn the face and arms of a child and thus caused its death. Here we have a strict application of the *lex talionis,* the primitive retributive principle of taking an eye for an eye and a tooth for a tooth. As if to make the travesty of justice complete, the sow was dressed in man's clothes and executed on the public square near the city-hall at an expense to the state of ten sous and ten deniers, besides a pair of gloves to the hangman. The executioner was provided with new gloves in order that he might come from the discharge of his duty, metaphorically at least, with clean hands, thus indicating that, as a minister of justice, he incurred no guilt in shedding blood. He was no common pig-killer, but a public functionary, a "master of high works" (*maître des hautes œuvres*), as he was officially styled. (*Vide* Appendix G.)

We may add that the west wall of the south

branch of the transept in the Church of the
Holy Trinity (*Sainte-Trinité*) at Falaise in
Normandy was formerly adorned with a fresco-
painting of this execution, which is mentioned
in *Statistique de Falaise* (1827, t. I. 83), and
more fully described by l'Abbé Pierre-Gilles
Langevin, in his *Recherches Historiques sur
Falaise* (1814, p. 146). In a Supplement (p. 12)
to this work, published several years later, the
Abbé states that, about the year 1820, the entire
church, including the fresco, was whitewashed,
so that the picture has since then been invisible,
and, so far as can be ascertained, no engraving
or other copy of it has ever been made. Unfortunately, too, as the same writer informs us,
la châsse de la bannière (banner-holder) was
fastened to the wall of the church on this very
spot, thus covering and permanently destroying
at least a portion of the painting.

In 1394, a pig was found guilty of " having
killed and murdered a child in the parish of
Roumaygne, in the county of Mortaing, for
which deed the said pig was condemned to be
haled and hanged by Jehan Petit, lieutenant of
the bailiff." The work was really done by the
hangman (*pendart*), Jehan Micton, who received
for his services the sum of " fifty souls tournois."
(*Vide* Appendix H.) In another case the deputy
bailiff of Mantes and Meullant presented a bill,
dated March 15, 1403, which contained the
following items of expense incurred for the in-

carceration and execution of an infanticide
sow :

    " Cost of keeping her in jail, six sols parisis.

    " Item, to the master of high works, who came
from Paris to Meullant to perform the said
execution by comand and authority of the
said bailiff, our master, and of the procurator of the king, fifty-four sols parisis.

    " Item, for a carriage to take her to justice, six
sols parisis.

    " Item, for cords to bind and hale her, two
sols eight deniers parisis.

    " Item, for gloves, two deniers parisis."

This account, which amounted in all to sixty-
nine sols eight deniers parisis, was examined
and approved by the auditor of the court, De
Baudemont, who affixed to it his own seal with
signature and paraph and " in further confirmation and approbation thereof caused it to be
sealed with the seal of the Chatellany of Meullant, on the 15th day of March in the year
1403." (See Appendix I.) In the following
year a pig was executed at Rouvres for the same
offence.

Brutes and human criminals were confined in
the same prison and subjected to the same treatment. Thus " Toustain Pincheon, keeper of
the prisons of our lord the king in the town of
Pont de Larche," acknowledges the receipt,
" through the hand of the honourable and wise
man, Jehan Monnet, sheriff (*vicomte*) of the said

town, of nineteen sous six deniers tournois for
having found the king's bread for the prisoners
detained, by reason of crime, in the said prison."
The jailer gives the names of the persons in
custody, and concludes the list with " Item, one
pig, conducted into the said prison and kept
there from the 24th of June, 1408, inclusive, till
the 17th of the folowing July," when it was
hanged "for the crime of having murdered
and killed a little child " (*pource que icellui
porc avoit muldry et tue ung pettit enfant*). For
the pig's board the jailer charged two deniers
tournois a day, the same as for boarding
a man, thus placing the porker, even in respect
to its maintenance, on a footing of perfect
equality with the human prisoners. He also
puts into the account " ten deniers tournois for
a rope, found and furnished for the purpose of
tying the said pig that it might not escape."
The correctness of the charges is certified to by
" Jean Gaulvant, sworn tabellion of our lord
the king in the viscounty of Pont de Larche."
(*Vide* Appendix J.)   Again in 1474, the official
of the Bishop of Lausanne sentenced a pig to
be hanged "until death ensueth," for having
devoured an infant in its cradle in the vicinity
of Oron, and to remain suspended from the gallows for a certain length of time as a warning to
wrong-doers. It is also expressly stated that,
in 1585, the body of a pig, which had been
executed for the murder of a child at Saint-

Omer, at the hostelry of Mortier d'Or, was left hanging " for a long space " on a gibbet in a field near the highway. (Derheims: *Histoire de Saint-Omer*, p. 327.) A little later a similar spectacle met the eyes of Guy Pape, as he was going to Châlons-sur-Marne in Champagne, to pay homage to King Henry IV. In his own words: *dum ibam ad civitatem Cathalani in Campania ad Regem tunc ibi existentem, vidi quemdam porcum, in furcis suspensum, qui dicebatur occidisse quemdam puerum.* (Quaestio CCXXXVIII: *De poena bruti delinquentis.* Lugduni, MDCX.)

On the 5th of September, 1379, as two herds of swine, one belonging to the commune and the other to the priory of Saint-Marcel-le-Jeussey, were feeding together near that town, three sows of the communal herd, excited and enraged by the squealing of one of the porklings, rushed upon Perrinot Muet, the son of the swine-keeper, and before his father could come to his rescue, threw him to the ground and so severely injured him that he died soon afterwards. The three sows, after due process of law, were condemned to death; and as both the herds had hastened to the scene of the murder and by their cries and aggressive actions showed that they approved of the assault, and were ready and even eager to become *participes criminis,* they were arrested as accomplices and sentenced by the court to suffer the same penalty. But the prior,

Friar Humbert de Poutiers, not willing to endure the loss of his swine, sent an humble petition to Philip the Bold, then Duke of Burgundy, praying that both the herds, with the exception of the three sows actually guilty of the murder, might receive a full and free pardon. The duke lent a gracious ear to this supplication and ordered that the punishment should be remitted and the swine released. (*Vide* Appendix K.)

A peculiar custom is referred to in the *procès verbal* of the prosecution of a porker for infanticide, dated May 20, 1572. The murder was committed within the jurisdiction of the monastery of Moyen-Montier, where the case was tried and the accused sentenced to be " hanged and strangled on a gibbet." The prisoner was then bound with a cord and conducted to a cross near the cemetery, where it was formally given over to an executioner from Nancy. " From time immemorial," we are told, " the justiciary of the Lord Abbot of Moyen-Montier has been accustomed to consign to the provost of Saint-Diez, near this cross, condemned criminals, wholly naked, that they may be executed; but inasmuch as this pig is a brute beast, he has delivered the same bound with a cord, without prejudicing or in any wise impairing the right of the Lord Abbot to deliver condemned criminals wholly naked." The pig must not wear a rope unless the right to do without it be

10

expressly reserved, lest some human culprit, under similar circumstances, should claim to be entitled to raiment.

> "'Twill be recorded for a precedent;
> And many an error, by the same example
> Will rush into the state: it cannot be."

In the case of a mule condemned to be burned alive together with a man guilty of buggery, at Montpellier, in 1565, as the quadruped was vicious and inclined to kick (*vitiosus et calcitrosus*), the executioner cut off its feet before consigning it to the flames. This mutilation was an arbitrary and extra-judicial act, dictated solely by considerations of personal convenience. Hangmen often indulged in capricious and supererogatory cruelty in the exercise of their patibulary functions, and mediæval as well as later writers on criminal jurisprudence repeatedly complain of this evil and call for reform. Thus Damhouder, in his *Rerum Criminalium Praxis* (*cap. de carnifice*, p. 234), urges magistrates to be more careful in selecting persons for this important office, and not to choose evil-doers, "assiduous gamblers, public whoremongers, malicious back-biters, impious blasphemers, assassins, thieves, murderers, robbers, and other violators of the law as vindicators of justice. Indeed, these hardened wretches sometimes took the law into their own hands. For example, on the 9th of June, 1576, at Schweinfurt in Franconia, a sow, which had bitten off the ear and

torn the hand of a carpenter's child, was given
into custody, whereupon the hangman, without
legal authority, took it to the gallows-green
(Schindrasen) and there "hanged it publicly
to the disgrace and detriment of the city." For
this impudent usurpation of judiciary powers
Jack Ketch was forced to flee and never dared
return. Hence arose the proverbial phrase
Schweinfurter Sauhenker (Schweinfurt sow-
hangman), used to characterize a low and lawless
ruffian and vile fellow of the baser sort. It was
not the mere killing of the sow, but the execution without a judicial decision, the insult and
contempt of the magistracy and the judicatory
by arrogating their functions, that excited the
public wrath and official indignation.

Buggery (*offensa cujus nominatio crimen est,*
as it is euphemistically designated in legal documents) was uniformly punished by putting to
death both parties implicated, and usually by
burning them alive. The beast, too, is punished
and both are burned (*punitur etiam pecus et
ambo comburuntur*), says Guillielmus Benedic-
tinus, a writer on law, who lived about the end
of the fourteenth century. Thus, in 1546, a
man and a cow were hanged and then burned
by order of the parliament of Paris, the supreme
court of France. In 1466, the same tribunal
condemned a man and a sow to be burned at
Corbeil. Occasionally interment was substituted
for incremation. Thus in 1609, at Niederrad,

a man and a mare were executed and their bodies buried in the same carrion-pit. On the 12th of September, 1606, the mayor of Loens de Chartres, on complaint of the dean, canons, and chapter of the cathedral of Chartres, condemned a man named Guillaume Guyart to be "hanged and strangled on a gibbet in reparation and punishment of sodomy, whereof the said Guyart is declared accused, attainted and convicted." A bitch, his accomplice, was sentenced to be knocked on the head (*assommée*) by the executioner of high justice and "the dead bodies of both to be burned and reduced to ashes." It is furthermore added that if the said Guyart, who seems to have contumaciously given leg-bail, cannot be seized and apprehended in person, the sentence shall, in his case, be executed in effigy by attaching his likeness in painting to the gibbet. It was also decreed that all the property of the absconder should be confiscated and the sum of one hundred and fifty livres be adjudged to the plaintiffs, out of which the costs of the trial were to be defrayed. (*Vide* Appendix L.) This disgusting crime appears to have been very common; at least Ayrault in his *Ordre Judiciaire*, published in 1606, states that he has many times (*multoties*) seen brute beasts put to death for this cause. In his *Magnalia Christi Americana* (Book VI, (III), London, 1702) Cotton Mather records that "on June 6, 1662, at New Haven, there was a most

unparalleled wretch, one Potter by name, about
sixty years of age, executed for damnable Besti-
alities.'' He had been a member of the Church
for twenty years and was noted for his piety,
" devout in worship, gifted in prayer, forward
in edifying discourse among the religious, and
zealous in reforming the sins of other people."
Yet this monster, who is described as possessed
by an unclean devil, " lived in most infandous
Buggeries for no less than fifty years together,
and now at the gallows there were killed before
his eyes a cow, two heifers, three sheep and two
sows, with all of which he had committed his
brutalities. His wife had seen him confound-
ing himself with a bitch ten years before; and
he then excused himself as well as he could,
but conjured her to keep it secret." He afterwards hanged the bitch, probably as a sort of
vicarious atonement. According to this account
he must have begun to practice sodomy when
he was ten years of age, a vicious precocity
which the author would doubtless explain on
the theory of diabolical possession. In 1681, a
habitual sodomite, who had been wont to defile
himself with greyhounds, cows, swine, sheep
and all manner of beasts, was brought to trial
together with a mare, at Wünschelburg in
Silesia, where both were burned alive. In 1684,
on the 3rd of May, a bugger was beheaded at
Ottendorf, and the mare, his partner in crime,
knocked on the head; it was expressly enjoined

that in burning the bodies the man's should lie underneath that of the beast. In the following year, fourteen days before Christmas, a journeyman tailor, " who had committed the unnatural deed of carnal lewdness with a mare," was burned at Striga together with the mare.

For the same offence Benjamin Deschauffour was condemned, May 25, 1726, to be tied to a stake and there burned alive " together with the minutes of the trial;" his ashes were strewed to the wind and his estates seized and, after the deduction of a fine of three thousand livres, confiscated to the benefit of his Majesty. In the case of Jacques Ferron, who was taken in the act of coition with a she-ass at Vanvres in 1750, and after due process of law, sentenced to death, the animal was acquitted on the ground that she was the victim of violence and had not participated in her master's crime of her own free-will. The prior of the convent, who also performed the duties of parish priest, and the principal inhabitants of the commune of Vanvres signed a certificate stating that they had known the said she-ass for four years, and that she had always shown herself to be virtuous and well-behaved both at home and abroad and had never given occasion of scandal to any one, and that therefore " they were willing to bear witness that she is in word and deed and in all her habits of life a most honest creature." This document, given at Vanvres on Sept. 19, 1750, and signed by

" Pintuel Prieur Curé " and the other attestors, was produced during the trial and exerted a decisive influence upon the judgment of the court. As a piece of exculpatory evidence it may be regarded as unique in the annals of criminal prosecutions.

The Carolina or criminal code of the emperor Charles V., promulgated at the diet of Ratisbon in 1532, ordained that sodomy in all its forms and degrees should be punished with death by fire " according to common custom " (" *so ein Mensch mit einem Viehe, Mann mit Mann, Weib mit Weib, Unkeuschheit treibet, die haben auch das Leben verwircket, und man soll sie der gemeinen Gewohnheit nach mit dem Feuer vom Leben zum Tode richten.*" Art. 116.), but stipulated that, if for any reason the punishment of the sodomite should be mitigated, the same measure of mercy should be shown to the beast. This principle is reaffirmed by Benedict Carpzov in his *Pratica Nova Rerum Criminalium* (Wittenberg, 1635), in which he states that " if for any cause the sodomite shall be punished only with the sword, then the beast participant of his crime shall not be burned, but shall be struck dead and buried by the knacker or field-master (*Caviller oder Feldmeister*)." The bugger was also bound to compensate the owner for the loss of the animal, or, if he left no property, the value must be paid out of the public treasury. " If the criminal act was not fully consummated,

then the human offender was publicly scourged
and banished, and the animal, instead of being
killed, was put away out of sight in order that
no one might be scandalized thereby " [Jacobi
Döpleri, *Theatrum Poenarum Suppliciorum et
Executionum Criminalium, oder Schau-Platz
derer Leibes- und Lebens-Straffen,* etc. Sondershausen, 1693, II. p. 151.]

All Christian legislation on this subject is
simply an application and amplification of the
Mosaic law as recorded in Exodus xxii. 19 and
Leviticus xx. 13–16, just as the cruel persecu-
tions and prosecutions for witchcraft in mediæval
and modern times derive their authority and justification from the succinct and peremptory command : " Thou shalt not suffer a witch to live."
In the older criminal codes two kinds or degrees
of sodomy are mentioned, *gravius* and *gravissimum;* the former being condemned in the
thirteenth verse and the latter in the fifteenth
and sixteenth verses of Leviticus. Döpler tells
some strange stories of the results of the *peccatum gravissimum;* and the fact that a sober
writer on jurisprudence could believe and seriously narrate such absurdities, furnishes a
curious contribution to the history of human
credulity.

It is rather odd that Christian law-givers
should have adopted a Jewish code against
sexual intercourse with beasts and then enlarged
it so as to include the Jews themselves. The

question was gravely discussed by jurists,
whether cohabitation of a Christian with a
Jewess or *vice versa* constitutes sodomy. Damhouder (*Prax. Rer. Crim.* c., 96, n. 48) is of the
opinion that it does, and Nicolaus Boër (Decis.,
136, n. 5) cites the case of a certain Johannes
Alardus or Jean Alard, who kept a Jewess in
his house in Paris and had several children by
her; he was convicted of sodomy on account of
this relation and burned, together with his para-
mour, "since coition with a Jewess is precisely
the same as if a man should copulate with a
dog" (Döpl., *Theat.*, II. p. 157). Damhouder,
in the work just cited, includes Turks and
Saracens in the same category, "inasmuch as
such persons in the eye of the law and our holy
faith differ in no wise from beasts."

But to resume the subject of the perpetration
of felonious homicide by animals, on the 10th
of January, 1457, a sow was convicted of
"murder flagrantly committed on the person of
Jehan Martin, aged five years, the son of Jehan
Martin of Savigny," and sentenced to be
"hanged by the hind feet to a gallows-tree (*a
ung arbre esproné*)." Her six sucklings, being
found stained with blood, were included in the
indictment as accomplices; but "in lack of any
positive proof that they had assisted in mangling
the deceased, they were restored to their owner,
on condition that he should give bail for their
appearance, should further evidence be forth-

coming to prove their complicity in their mother's crime." Above three weeks later, on the 2nd of February, to wit "on the Friday after the feast of Our Lady the Virgin," the sucklings were again brought before the court; and, as their owner, Jehan Bailly, openly repudiated them and refused to be answerable in any wise for their future good conduct, they were declared, as vacant property, forfeited to the noble damsel Katherine de Barnault, Lady of Savigny. This case is particularly interesting on account of the completeness with which the *procès verbal* has been preserved. (See Appendix M.)

Sometimes a fine was imposed upon the owner of the offending animal, as was the case with Jehan Delalande and his wife, who were condemned, on the 18th of April, 1499, by the bailiff of the Abbey of Josaphat near Chartres, to pay a fine of eighteen francs and to be confined in prison until this sum should be paid, "on account of the murder of a child named Gilon, aged five and a half years or thereabouts, perpetrated by a porker, aged three months or thereabouts." The pig was condemned to be "hanged and executed by justice." The owners were punished because they were supposed to have been culpably negligent of the child, who had been confided to their care and keeping, and not because they had, in the eye of the law, any proprietary responsibility for the infanticidal animal. The mulct implied remissness on their part as guardians or foster-parents of the infant. In general, as we have seen, the owner of the blood-guilty beast was considered wholly blameless and sometimes even remunerated for his loss. (*Vide* Appendix N.)

According to the laws of the Bogos, a pastoral and nominally Christian tribe of Northern Abyssinia, a bull, cow or any other animal which kills a man is put to death; the owner of the homicidal beast is not held in any wise responsible for its crime, nevertheless he practically incurs a somewhat heavy penalty by not receiving any compensation for the loss of his property. This exercise of justice is quite common among the tribes of Central Africa. In Montenegro, horses, oxen and pigs have been recently tried for homicide and put to death, unless the owner redeemed them by paying a ransom.

On the 14th of June, 1494, a young pig was arrested for having "strangled and defaced a young child in its cradle, the son of Jehan Lenfant, a cowherd on the fee-farm of Clermont, and of Gillon his wife," and proceeded against "as justice and reason would desire and require." Several witnesses were examined, who testified "on their oath and conscience" that "on the morning of Easter Day, as the father was guarding cattle and his wife Gillon was absent in the village of Dizy, the infant being left alone in its cradle, the said pig entered during the said time the said house and disfigured and ate the face and neck of the said child, which, in consequence of the bites and defacements inflicted by the said pig, departed this life (*de ce siècle trépassa*)." The sentence pronounced by the judge was as follows, " We, in detestation and horror of the said crime, and to the end that an example may be made and justice maintained, have said, judged, sentenced, pronounced and appointed, that the said porker, now detained as a prisoner and confined in the said abbey, shall be by the master of high works hanged and strangled on a gibbet of wood near and adjoinant to the gallows and high place of execution belonging to the said monks, being contiguous to their fee-farm of Avin." The crime was committed " on the fee-farm of Cler-mont-lez-Montcornet, appertaining in all matters of high, mean and base justice to the monks of the order of Premonstrants," and the prosecution was conducted by " Jehan Levoisier, licenciate in law, the grand mayor of the church and monastery of St. Martin de Laon of the order of Premonstrants and the aldermen of the same place." The plaintiffs were the friars, who preferred charges against the pig and procured the evidence necessary to its conviction. (*Vide* Appendix O.)

In 1394, a pig was hanged at Mortaign for having sacrilegiously eaten a consecrated wafer; and in a case of infanticide, it is expressly stated in the plaintiff's declaration that the pig killed the child and ate of its flesh, "although it was Friday," and this violation of the *jejunium sextae*, prescribed by the Church, was urged by the prosecuting attorney and accepted by the court as a serious aggravation of the porker's offence.

Nothing would be easier than to multiply examples of this kind. Infanticidal swine were hanged in 1419 at Labergement-le-Duc, in 1420 at Brochon, in 1435 at Trochères, and in 1490 at Abbeville; the last-mentioned execution took place "under the auspices of the aldermanity and with the tolling of the bells." It was evidently regarded as a very solemn affair. The records of mediæval courts, the chronicles of mediæval cloisters, and the archives of mediæval cities, especially such as were under episcopal sovereignty and governed by ecclesiastical law, are full of such cases. The capital punishment of a dumb animal for its crimes seems to us so irrational and absurd, that we can hardly believe that sane and sober men were ever guilty of such folly; yet the idea was quite familiar to our ancestors even in Shakespeare's day, in the brilliant Elizabethan age of English literature, as is evident from a passage in Gratiano's invective against Shylock:

> "thy currish spirit
> Govern'd a wolf, who, hang'd for human slaughter,
> Even from the gallows did his fell soul fleet,
> And, whilst thou lay'st in thy unhallow'd dam,
> Infus'd itself in thee; for thy desires
> Are wolfish, bloody, starv'd, and ravenous."

That such cases usually came under the jurisdiction of monasteries and so-called spiritualities
and were tried by their peculiarly organized
tribunals, will not seem strange, when we remember that these religious establishments were
great landed proprietors and at one time owned
nearly one-third of all real estate in France.
The frequency with which pigs were brought to
trial and adjudged to death, was owing, in a
great measure, to the freedom with which they
were permitted to run about the streets and to
their immense number. The fact that they were
under the special protection of St. Anthony of
Padua conferred upon them a certain immunity,
so that they became a serious nuisance, not only
endangering the lives of children, but also
generating and disseminating diseases. It is
recorded that in 1131, as the Crown Prince
Philippe, son of Louis the Gross, was riding
through one of the principal streets of Paris,
a boar, belonging to an abbot, ran violently
between the legs of his horse, so that the prince
fell to the ground and was killed. In some cities,
like Grenoble in the sixteenth century, the
authorities treated them very much as we do
mad dogs, empowering the carnifex to seize and
slay them whenever found at large. On Nov.
20, 1664, the municipality of Naples passed an
ordinance that the pigs, which frequented the
streets and piazzas to the detriment and danger
of the inhabitants, should be removed from the
city to a wood or other uninhabited place or be

slaughtered within twelve days on pain of the penalties already prescribed and threatened, probably in the order issued on Nov. 3, of the same year. It would seem, however, that these ordinances did not produce the desired effect, or soon fell into abeyance, since another was promulgated four years later, on Nov. 29, 1668, expelling the pigs from the city and calling attention to the fact that they corrupted the atmosphere and thus imperiled the public health. Sanitary considerations and salutary measures of this kind were by no means common in the Middle Ages, but were a gradual outgrowth of the spirit of the Renaissance. It was with the revival of letters that men began to love cleanliness and to appreciate its hygienic value as well as its æsthetic beauty. Little heed was paid to such things in the " good old times " of earlier date, when the test of holiness was the number of years a person went unwashed, and the growth of the soul in sanctity was estimated by the thickness of the layers of filth on the body, as the age of the earth is determined by the strata which compose its crust.

The freedom of the city almost universally enjoyed by mediæval swine is still maintained by their descendants in many towns of Southern Italy and Sicily, where they ramble at will through the streets or assemble in council before the palace of the prefect (cf. D'Addosio, *Bestie Delinquenti,* pp. 23–5).

In the latter half of the sixteenth century the tribunals began to take preventive measures against the public nuisance by holding the inhabitants responsible for the injuries done to individuals by swine running at large and by threatening with corporal as well as pecuniary punishment all persons who left " such beasts without a good and sure guard." Thus it is recorded that on the 27th of March, 1567, " a sow with a black snout," " for the cruelty and ferocity " shown in murdering a little child four months old, having " eaten and devoured the head, the left hand and the part above the right breast of the said infant," was condemned to be " exterminated to death, and to this end to be hanged by the executioner of high justice on a tree within the metes and bounds of the said judicature on the highway from Saint-Firmin to Senlis." The court of the judicatory of Senlis, which pronounced this sentence on complaint of the procurator of the seigniory of Saint-Nicolas, also forbade all the inhabitants and subjects of the said seignioralty to permit the like beasts to go unguarded on pain of an arbitrary fine and of corporal chastisement in default of payment. (*Vide* Appendix P.)

But although pigs appear to have been the principal culprits, especially as regard infanticide, other quadrupeds were frequently called to answer for similar crimes. Thus, in 1314, a bull belonging to a farmer in the village of

Moisy, escaped into the highway, where it attacked a man and injured him so severely that
he died a few hours afterwards. The ferocious
animal was seized and imprisoned by the officers
of Charles, Count of Valois, and after being tried
and convicted was sentenced to be hanged. This
judgment of the court was confirmed by the
Parliament of Paris and the execution took place
at Moisy-le-Temple on the common gallows.
An appeal based upon the incompetency of the
court was then made by the Procurator of the
Order of the Hospital of the Ville de Moisy to
the Parliament of La Chandeleur, which decided
that the bull had met with its deserts and been
justly put to death, but that the Count of Valois
had no jurisdiction on the territory of Moisy,
and his officials no power to institute proceedings in this case. The sentence was right in
equity, but judicially and technically wrong, and
could not therefore serve as a precedent.

There is also extant an order issued by the
magistracy of Gisors in 1405, commanding payment to be made to the carpenter who had
erected the scaffold on which an ox had been
executed " for its demerits." Again on the
16th of May, 1499, the judicial authorities of
the Cistercian Abbey of Beaupré near Beauvais
condemned a red bull to be " executed until
death inclusively," for having " killed with
furiosity a lad of fourteen or fifteen years of age,
named Lucas Dupont," who was employed in
tending the horned cattle of the farmer Jean

11

Boullet. (*Vide* Appendix Q.) In 1389, the
Carthusians of Dijon caused a horse to be condemned to death for homicide; and as late as
1697 a mare was burned by the decision and
decree of the Parliament of Aix, which, it must
be remembered, was not a legislative body, but
a supreme court of judicature, thus differing in
its functions from the States General, the only
law-making and representative assembly in
France, that may be said to have corresponded
in the slightest degree to the modern conception
of a parliament.

In 1474, the magistrates of Bâle sentenced a
cock to be burned at the stake " for the heinous
and unnatural crime of laying an egg." The
auto da fé was held on a height near the city
called the Kohlenberg, with as great solemnity
as would have been observed in consigning a
heretic to the flames, and was witnessed by an
immense crowd of townsmen and peasants.
The statement made by Gross in his *Kurze
Basler Chronik*, that the executioner on cutting
open the cock found three more eggs in him, is
of course absurd; we have to do in this case
not with a freak of nature, but with the freak of
an excited imagination tainted with superstition.
Other instances of this kind have been recorded,
one in the Swiss Prättigau as late as 1730, although in many cases the execution of the galli-
naceous malefactor was more summary and less
ceremonious than at Bâle.

The *oeuf coquatri* was supposed to be the product of a very old cock and to furnish the most active ingredient of witch ointment. When hatched by a serpent or a toad, or by the heat of the sun it brought forth a cockatrice or basilisk, which would hide in the roof of the house and with its baneful breath and " death-darting eye " destroy all the inmates. Many naturalists believed this fable as late as the eighteenth century, and in 1710 the French savant Lapeyronie deemed this absurd notion worthy of serious refutation, and read a paper, entitled " Observation sur les petits oeufs de poule sans jaune, que l'on appelle vulgairement oeufs de Coq," before the Academy of Sciences in order to prove that cocks never lay and that the small and yolkless eggs attributed to them owe their peculiar shape and condition to a disease of the hen resulting in a hydropic malformation of the oviduct. A farmer brought him several specimens of this sort, somewhat larger than a pigeon's egg, and assured him that they had been laid by a cock in his own barnyard. On opening one of them, M. Lapeyronie was surprised to find only a very slight trace of the yolk resembling " a small serpent coiled." He now began to suspect that the cock might be an hermaphrodite, but on killing and dissecting it discovered nothing in support of this theory, the internal organs being all perfectly healthy and normal. But although the unfortunate chanticleer had fallen a victim to the scientific investigation of

a popular delusion, the eggs in question continued to be produced, until the farmer by care-
fully watching the fowls detected the hen that
laid them. The dissection showed that the
pressure of a bladder of serous fluid against the
oviduct had so contracted it, that the egg in
passing had the yolk squeezed out of it, leaving
merely a yellowish discoloration that looked like
a worm. Another peculiarity of this hen was
that she crowed like "a hoarse cock" (*un coq
enroué*), only more violently; a phenomenon
also a source of terror to the superstitious, but
ascribed by M. Lapeyronie to the same morbid
state of the oviduct and the consequent pain
caused by the passage of the egg (*Mémoires de
l'Académie de Sciences*. Paris, 1710, pp. 553–
60.)

A Greek physiologus of the twelfth century,
written in verse, calls the animal hatched from
the egg of an old cock επτειναρια, a name which
would imply some sort of winged creature. It
was "sighted like the basilisk," and endowed
also in other respects with the same fatal qualities.

In the case of a valuable animal, such as an
ox or a horse, the severity of retaliatory justice
was often tempered by economical considerations and the culprit confiscated, but not capitally punished. Thus as early as the twelfth
century it is expressly stated that "it is the law
and custom in Burgundy that if an ox or a
horse commit one or several homicides, it shall

not be condemned to death, but shall be taken by the Seignior within whose jurisdiction the deed was perpetrated or by his servitors and be confiscated to him and shall be sold and appropriated to the profit of the said Seignior; but if other beasts or Jews do it, they shall be hanged by the hind feet" (Coustumes et Stilles de Bourgoigne, § 197 in Giraud: *Essai sur l'Histoire du Droit Francais,* II. p. 302; quoted by Amira). It was a cruel irony of the law that conferred upon pigs and Jews a perfect equality of rights by sending them both to the scaffold.

Animals were put on a par with old crones in bearing their full share of persecution during the witchcraft delusion. Pigs suffered most in this respect, since they were assumed to be peculiarly attractive to devils, and therefore particularly liable to diabolical possession, as is evident from the legion that went out of the lunatic and were permitted, at their own request, to enter into the Gadarene herd of swine. But Beelzebub did not disdain to become incarnate in all sorts of creatures, such as cats, dogs of high and low degree, wolves, night-birds and indeed in any beast, especially if it chanced to be black. Goats, it is well known, were not a too stinking habitation for him, and even to dwell in skunks he did not despise. The perpetual smell of burning sulphur in his subterranean abode may render him proof against any less suffocating form of stench. The Bible represents Satan as going about as a roaring lion; and according to the highest ecclesiastical authorities he has appeared visibly as a raven, a porcupine, a toad and a gnat. Indeed, there is hardly a living creature in which he has not deigned to disport himself from a blue-bottle to a bishop, to say nothing of his " appearing invisibly at times " (*aliquando invisibiliter apparens*), if we may believe what the learned polyhistor Tritheim tells of his apparitions. As all animals were considered embodiments of devils, it was perfectly logical and consistent that the Prince of Darkness should reveal himself to mortal ken as a mongrel epitome of many beasts—snake, cat, dog, pig, ape, buck and horse each contributing some characteristic part to his incarnation.

It was during the latter half of the seventeenth century, when, as we have seen, criminal prosecutions of animals were still quite frequent and the penalties inflicted extremely cruel, that Racine caricatured them in Les Plaideurs, where a dog is tried for stealing and eating a capon. Dandin solemnly takes his seat as judge, and declares his determination to " close his eyes to bribes and his ears to brigue." Petit Jean prosecutes and L'Intime appears for the defence. Both address the court in florid and high-flown rhetoric and display rare erudition in quoting Aristotle, Pausanias and other ancient as well

as modern authorities. The accused is condemned to the galleys. Thereupon the counsel
for the defendant brings in a litter of puppies,
pauvres enfants qu'on veut rendre orphelins,
and appeals to the compassion and implores the
clemency of the judge. Dandin's feelings are
touched, for he, too, is a father; as a public
officer, also, he is moved by the economical consideration of the expense to the state of keeping
the offspring of the culprit in a foundling hospital, in case they should be deprived of paternal
support. To the contemporaries of Racine the
representation of a scene like this had a significance, which we fail to appreciate. It strikes us
as simply farcical and not very funny; to them
it was a mirror reflecting a characteristic feature
of the time and ridiculing a grave judicial abuse,
as Cervantes, a century earlier, burlesqued the
institution of chivalry in the adventures of Don
Quixote. (See Appendix R.)

Lex talionis is the oldest kind of law and the
most deeply rooted in human nature. To the
primitive man and the savage, tit for tat is an
ethical axiom, which it would be thought immoral as well as cowardly not to put into practice. No principle is held more firmly or acted
upon more universally than that of literal and
exact retributions in man's dealings with his
fellows—the iron rule of doing unto others the
wrongs which others have done unto you.
Hebrew legislation demanded " life for life, eye
for eye, tooth for tooth, hand for hand, foot for

foot, burning for burning, wound for wound, stripe for stripe." An old Anglo-Saxon law made this retaliatory principle of *membrum pro membro* the penalty of all crimes of personal violence, including rape; even a lascivious eye was to be plucked out, in accordance with the doctrine that " whosoever looketh on a woman to lust after her hath committed adultery with her already in his heart." ["Corruptor puniatur in eo in quo deliquat: oculos igitur amittat, propter aspectum decoris, quo virginem concupivit; amittat et testiculos, qui calorem stupri induxerunt." Cf. Bracton, 147*b*; Reeves, I. 481.] This was believed to be God's method of punishment, smiting with disease or miraculously destroying the bodily organs, which were the instruments of sin. Thus Stengelius (*De Judiciis Divinis,* II. 26, 27) records how a thunderbolt was hurled by the divine hand in such a manner as to castrate a lascivious priest : *impurus et saltator sacerdos fulmine castratus.* The same sort of retributive justice was recognized by the Institutes of Manu, which punished a thief by the amputation or mutilation of his fingers.

In the covenant with Noah it was declared that human blood should be required not only "at the hand of man," but also "at the hand of every beast;" and it was subsequently enacted, in accordance with this fundamental principle, that "if an ox gore a man or a woman that they die, then the ox shall be surely

stoned, and his flesh shall not be eaten." To
eat a creature which had become the peer of
man in blood-guiltiness and in judicial punishment, would savour of anthropophagy. This
decision of Jewish law-givers as to the use of
the flesh of otherwise edible animals condemned
to death for crime has nearly always been
followed. Thus when, in 1553, several swine
were executed for child-murder at Frankfort on
the Main, their carcasses, although doubtless as
good pork as could be found in the shambles,
were thrown into the river. Usually, however,
they were buried under the gallows or in whatever spot was set apart for interring the dead
bodies of human criminals. At Ghent, however, in 1578, after judicial sentence of death
had been pronounced on a cow, she was
slaughtered and her flesh sold as butcher's meat,
half of the proceeds of the sale being given as
compensation to the injured party and the other
half to the city treasury for distribution among
the poor; but her head was struck off and stuck
on a stake near the gallows, to indicate that she
had been capitally punished. The thrifty Flem-
ings did not permit the moral depravity to taint
the material substance of the bovine culprit and
impair the excellence of the beef.

On the other hand, the Law Faculty of the
University of Leipsic decided that a cow, which
had pushed a woman and thereby caused her
death at Machern in Saxony, July 20, 1621,

should be taken to a secluded and barren place and there killed and buried "unflayed." In this case the flesh of the homicidal animal was not to be eaten nor the hide converted into leather. (*Vide* Appendix S.)

In this connection it may be interesting to mention a decision of the Ecclesiastical Court (*geistlicher Convent*) of Berne, given in 1666 and recorded in Türler's *Strafrechtliche Gutachten des geistlichen Konvents der Stadt Bern* (*Zeitschrift für schweiz. Strafrecht,* Bd. III., Heft 5. Quoted by Tobler). An insane man was tried for murder and the prosecutor seems to have urged that the lack of moral responsibility did not suffice to relieve the accused of legal responsibility and to free him from punishment, citing as pertinent to the case the Mosaic law, which inflicted the death penalty on an ox for the like offence. On this point the court replied: "In the first place, that specifically Jewish law is not binding upon other governments, and is not observed by them either as regards oxen or horses. Again, even if the Jewish law should be really applicable to all men, it could not be appealed to in the present case, since it is not permissible to draw an inference *a bove ad hominem.* Inasmuch as no law is given to the ox, it cannot violate any, in other words, cannot sin and therefore cannot be punished. On the other hand, death is a severe penalty for man. Nevertheless if God commanded that the 'goring ox' should be killed, this was done in order to excite aversion to the deed, to prevent the animal from injuring others, and in this manner to punish the owner of the beast. This fact, however, proves nothing touching the case now before us; for, although God enacted a law for the ox, he did not enact any for the insane man, and the distinction between the goring ox and the maniac must be observed. An ox is created for man's sake, and can therefore be killed for his sake; and in doing this there is no question of right or wrong as regards the ox; on the other hand, it is not permissible to kill a man, unless he has deserved death as a punishment." The remarkable points in this decision are, first, the abrogation of a biblical enactment by an ecclesiastical court of the seventeenth century, and, secondly, the discussion of a criminal act from a psychiatrical point of view and the admission of extenuating and exculpating circumstances derived from this source.

The Koran holds every beast and fowl accountable for injuries done to each other, but reserves their punishment for the life to come. Among the Kukis, if a man falls from a tree and is killed, it is the sacred duty of the next of kin to fell the tree, and cut it up and scatter the chips abroad. The spirit of the tree was supposed to have caused the mishap, and the blood of the slain was not thought to be thoroughly avenged until the offending object had been

effaced from the earth. A survival of this notion
was the custom of burning heretics and flinging
their ashes to the four winds or casting them
upon rivers running into the sea. The laws of
Drakôn and Erechtheus required weapons and
all other objects, by which a person had lost
his life, to be publicly condemned and thrown
beyond the Athenian boundaries. This sentence
of banishment, then regarded as one of the
severest that could be inflicted, was pronounced
upon a sword, which had killed a priest, the
wielder of the same being unknown; and also
upon a bust of the elegiac poet Theognis, which
had fallen on a man and caused his death. Even
in cases which, one would think, might be regarded as justifiable homicide in self-defence, no
such ground of exculpation seems to have been
admitted. Thus the statue erected by the Athenians in honour of the famous athlete, Nikôn of
Thasos, was assailed by his envious foes and
pushed from its pedestal. In falling it crushed
one of its assailants, and was therefore brought
before the proper tribunal and sentenced to be
cast into the sea. Judicial proceedings of this
kind were called ἀψύχων δίκαι (prosecutions of
lifeless things) and were conducted before the
Athenian law-court known as the Prytaneion;
they are alluded to by Æschines, Pausanias,
Demosthenes, and other writers, and briefly described in the *Onomasticon* of Julius Pollux and
the *Lexicon Decem Oratorum Graecorum* of
Valerius Harpokration.

Strictly speaking, the term ἄψῦχον should be applied only to an inanimate object and not to the brute, which was more correctly called ἄφωνον (dumb); but this distinction was not always observed either in common parlance or in legal phraseology. The law on this point as formulated and expounded by Plato (*De Leg.*, IX. 12) was as follows: "If a draught animal or any other beast kill a person, unless it be in a combat authorized and instituted by the state, the kinsmen of the slain shall prosecute the said homicide for murder, and the overseers of the public lands (ἀγρονόμοι), as many as may be commissioned by the said kinsmen, shall adjudicate upon the case and send the offender beyond the boundaries of the country (ἐξορίζειν, exterminate in the literal and original sense of the term). If a lifeless thing shall deprive a person of life, provided it may not be a thunderbolt (κεραυνός) or other missile (βέλος) hurled by a god, but an object which the said person may have run against or by which he may have been struck and slain, then the kinsman immediate to the deceased shall appoint the nearest neighbour as judge in order to purify himself as well as his next of kin from blood-guiltiness, but the culprit (τὸ ὄφλον) shall be put beyond the boundaries, in the same manner as if it were an animal." In the same section it is enacted that if a person be found dead and the murderer be unknown, then proclamation shall be made by a herald on the market-place forbidding the murderer to enter any sanctuary or the land of the slain, and declaring that, if discovered, he shall be put to death and his body be thrown unburied beyond the boundaries of the country of the person killed. The object of these measures was to appease the Erinnys or avenging spirit of the deceased, and to avert the calamities which would otherwise be brought upon the land, in accordance with the strict law of retribution demanding blood for blood, no matter whether it may have been shed wilfully or accidentally. [Cf. Æschylus, *Cho.*, 395, where this law ($\nu\acute{o}\mu os$) is clearly and strongly affirmed.] The same superstitious feeling leads the hunters of many savage tribes to beg pardon of bears and other wild animals for killing them and to purify themselves by religious rites from the taint incurred by such an act, the $\mu\acute{\iota}a\sigma\mu a$ of murder, as the Greeks called it.

Quite recently in China fifteen wooden idols were tried and condemned to decapitation for having caused the death of a man of high military rank. On complaint of the family of the deceased the viceroy residing at Fouchow ordered the culprits to be taken out of the temple and brought before the criminal court of that city, which after due process of law sentenced them to have their heads severed from their bodies and then to be thrown into a pond. The execution is reported to have taken place in the presence of a large concourse of approving spectators and "amid the loud execrations of the

masses," who seem in their excitement to have
" lost their heads " as well as the hapless deities.

When the Russian prince Dimitri, the son of
Ivan II., was assassinated on May 15, 1591, at
Uglich, his place of exile, the great bell of that
town rang the signal of insurrection. For this
serious political offence the bell was sentenced
to perpetual banishment in Siberia, and con-
veyed with other exiles to Tobolsk. After a
long period of solitary confinement it was partially purged of its iniquity by conjuration and
re-consecration and suspended in the tower of a
church in the Siberian capital; but not until 1892
was it fully pardoned and restored to its original
place in Uglich. A like sentence was imposed
by a Russian tribunal on a butting ram in the
latter half of the seventeenth century.

Mathias Abele von Lilienberg, in his *Metamorphosis Telae Judiciariae,* of which the eighth
edition was published at Nuremberg in 1712,
states that a drummer's dog in an Austrian
garrison town bit a member of the municipal
council in the right leg. The drummer was sued
for damages, but refused to be responsible for the
snappish cur and delivered it over to the arm of
justice. Thereupon he was released, and the
dog sentenced to one year's incarceration in the
Narrenkötterlein, a sort of pillory or iron cage
standing on the market-place, in which blasphemers, evil-livers, rowdies and other peace-
breakers were commonly confined. [The Narrenkötterlein, Narrenköderl or Kotter formerly

on the chief public squares in Vienna are described as " Menschenkäfige mit Gittern von Eisen und Holz, bestimmt das darin versperrte Individuum dem Spotte des Pöbels preiszugeben (zu narren)." Schläger : *Wiener Skizzen aus dem Mittelalter,* II. 245.] Mornacius also relates that several mad dogs, which attacked and tore in pieces a Franciscan novice in 1610, were " by sentence and decree of the court put to death." It is surely reasonable enough that mad dogs should be killed; the remarkable feature of the case is that they should be formally tried and convicted as murderers by a legal tribunal, and that no account should have been taken of their rabies as an extenuating circumstance or ground of acquittal. In such a case the plea of insanity would certainly seem to be naturally suggested and perfectly valid.

On the other hand, it is expressly declared in the Avesta that a mad dog shall not be permitted to plead insanity in exculpation of itself, but shall be " punished with the punishment of a conscious and premeditated offence (*baodho-varsta*), *i.e.* by progressive mutilation, corresponding to the number of persons or beasts it has bitten, beginning with the loss of its ears, extending to the crippling of its feet and ending with the amputation of its tail. This cruel and absurd enactment is wholly inconsistent with the kindly spirit shown in the Avesta towards all animals recognized as the creatures of Ahuramazda, and especially with the many measures

taken by the Indo-Aryans as a pastoral people
for the protection of the dog. Indeed, a paragraph immediately following in the same chapter
commands the Mazdayasnians to treat such a
rabid dog humanely, and to " wait upon him
with medicaments and to try to heal him, just
as they would care for a righteous man." On
this important point Avestan legislation is so
inconsistent and self-contradictory that one may
justly suspect the harsh enactments to be later
interpolations.

A curious example of imputed crime and its
penal consequences is seen in the Roman custom
of celebrating the anniversary of the preservation of the Capitol from the night-attack of the
Gauls, not only by paying honour to the descendants of the sacred geese, whose cries gave
warning of the enemy's approach, adorning them
with jewels and carrying them about in litters,
but also by crucifying a dog, as a punishment for
the want of vigilance shown by its progenitors on
that occasion. This imputation of merit and demerit was really no more absurd than to visit the
sins of the fathers on the children, as prescribed
by Jewish and other ancient lawgivers, or to
decree corruption of blood in persons attainted of
treason, as is still the practice of modern states,
or any other theory of inherited guilt or scheme
of vicarious atonement, that sets the sin of the
federal head of the race to the account of his
remotest posterity and relieves them from its
penalties only through the suffering and death

12

of a wholly innocent person. They are all applications of the barbarous principle, which, in primitive society, with its gross conceptions of justice, made the entire tribe responsible for the conduct of each of its members. The vendetta, which continues to be the unwritten but inviolable code of many semi-civilized communities, is based upon the same conception of consanguineous solidarity for the perpetration and avenging of crime.

According to an old Anglo-Saxon law, abolished by King Canute, in case stolen property was found in the house of a thief, his wife and family, even to the infant in the cradle, though it had never taken food (*þeâh hit nafre metes ne âbîte*), were punished as partakers of his guilt. The *Schwabenspiegel,* the oldest digest of South German law, treated as accessaries all the domestic animals found in a house, in which a crime of violence had been committed, and punished them with death. [" Man soll allez daz tötden daz in den huze ist gevonden : leuten und vie, ros und rinder, hunde und katzen, ganzen und hundre." § 290.]

Cicero approved of such penalties for political crimes as " severe but wise enactments, since the father is thereby bound to the interests of the state by the strongest of ties, namely, love for his children." Roman law under the empire punished treason with death and then added : " As to the sons of traitors, they ought to suffer the same penalty as their parents, since it is

highly probable that they will sometime be
guilty of the same crime themselves; nevertheless, as a special act of clemency, we grant
them their lives, but, at the same time, declare
them to be incapable of inheriting anything from
father or mother or of receiving any gift or
bequest in consequence of any devise or testament of kinsmen or friends. Branded with
hereditary infamy and excluded from all hope of
honour or of property, may they suffer the
torture of disgrace and poverty until they shall
look upon life as a curse and long for death as
a kind release." This atrocious edict of the
emperors Arcadius and Honorius has its counter-
part in the still more radical code of Pachacutez,
the Justinian of the ancient Peruvians, which
punished adultery with the wife of an Inca by
putting to death not only the adulteress and her
seducer, but also the children, slaves and kindred
of the culprits, as well as all the inhabitants of
the city in which the crime was committed,
while the city itself was to be razed and the site
covered with stones.

The principle enunciated by Cicero has also
been accepted by modern legislators as applicable to high treason. Thus, when Tschech, the
burgomaster of Storkow, attempted to take the
life of Frederic William of Prussia, July 26,
1844, he was tried and executed Dec. 14 of
the same year. On the day after his execution
his only daughter, Elizabeth, was arrested, and
to her inquiry by what right she had been

deprived of her freedom, the authorities replied that, " according to Prussian law the children of a person convicted of high treason and all the members of his family, especially if they seemed to be dangerous and to share the opinions of their father, can be imprisoned for life or banished from the country." The young lady was then exiled to Westphalia, and there placed in the custody of an extremely austere parson, until she finally escaped to France, and afterwards to Switzerland, where she spent the rest of her days.

When the prefects Tatian and Proculus fell into disgrace, Lycia, their native land, was deprived of the autonomy it had hitherto enjoyed as a Roman province, and its inhabitants were disfranchised and declared incapable of holding any office under the empire. So, too, when Joshua discovered some of the spoils of Jericho hidden in the tent of Achan, not only the thief himself, but also " his sons, and his daughters, and his oxen, and his asses, and his sheep, and his tent, and all that he had," were brought into the valley of Achor, and there stoned with stones and burned with fire. About this time, however, such holocausts of justice were suppressed among the Jews, and a law enacted that henceforth " the fathers shall not be put to death for the children, neither shall the children be put to death for the fathers, every man shall be put to death for his own sin;" or, as Jeremiah expresses it figuratively, the children's teeth were to be no longer set on edge by the sour grapes which their fathers had eaten. Yet the persistency of time-honoured custom and its power of overriding new statutes are seen in the fact that, several centuries later, at the request of the Gibeonites, whom it had become desirable to conciliate, David did not scruple to deliver up to them seven of Saul's sons to be hanged for the evil which their father had wrought in slaying these foes of Israel. It would have been a parallel case if Bismarck had sought to win the friendship and favour of the French by giving into their hands the descendants of Blücher to be guillotined on the Place de la Concorde, or, after having made a political pilgrimage to Canossa, should surrender the children of Dr. Falk to be racked and burned at the stake by the ultramontanes.

According to the current orthodox theology, treason against God, committed by our common progenitor, worked "corruption of blood" in the whole human race, all the children of men being attainted with guilt in consequence of the act of their first parent. This crude and brutal conception of justice is the survival of a primitive and barbarous state of society, and it is curious to observe how the most highly civilized peoples, who have outgrown this notion and set it aside in the secular relations of man to man, still cling to it as something sacred and sublime in the spiritual relations of man to the deity. Only the all-wise and all-powerful sovereign of the universe is supposed to continue to administer law and justice on principles which common-sense and the enlightened opinion of mankind have long since abrogated and banished from earthly legislation. Thus the divine government, instead of keeping pace with the progress of human institutions, still corresponds to the ideals of right and retribution entertained by savage tribes and the lowest types of mankind.

The horrible mutilations to which criminals were formerly subjected, originated in an endeavour to administer strictly even-handed justice. What could be fairer or more fit than to punish perjury by cutting off the two fingers which the perjurer had held up in taking the violated oath? It was a popular belief that the fingers of an undetected perjurer would grow out of the grave after death, seeking retributive amputation, as a plant seeks the light, and that his ghost would never rest until this penalty had been inflicted. (See Heinrich Roch : *Schles. Chron.*, p. 267, where a case of this kind is recorded.) The Carolina (*constitutio criminalis Carolina*), although in many respects an advance on mediæval penal legislation, doomed incendiaries to be burned alive; and an old law, cited by Döpler (*Theat. Poen.*, II. 271), condemned a man who had dug up and removed a boundary stone to be buried in the earth up to his neck and to have his head plowed off with a new plow, thus symbolizing in his own person the grave

offence which he had committed. Ivan Basilovitch, a Muscovite prince, ordered that an ambas-
sador, who did not uncover in his presence,
should have his hat nailed to his head; and it is
a feeble survival of the same idea of proper
punishment that makes the American farmer
nail the dead hawk to his barn-door, just as in
former times it was customary to crucify highway robbers at cross-roads.

According to an old Roman law ascribed to
Numa Pompilius, the oxen which plowed up
a boundary stone, as well as their driver, were
sacrificed to Jupiter Terminus. In the early
development of agriculture, and the transition
from communal to personal property in land, this
severe enactment was deemed necessary to the
protection of the " sacra saxa," by which the
boundary lines of the fields were defined. Only
by making the violation of enclosed ground a
sacrilege was it possible to prevent encroach-
ments upon it, so strong was the lingering prejudice against individual possessions of this kind
running in the blood of a people descended from
nomadic tribes of herdsmen, who regarded
sedentary communities engaged in tilling the
soil as their direst foes. The lawgiver knew
very well that the oxen were involuntary agents,
and that the plowman alone was culpable; but
when a religious atonement is to be made and an
angry god appeased, moral distinctions determining degrees of responsibility are uniformly
ignored, and the innocent are doomed to suffer

with the guilty. The oxen were tainted by the performance of an act, in which the exercise of their will was not involved, and must therefore be consigned to the offended deity. The same is true of the plowman, who did not escape immolation even when the *motio termini* or displacement of the boundary stone occurred unintentionally.

That the feeling, which found expression in such enactments and usages and survives in schemes of expiation and vicarious sacrifice, lies scarcely skin-deep under the polished surface of our civilization, is evident from the force and suddenness with which it breaks out under strong excitement, as when Cincinnati rioters burn the court-house because they suspect the judges of venality and are dissatisfied with the verdicts of the juries. The primitive man and the savage, like the low and ignorant masses of civilized communities, do not take into consideration whether the objects from which they suffer injury are intelligent agents or not, but wreak their vengeance on stocks and stones and brutes, obeying only the rude instinct of revenge. The power of restraining these aboriginal propensities, and of nicely analyzing actions and studying mental conditions in order to ascertain degrees of moral responsibility, presupposes a high degree of mental development and refinement and great acuteness of psychological perception, and is, in fact, only a recent acquisition of a small minority of the

human race. The vast bulk of mankind will
have to pass through a long process of intellectual evolution, and rise far above their present
place in the ascending scale of culture before
they attain it.

For this reason Lombroso would abolish trial
by jury, which seems to him not a sign of progress towards better judicatory methods, but a
clumsy survival of primitive justice as administered by barbarous tribes and even gregarious
animals. It makes the administration of justice
dependent upon popular prejudice and passion,
and finds its most violent expression or explosion in lynch law, which is only trial by a jury
of the whole community gone mad. It would
certainly be a dismal farce to apply to the
criminal classes the principle that every man
must be judged by his peers. In the cantonal
courts of Switzerland the verdict of the jury is
uniformly in favour of the native against the
foreigner, no matter what the merits of the case
may be; and this outrageous perversion of right
and equity is called patriotism, a term which
conveniently sums up and euphemizes the
general sentiment of Helvetian innkeepers and
tradesmen that "the stranger within their
gates" is their legitimate spoil, and has no other
raison d'être. In Italy, especially in Naples
and Sicily, a thief may be sometimes condemned, but a murderer is almost invariably
acquitted by the jury, whose decision expresses
the corrupted moral sense of a people accus-

tomed to admire the bandit as a hero and to consider brigandage a highly honourable profession.

The childish disposition to punish irrational creatures and inanimate objects, which is common to the infancy of individuals and of races, has left a distinct trace of itself in that peculiar institution of English law known as deodand, and derived partly from Jewish and partly from old German usages and traditions. " If a horse," says Blackstone, " or any other animal, of its own motion kill as well an infant as an adult, or if a cart run over him, they shall in either case be forfeited as deodand." If a man, in driving a cart, tumble to the ground and lose his life by the wheel passing over him, if a tree fall on a man and cause his death, or if a horse kick his keeper and kill him, then the wheel, the tree and the horse are deodands *pro rege,* and are to be sold for the benefit of the poor.

Omnia quae movent ad mortem sunt Deo danda is the principle laid down by Bracton. If therefore a cart-wheel run over a man and kill him, not only is the wheel, but also the whole cart to be declared deodand, because the momentum of the cart in motion contributed to the man's death; but if the shaft fall upon a man and kill him, then only the shaft is deodand, since the cart did not participate in the crime. It is also stated, curiously enough, that if an infant fall from a cart not in motion and be killed, neither the horse nor the cart shall be declared deodand; not so, however, if an adult come to his death in this manner. The ground of this distinction is not quite clear; although it may arise from the assumption that the child had no business there, or that such an accident could not have happened to an adult, unless there was something irregular and perverse in the conduct of the animal or the vehicle. In the archives of Maryland, edited by Dr. William Hand Browne and Miss Harrison in 1887, mention is made of an inquest held January 31, 1637, on the body of a planter, who "by the fall of a tree had his bloud bulke broken." "And furthermore the Jurors aforesaid upon their oath aforesaid say that the said tree moved to the death of the said John Bryant; and therefore find the said tree forfeited to the Lord Proprietor."

According to an old Anglo-Saxon law a sword or other object by which a man had been slain, was not regarded as pure (*gesund*) until the crime had been expiated, and therefore could not be used, but must be set apart as a sacrifice. A sword-cutler would not take such a weapon to polish or repair without a certificate that it was *gesund* or free from homicidal taint, so as not to render himself liable for any harm it might inflict, since it was supposed to exert a certain magical and malicious influence. Also an ancient municipal law of the city of Schleswig stipulated that the builder of a house should be held responsible in case any one should be killed by a beam, block, rafter or other piece of timber, and pay a fine of nine marks, or give the object that had committed the manslaughter to the family or kinsmen of the slain. If he failed to do so and built the contaminated timber into the edifice, then the owner had to atone for the homicide with the whole house. (Cf. Heinrich Brunner: *Deutsche Rechtsgeschichte,* II. p. 557, Anm. 31.) A modern survival of this legal principle is the notion, current especially among criminals, that any part of the body of a deceased person, or better still of an executed murderer, exerts a magical and protective power or brings good luck. It is by no means uncommon among the peasants and lower classes of Europe to put the finger of a dead thief under the threshold in order to protect the house homœpathically against theft. The persistency of this superstition is shown by the fact that a farmer's hired man named Sier and belonging to the hamlet of Heumaden, was tried at Weiden in Bavaria, May 23, 1894, and convicted of having exhumed the body of a newly buried child in the churchyard of Moosbach and taken out one of its eyes, which he supposed would render him invisible to mortal sight like the famous *tarnkappe* of old German mythology, and thus enable him to indulge with impunity his propensity to steal. For this sacrilege he was sentenced to one year and two months' imprisonment and to the loss of civil rights for three years.

In some of the Scottish islands it is the custom to beach a boat, from which a fisherman had been drowned, cursing it for its misdeed and letting it dry and fall to pieces in the sun. The boat is guilty of manslaughter and must no longer be permitted to sail the sea with innocent craft. Scotch law does not seem to have recognized deodand in the strictly etymological sense of the term, but only escheat, in other words, the confiscated objects were not necessarily appled to pious purposes—*pro anima regis et omnium fidelium defunctorum*—but were simply forfeited to the king or to the state. This form of confiscation never prevailed so generally in Central and Eastern, as in Western Europe. Some German communities and territorial sovereigns introduced it from France, but so modified the practical application of the principle as to award to the injured party the greater portion, in Lüneburg, for example, two-thirds of the value of the confiscated animal or object. (*Vide* Kraut's *Stadtrecht von Lüneburg*, No. XCVII. Cited by Von Amira, p. 594.)

Blackstone's theories of the origin of deodands are exceedingly vague and unsatisfactory. Evidently the learned author of the *Commentaries* could give no consistent explanation of these vestiges of ancient criminal legislation. His statement that they were intended to punish the owner of the forfeited property for his negligence, and his further assertion that they were " designed, in the blind days of popery, as an expiation for the souls of such as were snatched away by sudden death," are equally incorrect.

In most cases the owner was perfectly innocent and very frequently was himself the victim of the accident. He suffered only incidentally from a penalty imposed for a wholly different purpose, just as a slaveholder incurs loss when his human chattel commits murder and is hanged for it. The primal object was to atone for the taking of life in accordance with certain crude conceptions of retribution. Under hierarchical governments the prominent idea was to appease the wrath of God, who otherwise might visit mankind with famine and pestilence and divers retaliatory scourges. For the same reason the property of a suicide was deodand. Thus the wife and children of the deceased, who may be supposed to have already suffered most from the fatal act, were subjected to additional punishment for it by being robbed of their rightful inheritance. Yet this was by no means the intention of the lawmakers, who simply wished to prescribe an adequate atonement for a grievous offence, and in seeking to accomplish this main purpose, ignored the effect of their action upon the fortunes of the heirs or deemed it a matter of minor consideration.

Ancient legislators uniformly regarded a *felo de se* as a criminal against society and treated him as a kind of traitor. The man had enjoyed the support and protection of the body-politic during his infancy and youth, and, by taking his own life, he shook off the responsibilities and shirked the duties devolving upon him as an adult member of the commonwealth. This is why self-murder was called felony and as such involved forfeiture of goods. Calchas would not permit the body of "the mad Ajax," who died by his own hand, to be burned; and the Christian Church of to-day refuses to bury in consecrated ground with religious rites any person who deliberately cuts short the thread of his existence and thus commits treason against the Most High. The Athenians ignominiously lopped off the hand of a suicide and buried the guilty instrument of his death, as an accursed thing, apart from the rest of the interred or incremated body. In some communities all persons over sixty years of age have been left free to kill themselves, if they wished to do so. They had performed the duties of citizenship and of procreation and were permitted to retire in this way, if they saw fit. In very ancient times, the magistrates of Massalia (Marseilles, then a Greek colony) are said to have kept on hand a supply of poison to be given to any citizen, who, on due examination, was found to have good and sufficient reason for taking his own life. Suicide was thus legalized and facilitated, and thereby rendered honourable, and was perhaps found more convenient and economical than to grant pensions or to support paupers. It was a summary method of getting rid of those who had finished the struggle for existence or failed in it, and in either case might be a burden to themselves or to the state. On the other hand, when a suicidal mania seized upon the maidens of Miletos, an Ionian city in Caria, and threatened to produce a dearth of wives and mothers, the municipal authorities decreed that the bodies of all such persons should be exposed naked in the market-place, in order that virgin modesty and shame might overcome the desire of death, and check a self-destructive passion extremely detrimental to the Milesian commonwealth.

It is true, as Blackstone asserts, that the Church claimed deodands as her due and put the price of them into her own coffers; but this fact does not explain their origin. They were an expression of the same feeling that led the public authorities to fill up a well, in which a person had been drowned, not as a precautionary measure, but as a solemn act of expiation; or that condemned and confiscated a ship, which, by lurching, had thrown a man overboard and caused his death.

Deodands were not abolished in England until the reign of Queen Victoria. With the exception of some vestiges of primitive legislation still lingering in maritime law, they are, in modern codes, one of the latest applications of a penal principle, which, in Athens, expatriated stocks and stones, and in other countries of Europe excommunicated bugs and sent beasts to the stake and to the gallows.

CHAPTER II

MEDIÆVAL AND MODERN PENOLOGY

A STRIKING and significant indication of the remarkable change that has come over the spirit of legislation, and more especially of criminal jurisprudence, in comparatively recent times, is the fact that whereas, a few generations ago, law-givers and courts of justice still continued to treat brutes as men responsible for their misdeeds, and to punish them capitally as malefactors, the tendency now-a-days is to regard men as brutes, acting automatically or under an insane and irresistible impulse to evil, and to plead this innate and constitutional proclivity, in prosecution for murder, as an extenuating or even wholly exculpating circumstance. Some persons even maintain, as we have already seen, that such criminals are diabolically possessed and thus account for their inveterate and otherwise incredible perversity on the theory held by the highest authorities in the Middle Ages concerning the nature of noxious animals.

Mediæval jurists and judges did not stop to solve intricate problems of psycho-pathology nor

13

to sift the expert evidence of the psychiater.
The legal maxim : *Si duo faciunt idem non est
idem* (if two do the same thing, it is not the
same) was too fine a distinction for them, even
when one of the doers was a brute beast.   The
puzzling knots, which we seek painfully to untie
and often succeed only in hopelessly tangling,
they boldly cut with executioner's sword.   They
dealt directly with overt acts and administered
justice with a rude and retaliative hand, more
accustomed and better adapted to clinch a fist
and strike a blow than to weigh motives nicely
in a balance, to measure gradations of culpability, or to detect delicate differences in the
psychical texture and spiritual qualities of deeds.
They put implicit faith in Jack Cade's prescription of " hempen caudle " and " pap of hatchet "
as radical remedies for all forms and degrees of
criminal alienation and murderous aberration of
mind.   Phlebotomy was the catholicon of the
physician and the craze of the jurist; blood-
letting was regarded as the only infallible cure
for all the ills that afflict the human and the
social body.   Doctors of physic and doctors of
law vied with each other in applying this
panacea.   The red-streaked pole of the barber-
surgeon and the reeking scaffold, symbols of
venesection as a means of promoting the physical
and moral health of the community, were the
appropriate signs of medicine and jurisprudence.
Hygeia and Justicia, instead of being repre-

sented by graceful females feeding the emblematic serpent of recuperation or holding with firm and even hand the well-poised scales of equity, would have been more fitly typified by two enormous leeches gorged with blood.

Even the dead, who should have been hanged, but escaped their due punishment, could not rest in their graves until the corpse had suffered the proper legal penalty at the hands of the public executioner. Their restless ghosts wandered about as vampires or other malicious spooks until their crimes had been expiated by digging up their bodies and suspending them from the gallows. Culprits, who died on the rack or in prison, were brought to the scaffold as though they were still alive. In 1685, a were-wolf, supposed to be the incarnation of a deceased burgomaster of Ansbach, did much harm in the neighbourhood of that city, preying upon the herds and even devouring women and children. With great difficulty the ravenous beast was finally killed; its carcass was then clad in a tight suit of flesh-coloured cere-cloth, resembling in tint the human skin, and adorned with a chestnut brown wig and a long whitish beard; the snout of the beast was cut off and a mask of the burgomaster's features substituted for it, and the counterfeit presentment thus produced was hanged by order of the court. The pelt of the strangely transmogrified wolf was stuffed and preserved in the margrave's cabinet of curiosities as a memorial of the marvellous event and as ocular proof of the existence of were-wolves.

In Hungary and the Slavic countries of Eastern Europe the public execution of vampires was formerly of frequent occurrence, and the superstition, which gave rise to such proceedings, still prevails among the rural population of those semi-civilized lands. In 1337, a herdsman near the town of Cadan came forth from his grave every night, visiting the villages, terrifying the inhabitants, conversing affably with some and murdering others. Every person, with whom he associated, was doomed to die within eight days and to wander as a vampire after death. In order to keep him in his grave a stake was driven through his body, but he only laughed at this clumsy attempt to impale a ghost, saying : "You have really rendered me a great service by providing me with a staff, with which to ward off the dogs when I go out to walk." At length it was decided to give him over to two public executioners to be burned. We are informed that when the fire began to take effect, "he drew up his feet, bellowed for a while like a bull and hee-hawed like an ass, until one of the executioners stabbed him in the side, so that the blood oozed out and the evil finally ceased."

Again in 1345, in the town of Lewin, a potter's wife, who was reputed to be a witch, died and, owing to suspicions of her pact with Satan, was refused burial in consecrated ground and dumped

into a ditch like a dog. The event proved that
she was not a good Christian, for instead of
remaining quietly in her grave, such as it was,
she roamed about in the form of divers unclean
beasts, causing much terror and slaying sundry
persons. Thereupon she was exhumed and it
was found that she had chewed and swallowed
one half of her face-cloth, which, on being pulled
out of her throat, showed stains of blood. A
stake was driven through her breast, but this
precautionary measure only made matters worse.
She now walked abroad with the stake in her
hand and killed quite a number of people with
this formidable weapon. She was then taken
up a second time and burned, whereupon she
ceased from troubling. The efficacy of this post-
mortem *auto da fé* was accepted as conclusive
proof that her neighbours had neglected to perform their whole religious duty in not having
burned her when she was alive, and were thus
punished for their remissness.

Döpler cites also the case of Stephen Hübner
of Trautenau, who wandered about after death
as a vampire, frightening and strangling several
individuals. By order of the court his body was
disinterred and decapitated under the gallows-
tree. When his head was struck off, a stream of
blood spurted forth, although he had been already
five months buried. His remains were reduced
to ashes and nothing more was heard of him.

In 1573, the parliament of Dôle published a

decree permitting the inhabitants of the Franche Comté to pursue and kill a were-wolf or loup-garou, which infested that province; "notwithstanding the existing laws concerning the chase," the people were empowered to "assemble with javelins, halberds, pikes, arquebuses and clubs to hunt and pursue the said were-wolf in all places, where they could find it, and to take, bind and kill it, without incurring any fine or other penalty." The hunt seems to have been successful, if we may judge from the fact that the same tribunal in the following year (1574) condemned to be burned a man named Gilles Garnier, who ran on all fours in the forest and fields and devoured little children "even on Friday." The poor lycanthrope, it appears, had as slight respect for ecclesiastical fasts as the French pig already mentioned, which was not restrained by any feeling of piety from eating infants on a *jour maigre*.

Henry VIII. of England summoned Thomas à Becket to appear before the Star Chamber to answer for his crimes and then had him condemned as a traitor, and his bones, that had been nearly four centuries in the tomb and worshipped as holy relics by countless pilgrims, burned and scattered to the winds.

When Stephen VI. succeeded to the tiara in 896, one of his first acts was to cause the body of his predecessor, Formosus, to be exhumed and brought to trial on the charge of having unlawfully and sacrilegiously usurped the papal dignity. A writ of summons was issued in due form and the corpse of the octogenarian pope, which had lain already eight months in the grave, was dug up, re-arrayed in full pontificals and seated on a throne in the council-hall of St. Peter's, where a synod had been convened to adjudicate upon the case. No legal formality was omitted in this strange procedure and a deacon was appointed to defend the accused, although the synodical jury was known to be packed and the verdict predetermined. Formosus was found guilty and condemned to deposition. No sooner was the sentence pronounced than the executioners thrust him from the throne, stripped him of his pontifical robes and other ensigns of office, cut off the three benedictory fingers of his right hand, dragged him by the feet out of the judgment-hall and threw his body " as a pestilential thing " (*uti quoddam mephiticum*) into the Tiber. Not until several months later, after Stephen himself had been strangled in prison, were the mutilated and putrefied remains of Formosus taken out of the water and restored to the tomb. The Athenian Prytaneum, as we have already seen, was guilty of the childishness of prosecuting inanimate objects, but it never violated the sepulchre for the purpose of inflicting post-humous punishment on corpses. The perpetration of this brutality was reserved for the Papal See.

From the standpoint of ancient and mediæval jurisprudents the overt act alone was assumed to constitute the crime; the mental condition of the criminal was never or a least very seldom taken into consideration. It is remarkable how long this crude and superficial conception of justice prevailed, and how very recently even the first attempts have been made to establish penal codes on a philosophic basis. The punishableness of an offence is now generally recognized as depending solely upon the sanity and rationality of the offender. Crime, morally and legally considered, presupposes, not perfect, for such a thing does not exist, but normal freedom of the will on the part of the agent. Where this element is wanting, there is no culpabilty, whatever may have been the consequences of the act. Modern criminal law looks primarily to the psychical origin of the deed, and only secondarily to its physical effects; mediæval criminal law ignored the origin altogether, and regarded exclusively the effects, which it dealt with on the homœopenal principle of *similia similibus puniantur,* for the most part blindly and brutally applied.

Mancini, Lombroso, Garofalo, Albrecht, Benedikt, Büchner, Moleschott, Despine, Fouillée, Letourneau, Maudsley, Bruce Thompson, Nicholson, Minzloff, Notovich and other European criminal lawyers, physiologists and anthropologists have devoted themselves with peculiar

zeal and rare acuteness to the study and solution
of obscure and perplexing problems of psycho-
pathological jurisprudence, and have drawn nice
and often overnice distinctions in determining
degrees of personal responsibility. Judicial procedure no longer stops with testimony establishing the bald facts in the case, but admits also the
evidence of the expert alienist in order to ascertain to what extent the will of the accused
was free or functionally normal in its operation.
Here it is not a question of raving madness or
of drivelling idiocy, perceptible to the coarsest
understanding and the crassest ignorance; but
the slightest morbid disturbance, impairing the
full and healthy exercise of the mental faculties,
must be examined and estimated. If " privation
of mind " and " irresistible force," says Zupetta,
are exculpatory, then " partial vitiation of mind "
and " semi-irresistible force " are entitled to the
same or at least to proportional consideration.
There are states of being which are mutually
contradictory and exclusive and cannot co-exist,
such as life and death. A partial state of life
or death is impossible; such expressions as half-
alive and half-dead are hyperbolical figures of
speech used for purely rhetorical purposes; taken
literally, they are simply absurd. It is not so,
however, with states of mind. The intellect,
whose soundness is the first condition of accountability, may be perfectly clear, manifesting itself
in all its fulness and power, or it may be parti-

ally obscured. So, too, the will, whose self-determination is the second condition of accountability, may assert itself with complete freedom and untrammelled force, or it may act under stress and with imperfect volition. Moral coercion, whether arising from external influences, abnormities of the physical organism or defects of the mental constitution, is not less real because it is not easy to detect and may not be wholly irresistible. For this reason, it involves no contradiction in terms and is not absurd to call an action half-conscious, half-voluntary, or half-constrained. "Partial vitiation of mind" is a state distinctly recognized in psychiatrical science. In like manner, there is no essential incongruity in affirming that an impulse may be the result of a "semi-irresistible force." But these mental conditions and forces do not manifest themselves with equal obviousness and intensity in all cases; sometimes they are scarcely appreciable; again they verge upon "absolute privation of mind" and "wholly irresistible force;" and it is the duty of the judge to adjust the penalty to the gradations of guilt as determined by the greater or less freedom of the agent.

The same process of reasoning would lead to the admission of quasi-vitiations of mind and quasi-irresistible forces as grounds of exculpation. Thus one might go on analyzing and refining away human responsibility, and reducing all crime to resultants of mental derangement, until every malefactor would come to be looked upon, not as a culprit to be delivered over to the sharp stroke of the headsman or the safe custody of the jailer, but as an unfortunate victim of morbid states and uncontrollable impulses, to be consigned to the sympathetic care of the psychiater.

Italian anthropologists and jurisprudents have been foremost and gone farthest, both theoretically and practically, in this reaction from mediæval conceptions of crime and its proper punishment. This violent recoil from extreme cruelty to excessive commiseration is due, in a great measure, to the Italian temperament, to a peculiar gentleness and impressionableness of character, which, combined with an instinctive aversion to whatever shocks the senses and mars the pleasure of the moment, are apt to degenerate into shallow sentimentality and sickly sensibility, thereby enfeebling and perverting the moral sense and distorting all ideas of right and justice. To minds thus constituted the cool and deliberate condemnation of a human being to the gallows is an atrocity, in comparison with which a fatal stab in the heat of passion or under strong provocation seems a light and venial transgression. This maudlin sympathy with the guilty living man, who is in danger of suffering for his crime, to the entire forgetfulness of the innocent dead man, the victim of his anger or cupidity, pervades all classes of society, and has stimulated the ingenuity of lawyers and legislators to discover mitigating moments and extenuating circumstances and other means of loosening and enlarging the intricate meshes of the penal code so as to permit the culprit to escape. To this end they eagerly seized upon the doctrine of evolution and endeavoured to seek the origin of crime in hereditary propensities, atavistic recurrences, physical degeneracies and other organic fatalities, for which no one can be held personally responsible, and constructed upon the basis of the most recent scientific researches a penological system giving free scope and full gratification to this pitying and palliating disposition.

But, although the Italians have been pioneers in this movement, it has not been confined to them; it extends to all civilized nations, and expresses a general tendency of the age. Even the Germans, those leaders in theory and laggards in practice, whose studies and speculations have illustrated all forms and phases of judicial procedure, but who adhere so conservatively to ancient methods and resist so stubbornly the tides of reform in their own courts have yielded on this point. They no longer regard insanity and idiocy as the only grounds of exemption from punishment, but include in the same category " all morbid disturbances of mental activity," and " all states of mind in which the free determination of the will is not indeed wholly destroyed, but only partially impaired." In order to realize the radical changes that have taken place in this direction within a relatively recent period, it will suffice merely to compare the present criminal code of the German Empire with the Austrian code of 1803, the Bavarian code of 1813, and the Prussian code of 1851. It must be remembered, too, that these changes have been effected under the drift of public opinion in spite of the political preponderance of Prussia and her strong bureaucratic influence, which has always been exerted in favour of severe penalties, and shown slight consideration for individual frailties and criminal idiosyncrasies in inflicting punishment. As the stronghold of a stolid and supercilious squirearchy (Junkerthum) in Germany, Prussia has stubbornly resisted to the last every reformatory movement in civil and social, and especially in criminal legislation.

A recent decision of the supreme court of the German Empire (pronounced in the summer of 1894) seems to put a check upon this tendency by rejecting the plea of " moral insanity " in the extenuation of crime. As a matter of fact, however, the question whether such a state of mind as " moral insanity " exists or can exist has not yet been settled; and so long as psychiaters do not agree as to the actuality or possibility of this anomalous mental condition, courts of justice may very properly refuse to take it into consideration or to allow it to exert the slightest influence upon their judgment in the infliction of judicial punishment. Moral insanity, as usually defined, involves a disturbance of the moral perceptions and a derangement of the emotional nature, without impairing the distinctively intellectual faculties. The supposed victim of this hypothetical form of madness is capable of thinking logically and often shows remarkable astuteness in forming his plans and executing his criminal purposes, but seems utterly destitute of the moral sense and of all the finer feelings of humanity, performing the most atrocious deeds without hesitation and remembering them without the slightest compunction. In moral stolidity and the lack of susceptibility he is on a level with the lowest savage. German psychiaters, on the whole, are inclined to regard such persons, not as morally insane, but as morally degenerate and depraved; and German jurists and judges are not disposed to admit such vitiation of character as an extenuating circumstance, especially at a time when criminals of this class are on the increase and are banded together to overthrow civilized society and to introduce an era of anarchy and barbarism. The decision of the German judicatory is therefore not reactionary, but merely precautionary, and simply indicates a wise determination to keep the administration of criminal law unencumbered by theories, which science has not yet fully established and which at present can only serve to paralyze the arm of retributive justice.

Mediæval penal justice sought to inflict the

greatest possible amount of suffering on the offender and showed a diabolical fertility of invention in devising new methods of torture even for the pettiest trespasses. The monuments of this barbarity may now be seen in European museums in the form of racks, thumbkins, interlarded hares, Pomeranian bonnets, Spanish boots, scavenger's daughters, iron virgins and similar engines of cruelty. Until quite recently an iron virgin, with its interior full of long and sharp spikes, was exhibited in a subterranean passage at Nuremberg, on the very spot where it is supposed to have once performed its horrible functions; and in Munich this inhuman instrument of punishment was in actual use as late as the beginning of the nineteenth century. The criminal code of Maria Theresa, published in 1769, contained forty-five large copperplate engravings, illustrating the various modes of torture prescribed in the text for the purpose of extorting confession and evidently designed to serve as object lessons for the instruction of the tormentor and the intimidation of the accused. That Prussia was the first country in Germany to abolish judicial torture was due, not to the progressive spirit of the nation or of its tribunals, but solely to the superior enlightenment and energy of Frederic the Great, who effected this reform arbitrarily and against the will of jurists and judges by cabinet-orders issued in 1740 and 1745. Crimes which women are under peculiar temptation to commit, were punished with extraordinary severity. Thus the infanticide was buried alive, a small tube communicating with the outer air being placed in her mouth in order to prolong her life and her agony. A case of this kind is recorded in the proceedings of the " Malefiz-Gericht " or criminal court of Ensisheim in Alsatia under the date of February 3, 1570. In 1401, an apprentice, who stole from his master five pfennigs (then as now the smallest coin of Germany and worth about the fifth of a cent), was condemned to have both his ears cut off. Incredible barbarities of this kind were practised by some of the best and noblest men of that age. Thus Cardinal Carlo Borromeo, who was pre-eminent among his contemporaries for the purity of his life and the benevolence of his character, did not hesitate to condemn Fra Tommaso di Mileto, a Franciscan monk, to be walled up alive, because he entertained heretical notions concerning the sinfulness of eating meat on Friday, and expressed doubts touching the worship of images, indulgences, the supreme and infallible authority of the pope, and the real presence in the eucharist. This cruel sentence, a striking illustration of the words of Lucretius,

"Tantum religio potuit suadere malorum,"

was pronounced December 16, 1564, as follows :
" I condemn you to be walled up in a place

enclosed by four walls, where, with anguish of
heart and abundance of tears, you shall bewail
your sins and grievous offences committed
against the majesty of God, and the holy mother
Church and the religion of St. Francis, the
founder of your order.'' A bishop, who should
impose such a punishment now-a-days, would be
very properly declared insane and divested of his
office.

Much ridicule has been cast upon the so-called
'' Blue Laws '' of Connecticut on account of the
narrowness and pettiness of their prevailing
spirit. From our present point of view they are
absurd and in many respects atrocious, but compared with the penal codes of that time they
mark a great advance in human legislation.
They reduced the number of crimes, then
punishable in England by death, from two
hundred and twenty-three to fourteen. In the
mother-country, as late as the seventeenth
century, counterfeiters and issuers of false coin
were condemned to be boiled to death in oil by
slow degrees. The culprit was suspended over
the cauldron and gradually let down into it, first
boiling the feet, then the legs and so on, until all
the flesh was separated from the bones and the
body reduced to a skeleton. The Puritans of New
England, relentless as they were in their dealings
with sectaries, were never so ruthless as this;
nor is it probable that they would have inflicted
capital punishment upon their own '' stubborn

14

and rebellious sons," or upon persons who " worship any other God but the Lord God," had it not been for precedents recorded in laws enacted by a semi-civilized people thousands of years ago and supposed to have been dictated by divine wisdom. They failed to perceive the incongruity of attempting to rear a democratic commonwealth on theocratic foundations and made the fatal mistake of planning their structure after what they regarded as the perfect model of the Jewish Zion.

If we compare these barbarities with the law recently enacted by the legislature of the state of New York, whereby capital punishment is to be inflicted as quickly and painlessly as possible by means of electricity, we shall be able to appreciate the immense difference between the mediæval and the modern spirit in the conception and execution of penal justice.

A point of practical importance, which the criminal anthropologist has to consider is the relation of moral to penal responsibility. If there is no freedom of the will and the commission of crime is the necessary result of physiological idiosyncrasies, hereditary predispositions, brachycephalous, dolichocephalous or microcephalous peculiarities, anomalies of cerebral convolution, or other anatomical asymmetries, over which the individual has no control and by which his destiny is determined, then he is certainly not morally responsible for his conduct. But is he on this account to be exempt from punishment? The vast majority of criminalists answer this question unhesitatingly in the negative, declaring that penal legislation is independent of metaphysical opinion, and that punishment is proper and imperative so far as it is essential to the protection and preservation of society. If the infliction of the penalties depriving a man of his freedom or his life is found to secure these ends, it is the duty of the tribunals established for the administration of justice to impose them without troubling themselves about the mental condition of the culprit or stopping to discuss problems which belong to the province of the psychiater. Legal tribunals are not offices in which candidates for the insane asylum are examined or certificates of admission to reformatories issued, but are organized as a terror to evil-doers in the general interests of society, and all their decisions should have this object in view. If a madman is not hanged for murder, it is solely because such a procedure would exert no deterring influence upon other madmen; society protects itself, in cases of this kind, by depriving the dangerous individual of his liberty and thus preventing him from doing harm; but it has no right to inflict upon him wanton and superfluous suffering. Even if it should be deemed desirable to kill him, the method of his removal should be such as to cause the least possible pain and publicity.

Here, too, the welfare of society is the determinative factor.

This doctrine reduces confirmed criminals to the condition of ferocious beasts and venomous reptiles, and logically demands that they should be eliminated for precisely the same reason that noxious animals are exterminated, although neither the human nor the animal creatures are to blame for the perniciousness of their inborn proclivities and natural instincts. In the eyes of Courcelle-Seneuil a prison is a "kind of menagerie "; Naquet, the French chemist and senator, goes still farther, declaring that men are no more culpable for being criminal than vitriol is for being corrosive, and adding that it is our own fault if we put this stuff into our tea and are poisoned by it. The same writer maintains that " there is no more demerit in being perverse than in being cross-eyed or humpbacked." In a recent lecture on criminal jurisprudence and biology Professor Benedikt cites the case of a Moravian robber and murderer, whose brain was found on dissection to resemble that of a beast of prey and who was therefore, in the opinion of the eminent Viennese authority, no more responsible for his bloody deeds than is a lion or a tiger for its ravages. The corollary to this anatomical demonstration is that one should treat such a man as a lion or a tiger and shoot him on the spot. Atavistic relapses, defective cerebral development and other abnormities undoubtedly occur in criminals, whose acts may be traced, in some degree, to these physical imperfections and therefore be pathologically stimulated and partially necessitated by them. On the other hand, there are thousands of persons with equally small and unsymmetrical craniums, who do not commit crime, but remain respectable, safe, and useful members of society.

Lombroso discovers in habitual malefactors a tendency to tattoo their bodies; but this kind of cuticular ornamentation indicates merely a low development of the æsthetic sense, a barbarous conception of the beautiful or what would be called bad taste, and has not the slightest genetic or symptomatic connection with crime and the proclivity to perpetrate it. As a means of embellishing the exterior man it may be rude and unrefined, but after all it is only skin-deep, and does not extend to the moral character. Honest people of the lower classes take pleasure in disfiguring themselves in this way, and soldiers and sailors, who are very far from furnishing the largest percentage of criminals, are especially addicted to it, simply because they find ample leisure in the barracks and the forecastle to undergo this slow and painful process of what they deem adornment. According to Lombroso criminals have as a rule thick heads of hair and thin beards; but as the majority of them are comparatively young, these phenomena are by no means remarkable. He has also found that the hair of such persons is usually black or dark chestnut; had his investigations been carried on in Norway and Sweden instead of in Italy, he would have certainly come to the conclusion that flaxen hair is an index of a criminal character.

It would be difficult to deny the existence of a constitutionally criminal class, a persistently perverse element, which is the born foe of all law and order, at war with every form of social and political organization and whose permanent attitude of mind is that of the Irishman, who, on landing in New York, inquired: "Have ye a government here?" and, on receiving an affirmative answer, replied, "Then I'm agin' it." Criminal anthropologists have been especially earnest in their endeavours to define this pernicious type and to determine the physiological and physiognomical features, which characterize and constitute it. This line of research is unquestionably in the right direction, but as a reaction against barren scholastic speculations and brutal penal codes has been carried to excess by enthusiastic specialists and led to broad generalizations and hasty deductions from insufficient data. Taine's definition of man as "an animal of a higher species, that produces poems and systems of philosophy, as silk-worms spin cocoons and bees secrete honeycomb," applies with equal force to the vicious side of human nature. Criminal propensities, as well as creative powers, are the resultants of race, temperament, climate, food, organism, environment and other pre-natal and post-natal influences and agencies, to which the individual did not voluntarily subject himself and from which he cannot escape. The acts, therefore, which he performs, whether good or evil, are as independent of his will as the colour of his hair or the shape of his nose; for while they are apparently volitional impulses, the will itself, from which they seem to proceed, is determined by forces as fixed and free from his control as are those which render him blue-eyed or snub-nosed.

The penological application of this philosophical principle has given rise to numerous theories concerning the nature and origin of crime. Lombroso and his disciples, as we have already intimated, attribute it to atavism or the survival in the individual of the animal instincts and low morals of the aboriginal barbarian. The criminal is simply a savage let loose in a civilized community and ignoring the ethical conceptions developed by ages of culture and performing actions that would have seemed perfectly proper and praiseworthy in the eyes of our pre-historic ancestors. The hero of the Palæolithic age is the brigand and cut-throat of to-day. The criminal type is nothing but a reversion to the primitive type of the race, and the representatives of this school of anthropologists have been untiring in their efforts to discover physical and moral characteristics common to both : long arms like chimpanzees, four circumvolutions of the frontal lobes of the brain like the large carnivora, small cranial capacity like the cave-men, canine teeth like anthropoid apes and a simian nose. This analogy extends to the eyes, the ears, the hair, and even to the internal organs, the liver, the heart and the stomach, and the diseases by which they are affected. It has also been observed that assassins are brachycephalous and thieves dolichocephalous. Marro maintains that in many cases metaphors express real facts and embody the common conclusions of mankind based upon centuries of observation : swindlers have a foxy look, long-fingered persons are naturally thievish, whereas a club-fisted fellow is pretty sure to have a pugnacious disposition, and to be a born rough. Nevertheless social surroundings, educational influences and other outward circumstances are important factors, not so much in changing the character as in giving it direction; the same cerebral constitution and consequent innate predisposition may make a man a hero or a bravo, a dashing soldier like Phil Sheridan, or a daring robber like Fra Diavolo, according to the place of his birth and the nature of his environment.

In common discourse we speak of atrabiliary, spleeny, choleric, or even stomachous persons, but such expressions are, in most cases, survivals of antiquated beliefs concerning the functions of certain physical organs. Hypochondria has no more originary connection with the cartilage of the breastbone than with the cartilage of the ear. In the literal sense of the terms a large-brained man is not necessarily of superior intellectual power any more than a large-hearted man is naturally generous or a large-handed man instinctively grasping. So, too, the theory that intelligence and morality are in direct proportion to the size and symmetry of the encephalon is not sustained by facts; at least the exceptions to the rule are so many and so remarkable as to render it extremely misleading and therefore of little practical value as a scientific principle. Gambetta's brain, for example, weighed only 1294 grammes, being fifty-eight grammes less in weight than that of the average Parisian, and was so abnormally irregular in its configuration as to seem actually deformed. Any physiologist, says Dr. Manouvrier, who should come across such a skull in a museum, would unhesitatingly pronounce it to be that of a savage. The third frontal circumvolution of the left lobe of his brain had in the posterior part a supplementary fold said by some to be the organ of speech and by others to be the organ of theft; perhaps both combined in the ability of the orator to steal away men's hearts, as Antony says of the seductive eloquence of Brutus. The distinguished physiologist Bichat was an ardent advocate of this doctrine of the causal connection between cranial capacity and symmetry and vigorous and well-balanced mental faculties, but after his death his own cranium was found to be conspicuously lacking in the very characteristics which he deemed so essential to man as a moral and intellectual being. The late German professor Bischoff based his argument against the higher education of woman on the fact that the average female brain weighs only 1272 grammes, and asserted that a person with such a light encephalon must be organically incompetent to master the various branches of study taught in our universities. A post-mortem examination proved his own brain to be considerably inferior in weight to that of the average woman.

Careful investigations would doubtless furnish additional examples of this comical application of the *argumentum ad hominem* in refutation of the notion that intellectual capacity is determined by the bulk of the brain or the shape of the skull. Ugo Foscolo, one of the most celebrated of modern Italian poets, had a cranium, which, according to this standard of appreciation, ought to have belonged to an idiot. On the other hand, the brain of the " Hottentot Venus," examined by Gratiolet, far surpassed in the symmetry of both hemispheres and the perfection of its circumvolutions the normal brains of the Caucasian race. The same phenomenon has

been observed, although in a less striking
manner, occasionally in cretins and quite often
in criminals. Character is the resultant of a
multitude of combined forces, the great majority
of which are still unknown and perhaps unknow-
able quantities. The impulse given by each
must be exactly estimated in order to predeter-
mine the joint effect. No factor which contributes to its formation must be overlooked, and
the acceptance of any one of them, however important it may seem to be, as the basis on which
to reform and reconstruct our penal legislation,
would be premature and pernicious. This
hobby-horsical tendency, which is the vice of
every specialist, is now the besetting sin of
criminal anthropologists, each of whom is firmly
convinced that he can reach the goal only on his
own garran.

" The more advanced criminalists," says Professor Von Kirchenheim, "are becoming
thoroughly convinced that the penal codes of
to-day do not correspond to the criminal world
of to-day. No science has remained so deeply
rooted and grounded in scholasticism as jurisprudence; and this evil is most clearly perceptible in the province of criminal law. The
necessity of a change in our penal legislation
has already made itself widely felt. The contest
with crime must now be carried on in a different manner from what it was when men waged
war with bows and arrows; modern criminality

must be fought, as it were, with repeating rifles.'' In other words, we can never suppress crime by meeting it with bludgeons and boomerangs and other rude implements of barbarous warfare, but must encounter it with the finest and most effective weapons of precision, which the armoury of modern science can put into our hands. Society has outgrown the crude conception of punishment as mere retaliation or retribution incited by revenge. There is no doubt that even in the most enlightened countries, penology as a science is still in its infancy, and is only just beginning to feel the uncomfortable girding of its scanty swaddling-bands and blindly kicking itself free from them. That this first emancipatory effort should be somewhat clumsy, and occasionally attended by comical casualties and even serious disasters, lies in the very nature of the case. It is evident, too, that the antiquated and utterly irrational methods now employed for the suppression of crime tend directly to increase it. It is the aim of the positive, in distinction from the classical school of criminalists to discover the real causes of criminal actions, and thus to endeavour to eradicate or neutralize them. A casual criminal, for example, whom external conditions, accidental circumstances, sudden temptations or bad influences have led astray, should not be treated in the same manner, although guilty of the same overt act, as the habitual or constitutional criminal, whose wrong-doing arises from a diseased, ill-balanced or undeveloped mental or physical organization, and is therefore an inborn and perhaps irresistible proclivity. The latter is hardly responsible for his conduct, and the possibility of reforming him is slight. The only proper thing to do with such a culprit is to render him personally harmless to society either by death or perpetual incarceration, and to prevent him from propagating his kind. The law of the survival of the fittest through selection suggests as its necessary sequence the suppression of the unfittest through sterilization. Nature has her own effective and relentless method of attaining this desirable result; but man is constantly thwarting her beneficent purposes by all sorts of pernicious schemes originating in factitious sentimentalism and maudlin sympathy, which under the plea of philanthropy tend to foster and perpetuate moral monstrosities to the discomfort and detriment of civilized society and the permanent deterioration of the race. To sentence persons of this class to eight or ten years' imprisonment and then to turn them loose again as a constant source of peril to mankind, is the greatest folly that any tribunal can possibly commit. It is a wrong done both to the criminal and to the community of which he is a member. The penalties imposed by the law should be determined not solely by the enormity of the crime, but chiefly by the character of the criminal.

Paradoxical as such a conclusion may be, it is nevertheless a strictly logical deduction from the premises, that the more corrupt he is by his physical constitution and therefore the less culpable he is from a moral point of view, the more severe should be the sentence pronounced upon him. Where the vicious propensity is in the blood and beyond the reach of moral or penal purgations, the only safety is in the elimination of the individual, just as the only remedy for a gangrened limb is amputation. We ridicule ancient and mediæval courts of justice for prosecuting bugs and beasts, but future generations will condemn as equally absurd and outrageous our judicial treatment of human beings, who can no more help perpetrating deeds of violence, under given conditions, than locusts and caterpillars can help consuming crops to the injury of the husbandman, or wild beasts can help rending and devouring their prey. It is also interesting to know that in former times the animal was not punished capitally because it was supposed to have incurred guilt, but as a memorial of the occurrence, or in the language of canonical law: *Non propter culpam sed propter memoriam facti pecus occiditur.* It was put to death not because it was culpable, but because it was harmful; and this is the ground on which the radical wing of criminal anthropologists would repress and eliminate a vicious person without regard to his mental soundness or moral responsibility; to use Garofalo's metaphor he is a microbe injurious to the social organism and must be destroyed.

Lombroso carries his theory of the innateness, hereditability and ineradicableness of criminal propensities so far as to affirm that "education cannot change those who are born with perverse instincts," and to despair of correcting an obstinate bias of this sort even in a child. In accordance with this idea his disciple, Le Bon, proposes to "deport to distant countries all professional criminals or persistent relapsers into vice (*récidivistes*) together with their posterity," and would thus practically revive the barbarous principle of visiting the sins of the fathers upon the children, although he does not regard their conduct as sinful in the sense of being a voluntary transgression of the moral law, but as the result of a transmitted taint and organic deficiency, for which the individual is in no wise responsible. It is hardly necessary to add that this doctrine is not sustained by the statistics of reformatories, houses of refuge and similar institutions, which have now taken the place of the prison and the scaffold in the case of juvenile offenders.

Those who look upon crime as a pathological phenomenon find a striking illustration and strong confirmation of their views in violations of the law committed under the impulse of hypnotic suggestion. Some maintain that all acts originating in this manner are purely automatic, and acquit the person performing them of all moral and legal responsibility, since they express the will and purpose of the hypnotizer, who alone should be held accountable. Others hold that the man, who consents to be hypnotized and thus voluntarily surrenders his will-power and permits himself to be used as an instrument for the perpetration of crime, should be punished for his offences and not allowed to go scot-free by pleading the *force majeure* of hypnotic suggestion. The liability to punishment, it is justly argued, would be a safeguard to society by putting a wholesome and effective check on hypnotic experimentations. There is at least no reason why the hypnotized subject should not be called to account for accomplicity. Any passion may become automatic and irresistible by long indulgence and assiduous cultivation, so that the man is overmastered by it and cannot help yielding to it under strong temptation; but the victim of a vicious habit has no right to urge the force of an evil propensity in exculpation of himself. The inborn or inveterate badness of a man's character may explain, but cannot excuse his bad conduct in the impartial and inexorable eye of justice. So, too, he who sins against his own worthiness and dignity as a rational being by choosing to annul his power of self-determination as a voluntary agent and become a helpless tool in the hands of another,

ought not wholly to escape the consequences of
his folly. That the hypnotizer should be made
fully responsible for the realization of his suggestions, no representative of either the positive
or classical school of criminalists would probably
deny. To take a man's life by means of hypnotic
suggestion is as truly subornation to murder as
to hire an assassin to plunge a dagger into his
heart.

As regards hypnotism itself, it would be
strange enough if we should discover in it the
real scientific basis of witchcraft, and modern
legislation should prosecute and punish hypno-
tizers as mediæval legislation prosecuted and
punished sorcerers. The sympathetic influence
of a morbidly imaginative mind upon the body
in directing the currents of nervous energy and
increasing the flow of blood towards particular
points of the physical organism, so as to produce
stigmata and similar abnormal phenomena, has
long been recognized as an adequate explanation
of much mediæval and modern miracle-monger-
ing. It would now seem as if hypnotism, or
the magnetic influence of one man's will upon
another man's mind and body were destined
to furnish the key to still greater marvels and
reveal the true nature and origin of what has
hitherto passed for divine inspiration or diabolical
possession. Charcot, Renaut, Fowler and other
eminent neuropathologists have conclusively
shown that certain forms of hysteria sometimes

15

produce tumors, ulcers, muscular atrophy, paralysis of the limbs and like affections apparently organic, but really nervous. In such cases any kind of faith-cure, in which the patient has confidence, prayer, the laying on of hands, the water of Lourdes or of St. Ignatius, medals of St. Benedict, scapularies of the Virgin, seraphic girdles, a pilgrimage to the shrine of a saint or contact with a holy relic may prove far more efficacious than drugs and are therefore recommended by priests and occasionally even prescribed by physicians, who are far too enlightened to regard such healings as miraculous or supernatural. The success of scientific research in disclosing the physical basis of intellectual life is gradually undermining the foundations of so-called spiritualism, and rendering it more and more impossible to mistake symptoms of chlorosis and hysterical weakness for spiritual gifts and signs of God's special favour. Sickly women are no longer treated as seeresses and their vague and incoherent sayings treasured as oracular utterances.

One of the chief difficulties encountered by those who seek to frame and administer penal laws on psycho-pathological principles arises from the fact that no one has ever yet been able to give an exact and adequate definition of insanity. However easy it may be to recognize the grosser varieties of mental disorder, it is often impossible even for an expert to detect it in its subtler forms, or to draw a hard and fast line between sanity and insanity. An eminent alienist affirms that very few persons we meet in the counting-room, on the street or in society, or with whom we enjoy pleasant intercourse at their firesides, are of perfectly sound mind. Nearly every one is a little touched; some molecule of the brain has turned into a maggot; there is some topic that cannot be introduced without making the portals of the mind grate on their golden hinges,—some point at which we are forced to say,—

"O, that way madness lies ; let me shun that."

It is possible, however, that this very opinion may be a fixed idea or symptomatic eccentricity of the alienist himself. The theory that all men are monomaniacs may be merely his peculiar monomania. Still there is unquestionably this much truth in it, that nearly every person has developed some faculty at the expense of the others and thus destroyed his mental equilibrium. Every tendency of this kind, which is not checked or balanced and in some way rounded off in the growth of the character, becomes morbidly strong and leads to a sort of insanity. The specialist is always exposed to this danger of growing into a man of one idea; his monomania may be in the direction of valuable research or in the pursuit of a foolish whim, resulting in useful inventions or dissipating itself in chimerical projects; it may be a harmless crotchet or a vicious proclivity, philanthropic or misanthropic; it is, nevertheless, a bent or bias and so far a deviation from the norm of perfect intellectual rectitude.

A madman, says Coleridge, is one who " mistakes his thoughts for person and things." But here the frenzies of the lunatic intrench on the functions of the poet, who " of imagination all compact," takes his fancies for realities,

> " Turns them to shapes, and gives to airy nothing
> A local habitation and a name."

Coleridge's definition includes also the mythopœic faculty, the power of projecting creations of the mind and endowing them with objective actuality and independent existence, which in the infancy of the race peopled heaven and earth with phantasms, and still croons over cradles and babbles of brownie and fairy in nurseries and chimney-corners. No progress of science can wholly eradicate this tendency to mythologize. In the absence of better material, it seizes upon the most prosaic and practical improvements in modern household life and clothes them with poetry and legend. The imaginative child of New York or Boston, after feeding the mind on fairy tales, converts the ordinary gas-pipe into the den of a dragon, which puts forth its fiery tongue when the knob is turned. The sleeping figure of a virgin carved in marble and copied from an ancient Greek sculpture of Ariadne, which reposes on an arch in the park of Sans-souci at Potsdam, has been transformed by the popular imagination into an enchanted princess, who will awake as soon as a horseman succeeds in springing over it three times with his steed. So vivid is the belief in this story that many good Christians never pass through the archway without making the sign of the cross as a prophylactic against possible demonic influences. The Suabian peasant still believes that the railroad is a device of the devil, who is entitled by contract to a tollage of one passenger on every train; he is in a constant state of anxiety lest his turn may come on the next trip and always wears a crucifix as the best means, so far as his own person is concerned, of cheating the devil of his due. As the Church has uniformly consigned great inventors to the infernal regions, his Satanic Majesty could have never had any lack of ingenious wits among his subjects capable of advising him in such matters.

An important consideration, which did not disturb the minds of mediæval jurists, nor stay the hand of strictly retributive justice, is the fact, now generally admitted, that crimes, like all other human actions, are subject to certain fixed laws, which seem to some extent to remove them from the province of free will and the power of individual determination. Professor Morselli has shown statistically that suicide, which we are wont to consider a wholly voluntary act, is really dependent upon a great variety of circumstances, over which man has no control : climate, seasons, months, days, state of crops, domestic, social, political, financial, economical, geographical and meteorological conditions, sun, moon, and stars all work together, impelling him to self-destruction or keeping him from it. Suicide increases when the earth is in aphelion, and decreases when it is in perihelion. Race and religion are also important factors in aggravating or mitigating the suicidal tendency, Germans and Protestants being most, and Semitic nations and Mohammedans, including those of Aryan and African blood, being least addicted to it. Suicide is, in fact, the resultant of a vast number of complicated and far-reaching forces, which we can neither trace nor measure, and of which the victims themselves are for the most part unconscious. To a very considerable degree, it is a question of environment in the broadest sense of the term; " an effect," says Morselli, " of the struggle for existence and of human selection, working according to the laws of evolution among civilized peoples." What is proved to be true of self-slaughter is equally so of murder and every other crime.

An additional reflection, that " must give us pause " in the presence of crime, is that some of the chief causes operating to produce the manifold evils afflicting society and threatening to subvert it, are due in a great measure to the present egoistic organization of our social and industrial system, the selfish and unscrupulous power of wealth directed and stimulated by superior intelligence and energy, on the one hand, and the brute forces of ignorance driven to despair by the disheartening and debasing pressure of poverty, on the other hand, arrayed against each other in fierce and bitter conflict. Much of the individual viciousness, which society is required to punish, springs directly from the unjust and injurious conditions of life, which society itself has created. It is the perception of this fact that disturbs the conscience, puzzles the will, and palsies the arm of the modern law-giver and executor of justice.

Mediæval legislators were not restrained by any scruples of this sort; they regarded the criminal, both human and animal, as the sole author of the crime, ascribing it simply to his own wickedness and never looking beyond the mere actual deed to the social influences, psychical and physical characteristics and inherited qualities, that impelled him with irresistible force to do iniquitous things. This was doubtless a very narrow, superficial and utterly unphilosophical view of human action and responsibility; the danger now-a-days lies in the opposite extreme, in the tendency to pity the vicious individual as the passive product and commiserable victim of unfortunate conditions, and while engaged in the laudable attempt to improve these conditions by working out broad and benevolent plans of permanent relief and reformation for the future amelioration of society, to relax penalties and to fail in providing by sufficiently stringent measures for its present security. Tribunals have only to do with individual criminals as their conduct affects the general welfare. In what manner their characters have been formed by ancestral agencies and other predispositions may be an interesting study to the psychologist and the sociologist, but does not concern the judge or the jurist in the discharge of their official functions. The problem of crime is therefore a very simple one, so far as the criminal lawyer has to deal with the concrete case, but very complex, when we look beyond the overt act to its genesis in the life of the race. The proper administration of penal justice is weakened and defeated by mixing itself up with psycho-pathological inquiries wholly foreign to it.

It is a curious coincidence that the theory of evolution, in its application to man's free agency, should arrive at essentially the same conclusion as the theology of Augustine and Calvin. Predestination, which the suffragan of Hippo and the Genevan divine attributed to the arbitrary decrees of God, evolution traces to the influences of heredity upon individuals, predetermining their bodily and mental constitutions. There is, however, a wide difference between these two doctrines in their workings. From the clutch of a deity "willing to show his wrath and to make his power known," no man can by any effort of his own effect his escape. Against this imperious and general sentence of damnation no process of development, no upward striving, no individual initiative can be of any avail. Evolution, on the contrary, promises a gradual release from low ancestral conditions—the original sin of the theologians—and opens up to the race a way of redemption, not only through natural selection and spontaneous variations resulting in higher and nobler types of mankind, but also through the modification of inherited traits by careful breeding, thorough discipline and the conscious and constant endeavour of every human being to improve and perfect himself. Salvation through the "election of grace" is by no means identical with salvation through the "survival of the fittest." The righteousness of those whom God has chosen as "the vessels of mercy whom he had afore prepared unto glory," may be and probably is "as filthy rags"; evolutionary science, on the contrary, recognizes and appreciates redeemable qualities by selecting, strengthening and propagating them and by this means aims ultimately to redeem the world. It imposes upon each man the duty and necessity of working out his own salvation, not with fear and trembling at the prospect of meeting an angry deity, but with hope and cheerfulness, knowing that the beneficent forces of nature

are working in him, as in all forms of organic
life, in obedience to the laws of development,
towards the goal of his highest possible perfection by gradually eliminating the heirloom of
the beast and the savage, and letting the instincts
of the tiger and the ape slowly die within him.
"The best man," said Socrates, "is he who
seeks most earnestly to perfect himself, and the
happiest man is he who has the fullest consciousness that he is perfecting himself." This utterance of the Athenian sage expresses the fundamental principle of the ethics of evolution,
according to which there can be no greater sin
than the neglect of self-culture, holding, as it
does, in the province of science a place corresponding in importance to that which the un-
pardonable sin against the Holy Ghost holds in
the province of theology. No one is blamable
for inheriting bad tendencies; but every one is
blamable for not striving to eradicate them. If
evil impulses prove to be irresistible, then society
must step in and render them harmless by depriving of life or liberty the unfortunate victims
of such propensities.

Again, if the mental and moral qualities of
the lower animals differ from those of man, not
in kind, but only in degree, and the human
mammal is descended from a stock of primates,
to which apes and bats belong, and dogs and
cats and pigs are more remotely akin, it is difficult to determine the point at which moral and

penal responsibility ceases in the descending,
or begins in the ascending scale of being. That
beasts and birds and even insects commit acts
of violence, which in human agents would be
called crimes, and which spring from the same
psychical causes and, as we have shown in
another work (*Evolutionary Ethics and Animal
Psychology*. New York: D. Appleton and
Co.; London: William Heinemann, 1898), are
punished by the herd, the flock or the swarm
in a more or less judicial manner, is undeniable.
The zoöpsychologist Lacassagne divides the
criminal offences of animals into six classes or
categories, the ground of the classification being
the motives which underlie and originate them.
The lowest or most rudimentary motive to crime
in both man and beast is hunger, the operation
of which is seen in the spectacle of one savage
killing another in order to get sole possession
of a wild beast slain by them in common, and
in the ferocity of two dogs fighting over a bone.
Perhaps the great majority of crimes afflicting
society at the present time have their origin in
this source. Next to the desire of the individual
to preserve himself comes the desire to preserve
his kind; this motive is commonly considered
a more generous impulse and is praised as par-
ental affection. This earliest and most primitive
of altruistic emotions is exceedingly strong in
the lower animals, especially in those whose offspring are comparatively helpless in infancy, as

is the case with all species of monkeys, and manifests itself not only in tender care of the young, but also in theft, robbery, and other acts of violence committed for their sake. The wanton love of destruction characterizes both beasts and men; there are roughs and vandals among the former as well as among the latter, who take a malicious delight in doing injury to persons and property. Vanity and the desire of " showing off " play no small part in the wrongdoings of apes and apish men and women. Other incentives to crime are ambition, sexual passion, gregariousness, the concentrated egoism and merciless brutality of a crowd even in the most civilized communities, the outrages so recklessly perpetrated by what a French jurist, M. Tarde, calls " that impulsive and maniac beast, the mob." It may be remarked, too, that the kinds of criminal actions, which civilization tends to diminish among men, domestication tends to diminish among the lower animals.

If these statements be correct, why should not animals be held penally responsible for their conduct as well as human beings? There are men apparently less intelligent than apes. Why then should the man be capitally punished and the ape not brought to trial? And if the ape be made responsible and punishable, why not the dog, the horse, the pig, and the cat? In other words, does evolutionary criminology justify the judicial proceedings instituted by mediæval courts against animals or regard the typical human criminal as having in this respect no supremacy over the beast? Does modern science take us back to the barbarities of the Middle Ages in matters of penal legislation, and in abolishing judicial procedure against quadrupedal beasts is it thereby logically forced to stay the hand of justice uplifted against bipedal brutes? The answer to these questions is unhesitatingly negative. Zoöpsychology is the key to anthropopsychology and enables us to get a clearer conception of the genesis of human crime by studying its manifestations in the lower creation; we thus see it in the process of becoming, acquire a more correct appreciation of its nature and origin and learn how to deal with it more rationally and effectively in bestial man.

Another point discussed by Plato and still seriously debated by writers on criminal jurisprudence is whether punishment is to be inflicted *quia peccatum est* or *ne peccetur;* in other words, whether the object of it should be retributive or preventive. The truth is, however, that both of these motives are operative and as determining causes are so closely intermixed that it is impossible to separate them. As the distinguished criminalist, Professor Von Liszt, has remarked one might as well ask whether a sick man takes medicine because he is ill or in order to get well. The penalty is imposed in consequence of the commission of a crime and also for the purpose of preventing a recurrence of it, and is therefore both retributory and reformatory. Punishment is defined by Laas as "ethicized and nationalized revenge, exercised by the state or body politic, which is alone impartial enough to pronounce just judgments and powerful enough to execute them." Civilization takes vengeance out of the hands of the injured individual and delegates it to the community or commonwealth, which has been outraged in his person. The underlying principle, however, is, in both cases, the same, and the idea of justice, as administered by the community, does not rise above that entertained by the aggregate or average of individuals composing it.

The recent growth of sociology and especially the scientific study of the laws of heredity thus tend, by exciting an intelligent interest in the psychological solution of such questions, to render men less positive and peremptory in their judicial decisions. The intellectual horizon is so greatly enlarged and so many possibilities are suggested, that it is difficult for conscientious persons, strongly affected by these speculations and honestly endeavouring to make an ethical or penal application of them, to come to a prompt and practical conclusion in any given case. The voice of decision loses its magisterial sternness and

"the native hue of resolution
Is sicklied o'er with the pale cast of thought."

If it be true, as Mr. Galton affirms, that legal ability is transmitted from father to son, criminal proclivity may be equally hereditary, and the judge and the culprit may have reached their relative positions through a line of ancestral influences, working according to immutable and inevasible laws of descent.

Schopenhauer maintained the theory of "responsibility for character," and not for actions, which are simply the outgrowth and expression of character. The same act may be good or bad according to the motives from which it springs. This distinction is constantly made both in ethics and in jurisprudence, and determines our moral judgments and judicial decisions. Yet the chief elements, which enter into a person's character and contribute to its formation, lie beyond his control or even his consciousness, and in many cases have done their work before his birth. Responsibility for character is equivalent to responsibility for all the inherited tendencies and prenatal influences, of which character is the resultant, and leads at last to the theological dogma of the imputation of sin all the way back to Adam as the federal head of the race, a doctrine which Schopenhauer would be the first to repudiate. Besides, evil propensities and criminal designs are recognizable and punishable only when embodied in overt acts. The law cannot deprive a man of life or liberty because he is known to be vicious

and depraved, although the police in the exercise of its protective and preventive functions
and as a means of providing for the general
security, may feel in duty bound to keep a watch-
ful eye on him and to make an occasional raid
on the dens and " dives " haunted by him and
his kind. There are also instances on record,
in which it is impossible to trace the culpable act
to any marked corruption of character.

A rather remarkable illustration of this fact is
furnished by the trial of Marie Jeanneret, which
took place at Geneva in Switzerland in 1868 and
which deservedly ranks high among the *causes
célèbres* of the present century, both as a legal
question and a problem of psycho-pathology.
[At the time when this trial occurred, the writer
directed attention to the peculiar and perplexing features of the case in *The Nation* for
January 7, 1869, p. 11.] Dumas in his novel
Le Comte de Monte Christo, describes the character and career of a young, refined and beautiful woman, moving in the best circles of Parisian
society, and yet poisoning successively six or
seven members of her own family; but even the
most imaginative and audacious of French
romancers did not dare to delineate such criminality without ascribing it to some apparently
adequate motive. Madame de Villefort administered deadly potions to her relatives under
the impulse of a morbidly intense maternal love,
which centred all her moral and intellectual

faculties on the idea of making her son the sole heir to a large estate. Affection and social ambition for her offspring incited her to the murder of her kin. But the invention, which created such a monster of sentimental depravity, has been far surpassed in real life by the exploits of Marie Jeanneret, a Swiss nurse, who took advantage of her professional position to give doses of poison to the sick persons confided to her care, from the effects of which seven of them died.

In the commission of this monotonous series of diabolical crimes, the culprit does not seem to have been animated either by animosity or cupidity. On the contrary, she always showed the warmest affection for her victims, and nursed them with the tenderest care and the most untiring devotion, as she watched the distressful workings of the fatal draught; nor did she derive the slightest material benefit from her course of conduct, but rather suffered considerable pecuniary loss by the death of her patients. The testimony of physicians and alienists furnished no evidence of insanity, nor did she show any signs of atavistic reversion, physiological abnormity or hereditary homicidal bent. Monomaniacs usually act fitfully and impulsively; but Marie Jeanneret always manifested the coolest premeditation and self-possession, never exhibiting the least hesitation or confusion, or the faintest trace of hallucination, but answered

16

with the greatest clearness and calmness every question put by the president of the court. Even M. Turrettini, the prosecuting attorney, in presenting the case to the jury, was unable to discover any rational principle on which to explain the conduct and urge the conviction of the accused; and after exhausting the common category of hypotheses and showing the inadequacy of each, he was driven by sheer stress of inexplicability to seek a motive in " *l'espèce de volupté qu'elle éprouverait à commettre un crime*," or what, in less elegant, but more vigorous Western vernacular, would be called " pure cussedness." Not only was such an explanation merely a circumlocutory confession of ignorance, but it was wholly inconsistent with the general character of the indictee.

Indeed, the persistent and pitiless perpetration of this one sort of crime by this woman, under circumstances which should have excited compassion in the hardest human heart, seems more like the working of some baneful and irrepressible force in nature, or the relentless operation of a destructive machine, than like the voluntary action of a free and responsible moral agent. M. Zurlinden, the counsel for the defendant, dwelt with emphasis upon this mysterious phase of the case and thus saved his client from the scaffold. The jury, after five hours' deliberation, rendered a verdict of " Guilty, with extenuating circumstances," as the result of which the accused was sentenced to twenty years' hard labour. As a matter of fact, there were no circumstances of an extenuating character except the utter inability of the jurors to discover any motive for the commission of such a succession of cold-blooded atrocities.

After fifteen years' imprisonment the convict died. During this whole period of incarceration she not only showed great intelligence and strict integrity, but was also remarkably kind and helpful to all with whom she came in contact. She instructed her fellow-convicts in needle-work and fine embroidery, loved to attend them in sickness, and by her general influence raised very perceptibly the tone of morals in the workhouse. If it be true, as asserted by Mynheer Heymanns, one of the latest expounders of Schopenhauer's ethics, that " a man is responsible for his actions only so far as his character finds expression in them, and is to be judged solely by his character," what shall be done in cases like the afore-mentioned, in which the criminal conduct is exceptional, and so far from being symptomatic of the general character stands out as an isolated and ugly excrescence and appalling abnormity ? According to this theory crime is to be punished only when it is the natural outgrowth and legitimate fruit of the criminal's individuality and society is to be left unprotected against all maleficence not traceable to such an origin.

There can be hardly any doubt that the Swiss nurse was a toxicomaniac, and that she had become infatuated with poisons, partly by watching their effects on her own system, and partly by reading about their properties in medical and botanical works, to the study of which she was passionately devoted. Did not Mithridates, if we may believe the statements of Galen, experiment with poisons on living persons? Why should she not follow such an illustrious example, especially as she never hesitated to take herself the potions she administered to others; the only difference being that habit had made her, like the famous King of Pontus, proof against their venom. She often attempted analyses of these substances, and in one instance was severely burned by the bursting of a crucible, in which she was endeavouring to obtain atropine from atropa belladonna or deadly nightshade. It was this terrible poison, which is endowed with exceedingly energetic qualities and is therefore used by physicians with extreme precaution, that seems to have had an irresistible fascination for her, growing into an insane desire to discover and test its occult virtues. She had read and heard of zealous scientists and illustrious physicians, who had experimented on themselves and on their disciples, and become the benefactors of mankind; why then should she not adopt the same method in the pursuit of truth and use for this purpose the physiological

material which her profession placed in her
hands?

However preposterous such reasoning on her
part may appear to us and however vaguely and
subconsciously the mental process may have
been carried on, it offers the only theory
adequate to explain all the facts and to account
for the almost incredible union of contradictory
traits in her character. The enthusiasm of the
experimenter overbore in her the native sympathy of the woman. She observed the writh-
ings of her poisoned victims with as " much
delight " as Professor Mantegazza confesses he
felt in studying the physiology of pain in the
dumb animals " shrieking and groaning " on
his tormentatore. " The physiologist," says
Claude Bernard, " is no ordinary man. He is
a savant, seized and possessed by a scientific
idea. He does not hear the cries of suffering
wrung from racked and lacerated creatures, nor
see the blood which flows. He has nothing
before his eyes but his idea and the organisms,
which are hiding the secrets he means to discover." Marie Jeanneret was a fanatic of this
kind. She, too, was a woman possessed with
ideas as witches were once supposed to be possessed with devils. Had she prudently confined
her experiments to the torture of helpless animals, she might perhaps have taken rank in the
scientific world with Brachet, Magendie and
other celebrated vivisectors, and been admitted

with honour to the Academy, instead of being thrust ignominiously into a penitentiary.

The assertion as regards any supposed case of madness, that "there's method in it," is popularly assumed to be equivalent to a denial of the existence of the madness altogether. But psycho-pathology affords no warrant for such an assumption. An individual, who commits murder under the impulse of morbid jealousy, pecuniary distress, social rancour, political or scientific fanaticism, or any other form of mono-mania, is not the less the victim of a mind diseased because he shows rational forethought in planning and executing the deed. His mental faculties may be perfectly healthy and normal in their operation up to the point of derangement, from which the fatal act proceeds. No chain is stronger than its weakest link; and this is equally true of physical and psychical concatenations. Under such circumstances the sane powers of the mind are all at the mercy of the one fault and are made to minister to this single infirmity.

According to English law a man is irre-sponsibly insane, when he has "such defect of reason from disease of the mind as not to know the nature and quality of the act he was doing, or, if he did know it, that he did not know he was doing what was wrong." This definition is very incomplete and covers only the most obvious forms of insanity; perhaps in the great majority of cases there is no "defect of reason" nor

" disease of mind " in the proper sense of these terms, but only a disturbance of the emotions or perversion of the will originating in physical disorder. Besides, it is undeniable that animal intelligence is capable of distinguishing between right and wrong and of comprehending what is punishable and what is not punishable. In general when a dog does wrong, he knows that he is doing wrong; and a monkey often takes delight in doing what is wrong simply because he knows it is wrong. If a monkey gets angry and kills a child, he obeys the same vicious propensity that impels a brutal man to commit murder. There is no greater " defect of reason " in one case than in the other. Why then should the monkey be summarily shot or knocked on the head, and the man arrested, tried, convicted and hanged by the constituted authorities? Simply because such a public prosecution and execution would not exert any influence whatever in preventing infanticide on the part of other monkeys; if it could be shown that a formal trial of the monkey would produce this salutary effect, then it certainly ought not to be omitted. The recent attempt to modify the English law so as to render all " certifiably insane " persons irresponsible for their actions, would result in the abolition of all punishment for crime, since many physicians regard every criminal as insane and would not hesitate to certify their opinion to the proper tribunal.

It is no easy task now-a-days for penal legislation to keep pace with psychiatral investigation and to adjust itself to the wide range and nice distinctions of modern psycho-pathology; nor is it necessary to do so. *Salus socialis suprema lex esto.* Society is bound to protect itself against every criminal assault, no matter what its source or character may be. This is the ultimate object not only of the prison and the scaffold, but also of all reformatories for juvenile offenders and vagabonds, who by judicious correction and instruction may perhaps be brought to amend their ways and thus be prevented from becoming a social danger by swelling the disorderly ranks of the permanently criminal classes. If a person proves to be unamenable to moral or penitential measures and remains an incorrigible transgressor, it is the duty of the community to set him aside by death or by life-long durance. Penal legislation does not aim primarily at the betterment of the individual; laws are enacted not for the purpose of making men good and noble, but solely for the purpose of rendering them safe members of society. This is effected by depriving the irremediably vicious of their liberty and, if necessary, also of their life.

The pardoning power, too, must be exercised with the utmost reserve and circumspection. The state does not look upon public offences as sins but as crimes. The introduction of the theological conception of delinquencies into the pro-

vince of civil government has always been the
vice of hierarchies and has never failed to work
immense mischief by leading inevitably to im-
pertinent intermeddling with matters of conscience and private opinion, putting a premium
on pretended repentance and like hypocrisies,
and converting the witness-box into a confes-
sional and the court of justice into a court of
inquisition. This has been uniformly the result
wherever a body of priests has become a body
of rulers, endowed with sovereignty in the
administration of secular affairs.

If it could be conclusively proved or even
rendered highly probable, that the capital
punishment of an ox, which had gored a man
to death, deterred other oxen from pushing with
their horns, it would be the unquestionable
right and imperative duty of our legislatures
and tribunals to re-enact and execute the old
Mosaic law on this subject. In like manner,
if it can be satisfactorily shown that the hanging of an admittedly insane person, who has
committed murder, prevents other insane persons from perpetrating the same crime, or tends
to diminish the number of those who go insane
in the same direction, it is clearly the duty of
society to hang such persons, whatever may be
the opinion of the alienist concerning their
moral responsibility. Nor is this merely a
hypothetical case or purely academical question. It is a well-established fact, that the

partially insane, especially those affected with " moral insanity " or so-called " cranks," have their intelligence intact, and are capable of exercising their reasoning powers freely and fully in laying their plans and in carrying out their designs. Indeed, criminals of this class are sometimes known to have entertained the thought that they would be acquitted on the ground of insanity, and have thereby been emboldened to do the deed; and it is by no means impossible, but highly probable, that a belief in the certainty of punishment would have acted as an effective deterrent. A case of this kind occurred in 1894 in England, where an inmate of a lunatic asylum deliberately murdered a lawyer, who was visiting the institution. The murderer declared that he had no grudge against his victim, but believed himself to be persecuted in general and wished to call attention to his wrongs by assassinating some official or prominent person. His method of redress was that of the ordinary anarchist; and his confession that he would not have dared to commit the act unless he had believed that as a certificated lunatic under confinement he ran no risk of being hanged, illustrates the point in question. There can be no doubt, for example, that the execution of Guiteau for the assassination of Garfield has greatly lessened the dangers of this kind to which the President of the United States is exposed; just as the swift and

severe punishment of the Chicago anarchists has
dampened the zeal and restrained the activity
of the fanatics, who labour under the delusion
that, in a free country, dynamite bombs are the
fittest means of disseminating reformatory
ideas and bringing about the social and political
regeneration of the world.

From this point of view it is hardly necessary to remark upon the absurdity of Lombroso's assertion that the jurists, who formerly
condemned and punished animals, were more
logical and consistent than those who now pass
sentence of death on cretins like Grandi or
cranks (*grafomani matteschi*) like Passannante
and Guiteau (*Archivio di Psichiatria*. Torino,
1881, Vol. II. Fasc. IV.), since he utterly
ignores the preventive character and purpose of
judicial punishment and its practical utility in
checking the homicidal propensities of such
persons, whereas the criminal prosecution and
capital punishment of a pig for infanticide will
not have the slightest effect in preventing
other pigs from mangling and devouring little
children.

That animals might be deterred from doing
violence to men by putting one of their kind to
death and suspending its body as a scarecrow is
maintained by a distinguished writer in the first
half of the sixteenth century, Hierolymus
Rosarius, the nuntius of Pope Clement VII. to
the court of Ferdinand I., then King of Hun-

gary, who states that in Africa crucified lions are placed near towns, and that other lions, however hungry they may be, are kept away through fear of the same punishment: *cujus pœnæ metu, licet urgeat fames, desinunt.* He records also that in riding from Cologne towards Düren, he and his companions saw in the vast forest two wolves in brogans hanging on a gallows, just like two thieves, as a warning to the rest of the pack: " Et nos ab Agrippina Colonia Duram versus equitantes in illa vasta silva, vidimus duos caligatos lupos non secus quam duos latrones, furcæ suspensos; *quo similis pœnæ formidine a maleficio reliqui deterreantur.*" In like manner the American farmer sets up a dead hawk as a deterrent for the protection of his hens. We may add that Rosarius entertained a high opinion of the intelligence and moral character of animals and wrote a book to prove their frequent superiority to men in the use of their rational faculties. This very clever and original work entitled: *Quod animalia bruta sæpe ratione utantur melius homine,* was first published by Gabriel Naudé at Paris in 1648; an enlarged edition was issued by Ribow at Helmstedt in 1728, with a dissertation on the soul in animals.

In the class of ill-poised minds, yclept cranks, just mentioned, the spirit of imitation is peculiarly strong and morbidly contagious. The celebrated psychiater, Baron Von Feuchtersleben, in his treatise *On the Diatetics of the Soul*, cites the case of a French soldier, who shot himself in a sentry-box; soon afterwards, several other soldiers took their lives in the same manner and in the same place. Napoleon I. ordered the sentry-box to be burned and thus put an end to the suicides. A similar instance is recorded by Max Simon in his *Hygiène de l'esprit,* in which he states that a workman hanged himself in the embrasure of a gate, and his example was followed directly by a dozen of his fellows, so that it was found necessary to wall up the gate in order to stop this strange epidemic. The same effect is produced by popular romances, in which the hero or heroine or both together dispose of themselves in this way; sometimes whole communities are thus infected by a single work of fiction; perhaps the most notable case of this kind in modern literature is the era of sentimentalism and suicidism which followed the publication of Goethe's *Werther.* It is well known, too, that another class of sensational novels, the plots of which consist in the development of criminal intrigues, tend to promote crime by rendering it fascinating and indicating an attractive and exciting method of perpetrating it. We have a recent and very striking instance of this kind in the origin and evolution of the notorious Dreyfus affair. In June 1893, a year and a half before the arrest of Dreyfus, a novel entitled

Les Deux Frères, by Louis Letang, appeared
in the Paris *Petit Journal,* the plot of which
may be concisely described as follows. A
young and capable officer, Captain Philippe
Dormelles, who holds a position of confidence
in the French department of war, is envied and
hated by two colleagues named Aurélien and
Daniel. Their enmity and jealousy finally become so intense that they conspire to effect his
ruin by accusing him of selling to a foreign
power the secrets of the national defence. It is
arranged that a compromising letter imitating
the handwriting of Dormelles and addressed to
a foreign military *attaché* shall be placed in the
secret archives, where it will fall into the hands
of the head of the department Lieutenant-
Colonel Alleward. Dormelles is arrested and
thrown into the prison Cherche-Midi, and at the
same time Daniel causes a violent article to be
inserted in a newspaper *Le Vigilant,* charg-
ing him with high treason, and seeking to excite
public opinion against him. This article concludes with the false statement that a search in
Dormelles' department had led to the discovery
of important documents referring to the fabrica-
tion of smokeless powder, and that thereupon
Dormelles had confessed his guilt. He is then
sentenced to the galleys, but his betrothed is
convinced of his innocence and finally succeeds
in detecting and exposing the forgeries. Lieu-
tenant-Colonel Alleward is arrested and com-

mits suicide in prison, not with a razor like
Henry, but with a revolver. One scene in the
novel describes the appearance of a veiled lady
on the very spot near the Champs Elysées,
where the mysterious veiled lady is said to have
appeared to Esterhazy three years later and for
much the same purpose. The French minister of
war, Mercier, was forced to proceed against
Dreyfus by the *Libre Patrole,* which published
lies about his confession, as *Le Vigilant* did
about Dormelles. The only rational explanation of this remarkable concurrence of events,
as they are narrated in the fiction and afterwards occurred in fact, is that the method of con-
ducting the conspiracy against Dreyfus and the
possibility of accomplishing it were suggested
by Letang's story, although the conspirators
doubtless did not anticipate that the logic of
events would render the results of their false-
hoods and forgeries as fatal to them as they were
to their prototypes in the novel. Every
scoundrel is firmly convinced that he can pattern
after his precursors in villainy, avoid their mistakes and commit the same crime without incurring the same penalty.

That paroxysms of epilepsy, hysterics and
various forms of frenzy are contagious and may
be easily communicated to nervous persons, who
witness them, has been clearly proved. Vicious
passions obey the same law of imitation even in
a still higher degree than tender emotions and

nervous diseases, and more than two centuries ago the illustrious jurisconsult, Samuel Pufendorf, laid down the general principle that he who for the first time commits a crime liable to spread by contagion and to become virulent, should be punished with extreme severity, in order that it may not infect others and create a moral pestilence.

The hemp cure is always a harsh cure, especially where there is any doubt as to the offender's mental soundness; but in view of the increasing frequency with which atrocious and wilful crime shelters itself under the plea of insanity and becomes an object of misdirected sympathy to maudlin sentimentalists, the adoption of radical and rigorous measures in the infliction of punishment were perhaps an experiment well worth trying. Meanwhile, let the psychiater continue his researches, and after we have passed through the present confused and perilous period of transition from gross and brutal mediæval conceptions of justice to refined and humanitarian modern conceptions of justice, we may, in due time, succeed in establishing our penal code and criminal procedure upon foundations that shall be both philosophically sound and practically safe.

APPENDIX

CONTAINING ORIGINAL DOCUMENTS

A

TESTIMOÑIALES ET REASSUMPTUM

Anno domini millesimo quingentesimo octuagesimo
septimo et die decima tertia mensis aprilis comparuit
in bancho actorum judicialium episcopatus Maurianne
honestus vir Franciscus Ameneti scindicus et procurator
procuratorioque nomine totius communitatis et parrochie
Sancti Julliani qui in causa quam pretendunt reassumere
prosequi aut de novo intentare coram reverendissimo
domino Maurianne episcopo et principe seu reverendo
domino generali ejus Vicario et Officiali contra Animalia
ad formam muscarum volantia coloris viridis communi
voce appellata Verpillions seu Amblevins facit constituit
elegit et creavit certum ac legitimum procuratorem totius
dicte communitatis et substituit vigore sui scindicatus de
quo fidem faciet egregium Petremandum Bertrandi causi-
dicum in curiis civitatis Maurianne presentem et accep-
tantem ad fines coram eodem reverendissimo Episcopo
et ejus Vicario generali comparendi et faciendi quicquid
circa negotiis ejusdem cause spectat et pertinet et prout
ipse scindicus facere posset si presens et personaliter
interesset cum electione domicillii et ceteris clausulis

relevationis ratihabitionis et aliis opportunis suo jura-
mento firmatis subque obligatione et hypotheca bonorum
suorum et dicte communitatis que conceduntur in bancho
die et anno premissis.

ORDINATIO

Anno domini millesimo quinquagesimo octuagesimo
septimo et die sabatti decima sexta maii comparuerunt
judicialiter coram nobis Vicario generali Maurianne
prefato Franciscus Ameneti conscindicus Sancti Julliani
cum egregio Petremando Bertrandi ejus procuratore producens testimoniales constitutionis facte eidem egregio
Bertrandi die tertia decima aprilis proxime fluxi petit sibi
provideri juxta supplicationem nobis porrectam parte
scindicorum et communitatis Sancti Julliani exordiente
Divino primitus implorato auxilio signatum *Franciscus Faeti*
contra Animalia bruta ad formam muscarum volantia
nuncupata Verpillions producens etiam acta et agitata
superioribus annis coram predecessoribus nostris maxime
de anno 1545 et die vicesima secunda mensis aprilis
unacum ordinatione nostra lata octava maii millesimo
quingentesimo octuagesimo sexto et ne contra Animalia
ipsis inauditis procedi videatur petunt sibi provideri de
advocato et procuratore pro defensione si quam habeant
aut habere possent dictorum Animalium se offerentes
ad solutionem salarii illis per nos assignandi. Inde et
nos Vicarius generalis Maurianne ne Animalia contra que
agitur indeffensa remaneant deputamus eisdem pro procuratore egregium Anthonium Fillioli licet absentem cui
injungimus ut salario moderato attenta oblatione conquer-
entium qui se offerunt satisfacere teneatur et debeat ipsa

Animalia protegere et defendere eorumque jura et ne de
consilio alicujus periti sint exempta ipsis providemus de
spectabili domino Petro Rembaudi advocatum (*sic*) cui
similiter injungimus ut debeat eorum jura defendere
salario moderato ut supra. Quamquidem deputationem
mandamus eis notifficari et ipsis auditis prout juris fuerit
ad ulteriora providebitur. Quo interim visa per nos
quadam ordinatione fuit fieri certas processiones et alias
devotiones in dicta ordinatione declaratas quas factas
fuisse non edocetur ideo ne irritetur Deus propter non
adempletionem devotionum in ipsa ordinatione narratarum
dicimus ipsas devotiones imprimis esse fiendas per
instantes et habitatores loci pro quo partes agunt quibus
factis postea ad ulteriora procedemus prout juris fuerit
decernentes literas in talibus necessarias per quas
comittimus curato seu vicario loci quathenus contenta
in dicta ordinatione in prono ecclesie publice declarare
habeat populumque monere et exortari ut illas adimpleant
infra terminum tam breve quam fieri poterit et de ipsis
attestationem nobis transmittere. Datum in civitate
Sancti Johannis Maurianne die anno permissis.

MEMORIALE

Anno premisso et die trigesima mensis maii comparuerunt judicialiter coram nobis Vicario generali
Maurianne prefato honestus Franciscus Ameneti conscindicus jurat venisse cum egregio Petremando Bertrandi
ejus procuratore producit et reproducit supplicationem
nobis porrectam retroacta et agitata contra eadem Animalia maxime designata in memoriali coram nobis tento

decima sexta maii literas eodem die curato Sancti Julliani
directas unacum attestatione signata *Romaneti* qua constat
clerum et incolas dicti loci proposse satisfecisse contentis
in eisdem literis ad formam ordinis in ipsis designato
petit sibi juxta et in actis antea requisita provideri et alia
uberius juxta cause merita et inthimari egregio Fillioli
procuratori ex adverso. Hinc egregius Fillioli procurator
dictorum Animalium brutorum petit communicationem
omnium et singularum productionum ex adverso cum
termino deliberandi defendendi et participandi cum
domino advocato premisso. Indi et nos Vicarius
generalis Maurianne prefatus communicatione superius
petita concessa partibus premissis diem assignamus
sabatti proximi sexta instantis mensis junii ad ibidem
judicialiter coram nobis comparandum et tunc per
dictum egregium Fillioli nomine quo supra quid voluerit
deliberare et defendere deliberandum et defendendum.
Datum in civitate Maurianne die et anno premissis.

R. D. GENERALI VICARIO ET OFFICIALI
EPISCOPATUS MAURIANÆ

Divino primitus implorato auxilio humiliter exponunt
syndici totius communitatis seu parrochie Sancti Julliani
cæterique homines ac sua interesse putantes et infra-
scriptis adherere cupientes quod cum alias ob forte
peccata et cætera commissa tanta multitudo bruti
animalis generis convoluntium vulgo tamen vocabulo
Amblevini seu Verpillion dicti per vineas et vinetum
ipsius parrochie accessisset damna quamplurima ibi per-
petrantis folia et pampinos rodendo et vastando ut ex
eis nulli saltem pauci fructus percipi poterant qui juri

cultorum satisffacere possint et quod magis et gravius
erat illa macula ad futura tempora trahendo vestigia nulli
palmites fructus afferentes produci poterant illi autem
flagitio antecessores amputare viam credentes prout divina
prudentia erat credendum porrectis precibus adversus
eadem Animalia et in eorum defensoris constituti per-
sonam debitis sumptis informationibus ac aliis formali-
tatibus necessariis prestitis sententia seu ordinatio pro-
lata comperitur cujus et divinæ potentiæ virtute præcibus
tamen et officiis divinis mediantibus illud flagitium et
inordinatus furor prefatorum brutorum Animalium cessa-
runt usque ad duos vel circa citra annos quod veluti
priscis temporibus rediere in eisdem vineis et vineto et
damna inextimabilia et incomprehensibilia afferre cep-
erunt ita ut pluribus partibus nulli fructus sperantur
percipi possetque in dies deterius evenire culpa forte
hominum minus orationibus et cultui divino vacantium
seu vota et debita non vere et integre reddentium que
tamen omnia divinæ cognitioni consistit et remittenda
veniunt eo quod Dei arcana cor hominis comprehendere
nequit.

Nihilominus cum certum sit gratiarum dona diversis
diversimode fore collata hominibus et potissimum
ecclesiastico ordini ut in nomine Jesu et virtute ejus
sanctissime passionis possit in terris ligare solvere et
flectere iterum ad R. V. recurrentes prius agitata reas-
sumendo et quatenus opus fuerit de novo procedendo
petunt in primis procuratorem aut defensorem ipsis
Animalibus constitui ob defectum præcedentis vita functi
quo facto et ut de expositis legitime constet debeatis
inquisitiones et visitationes locorum fieri per nos aut alium
idoneum commissarium cæterasque formalitates ad hæc
opportunas et requisitas exerceri ipso defensore legitime

vocato et audito nec non aliter prout magis equum visum
et compertum de jure extiterit procedere dignetur ad
expulsionem dictorum Animalium via interdicti sive
excommunicationis et alia debita censura ecclesiastica et
justa ipsius sanctas constitutiones ad quas et divinæ
clementiæ et mandatis suorum ministrorum se parituros
offerunt et submittunt omni superstitione semota quod si
stricta excommunicatione processum fuerit sunt parati
dare et prestare locum ad pabulum et escam recipiendos
ipsis Animalibus quemquidem locum exnunc relaxant et
declarant prout infra et alias jus et justitiam ministrari
omni meliori modo implorato benigno officio.

Fran. Faeti

Ego subsignatus curatus Sancti Julliani attestor quomodo sacro die Penthecostes decima septima mensis
maij anno domini millesimo quingentesimo octuagesimo
septimo ego accepi de manibus sindicorum mandatum
exortativum sive ordinationem R^{di} generalis Vicarii et
Officialis curie diocesis Maurianne datum in civitate
Sancti Johannis decima sexta mensis may anno quo
supra quod cum honore et reverentia juxta tenorem illius
die lune Penthecostes decima octava may in offertorio
magne misse parochialis populo ad divina audienda con-
gregato publicavi idem populum michi commissum ad
contritionem suorum peccaminum et ad devotionem juxta
meum posse et serie monui processiones missas obsecra-
tiones et orationes in predicto mandato contentas per tres
dies continuos videlicet vicesima vicesima prima vicesima
secunda predicti mensis cum ceteris presbiteris feci in
quibus processionibus scindici cum parrochianis utriusque
sexus per majorem partem circuitus vinearum interfuerunt

deprecantes Dei omnipotentis clementia pro extirpatione brutorum Animalium predictas vineas atque alios fructus terre devastantium vulgariter nuncupatas (*sic*) Verpilions seu Amblavins in predicto mandato mentionata sive nominata in quorum fidem ad requisitionem dictorum scindicorum qui hanc attestationem petierunt quam illis in exonus mei tradidi hac die vicesima quarta may anno quo supra.

Romanet

Franciscus de Crosa Canonicus et Cantor ecclesie cathedralis Sancti Johannis Maurianne in....... et temporalibus episcopatus Maurianne generalis Vicarius et Officialis dilecto sive vicario Sancti Julliani s........ in domino. Insequendo ordinationem per nos hodie date presentium latam in causa scindicorum Sancti Julliani agentium contra Animalia bruta ad formam muscarum volantia coloris viridis nuncupata Verpillions supplicata per quam inter cetera contenta in eadem dictum et ordinatum extitit devotiones et processiones fieri ordinatas per ordinationem latam ab antecessore nostro die octava maii anni millesimi quingentesimi quadragesimi sexti in eadem causa in primis et ante omnia esse fiendas per instantes et habitatores dicti loci Sancti Julliani. Igitur vobis mandamus et injungimus quathenus die dominico Penthecostes in prono vestra ecclesie parrochialis contenta in dicta ordinatione declarare habeatis populumque monere et extortari ut illa adimpleant infra terminum tam breve quod fieri poterit et de ipsis attestationem nobis transmittere. Tenor vero dicte ordinationis continentis devotiones sequitur et est talis.

Quia licet per testes de nostri mandato et commissarium per nos deputatum examinatos apparet Animalia

bruta contra que in hujusmodi causa parte prefatorum
supplicantium fuit supplicatum intulisse plura dampna
insupportabilia ipsis supplicantibus que tamen dampna
potius possunt attribuenda peccatis supplicantium deci-
mis Deo omnipotenti de jure primitivo et ejus ministris
non servientium et ipsum summum Deum diversimode
eorum peccatis non (*sic*) offendentium quibus causis
causantibus dampna fieri supplicantibus predictis non ut
fame et egestate moriantur sed magis ut convertantur
et eorum peccata deffluant ut tandem abundantiam
bonorum temporalium consequantur pro substentatione
eorum vite vivere et post hanc vitam humanam salutem
eternam habeant. Cum a principio ipse summus Deus
qui cuncta creavit fructus terre et anime vegetative
produci permiserit tam substentatione vite hominum
rationabilium et volatilium super terram viventium
quamobrem non sic repente procedendum est contra
prefata Animalia sic ut supra damnificantia ad fulmina-
tionem censurarum ecclesiasticarum Sancta Sede Apos-
tolica inconsulta sive ab eadem ad id potestatem haben-
tibus superioribus nostris sed potius recurrendum ad
misericordiam Dei nostri qui in quacumque hora in-
genuerit peccata propitius est ad misericordiam. Ipsi
quamobrem causis premissis et alliis a jure resultantibus
pronunciamus et declaramus inprimis fore et esse mo-
nendos et quos tenore presentium monemus et moneri
mandamus ut ad ipsum Dominum nostrum ex toto et
puro corde convertantur cum debita contrictione de peccatis commissis et proposito confitendi temporibus et
loco opportunis et ab eisdem de futuro abstinendi et de
cetero debite persolvendum Deo decimas de jure debitas
et ejus ministris quibus de jure sunt persolvende eidem
Domino Deo nostro per meritata sue sacratissime passio-

nis et intercessione Beate Marie Virginis et omnium
Sanctorum ejus humiliter exposcendo veniam et quibuscumque peccatis delictis et offensis contra ejus majes-
tatem divinam factis ut tandem ab afflictionibus prefatorum Animalium liberare dignetur et ipsa Animalia
loca non it . . . ipsis supplicantibus ceterisque christianis
transferre et al . . . secundem ejus voluntatem et aliter
exting . . . .
. . . . eisdem supplicantibus uno die dominico
in offertorio . . . . ut ipso
die dominico . . . . supplicantibus . . . .
. . . . per circuitum
vinearum ejusdem parrochie . . . . et per
loca cum aspersione aque benedicte pro effugandis prefatis
Animalibus tribus diebus immediate sequentibus signifi-
cationem et notificationem sic ut supra fiendas quibus processionibus durantibus decantari et celebrari mandamus
tres missas altas ante sive post quamlibet earum proces-
sionum ad devot. . . cleri et populi quarum prima primo
die decantabitur de Sancto Spiritu cum orationibus de
Beata Maria. . . . . *Deus Deus qui contritorum* et *A
cunctis nos quesumus Domine mentis et corporis* etc. et
una pro defunctis secundo die decantatis de Beata Maria
Virgine cum orationibus Sancti Spiritus Beate Marie
Virginis illis *Qui contritorum* et pro deffunctis. In
eisdem processionibus supra fiendis jubemus in eadem
ecclesia genibus flexis dici et decantari integriter *Veni
Creator Spiritus* quo hymno sic finito et dicto verceleto
Emitte Spiritum tuum et creabuntur etc. cum orationibus
Deus qui corda fidelium singulis diebus sic prout supra
fiat proces . . . decantando septem psalmos penitentiales
cum letaniis suffragii et orationibus inde sequentibus
mandamus moneri supplicantes prout supra ut in eisdem

missis processionibus et devotionibus sic ut supra fiendis
ad minus d. . de qualibet domo devote intersint dicendo
eorum Fidem catholicam et alias devotiones et orationes
. . . . cum fuerit humiliter et devote preces
et effundendo Domino Deo nostro ut per merita sue
sanctissime passionis et intercessionem Beatissime
Virginis Marie et omnium Sanctorum dignetur expellere
ipsa Animalia predicta a prefatis vineis ut de fructus
earumdem non corrodant nec. . . . . et
ibidem supplicantes a cunctis alliis adversitatibus liberare
ut tandem de eisdem fructibus debite vivere possint et
eorum necessitatibus subvenire et semper in omnibusque
glorificare laudare eumdem Dominum et Redemptorem
nostrum et in eodem fidem et spem nostram totaliter
cohibenda a devastatione prefatarum vinearum et nos
liberare a cunctis alliis adversitatibus dummodo sic ut
supra ejus mandata servaverimus et hoc absque allia
fulminatione censurarum ecclesiasticarum quas distu-
limus fulminare donec premissis debite adimpletis et
alliud a prefatis superioribus nostris habuerimus in
mandatis literas quatenus expediat in exequutionem
omnium et singulorum premissorum decernentes. . . . .
. . . . Post. . . . . . insertionem dicte ordinationis dicti scindici Sancti Julliani petierunt sibi concedi
literas quas concedimus datas in civitate Sancti Johannis
Maurianne die decima sexta mensis maii millesimo
quingentesimo octuagesimo septimo.

Franciscus de Crosa Vic.ˢ et Off.ˢ gen.ˡⁱˢ Maurianne.

FAURE

Per eumdem R. D. Maurianne generalem Vicarium et
Officialem.

(*locus sigilli.*)

MEMORIALE

Anno premisso et die quinta mensis junii comparuerunt judicialiter coram nobis Vicario generali Maurianne Franciscus Ameneti consindicus Sancti Julliani asserens venisse a loco sancti Julliani ad fines remittendi in manibus egregii Anthonii Fillioli procuratoris Animalium brutorum cedulam signatam *Rembaud* producendam pro deffensione dictorum Animalium quiquidem egregius Fillioli produxit realiter eandem cedulam incohantem *Approbando* etc. signatam *Rembaud* dicens concludens et fieri requirens pro ut in eadem cedula continetur. Hinc et egregius Petremandus Bertrandi procurator dictorum sindicorum Sancti Julliani agentium petiit copiam dicte cedule. Inde et nos Vicarius generalis Maurianne prefatus partibus premissis diem assignamus veneris proximam duodecimam presentis mensis junii nisi etc. ad ibidem coram nobis comparendum et tunc per dictum egregium Bertrandi nomine quo supra quid voluerit deliberare deliberandum eidem concedendo copiam dicte cedule per eum requisitam. Datum in civitate Sancti Johannis Maurianne die et anno premissis.

COPIA CEDULE

Approbando et in quantum de facta in medium adducendo ea que hoc in processu antea facto fuerunt et potissimum scedulam productam ex parte egregii Baudrici procuratoris Animalium signatam *Claudius Morellus* egregius Anthonius Fillioli procurator et eo nomine a

reverendo domino Vicario constitutus occasione tuen-
dorum ac deffendendorum Animalium de quibus hoc
in processo agitur ut in actis ad quæ impugn. . . . . . .
super relatio habeatur et brevibus agendo ac realiter
deffendendo excipit et opponit ac multum miratur de
hujusmodi processu tam contra personas agentium quam
contra insolitum et inusitatum modum et formam pro-
cedendi de eo saltem modo quo hactenus processum fuit
maxime cum agitur de excommunicatione Animalium
quod fieri non potest quia omnis excommunicatio aut
fertur ratione contumaciæ *cap. primo* et ibi Gr. *De
sententiis excommunicationis lib. 6.* at cum certum est
dicta animalia in contumacia constitui non posse quia
legitime citari non possunt per consequens via excommunicationis Agentes uti non possunt nec debent eo
maxime quod Deus ante hominis creationem ipsa
Animalia creavit ut habetur Genesi ib. *Producat terra
animam viventem in genere suo jumenta et reptilia et
bestias terre secundum species suas benedixitque eis dicens
crescite et multiplicamini et replete aquas maris avesque mul-
tiplicentur super terram* quod non fecisset nisi sub spe
quod dicta Animalia vita fruerentur tum quod ipse Deus
optimus maximus creator omnium Animalium tam
rationabilium quam irrationabilium cunctis Animalibus
suum dedit esse et vesci super terram unicuique secondum suam propriam naturam certum est et potissimum
plantas ad hoc creavit ut animalibus deservirent est
enim ordo naturalis quod plante sunt in nutrimentum
Animalium et. . . . . . quedam in nutrimentum aliorum
et omnia in. . . . . hominis. Genes: 9: ibi *Quasi
olera virentia tradidi vobis omnia a Deo* quod dicta
Animalia de quibus Adversantes conqueruntur modum
vivendi a legi ordinatum non videtur egredi tum quia

bruta sensu et usu rationis carentia que non secondum
legem divinam gentium canonicam vel civilem sed
secondum legem naturæ primordialis qua Animalia
cuncta docuit vivere solo instinctu naturæ vivunt et
ut ait Philosophus *actus activorum non operantur in
patienti.* . . . . tum quia jura naturalia sunt im-
mutabilia § *Sed naturalia Instit. : de jur natur. gent. et
civili.* ergo cum dicta Animalia solo instinctu naturæ
dicantur per consequens excommunicanda non veniunt.
Et quamvis dicta Animalia hominibus subjecta esse
dicantur ut habetur Ecclesiast: 17. ibi *Posuit timorem
illius super omnem carnem et bestiarum ac volatilium* non
idcirco adversus talia Animalia licet subjecta uti non debent excommunicatione nec ullo modo veniunt petita
executioni mandanda saltem modo petito presertim cum
ratio et æquitas dicta Animalia non regat. Et licet juribus
divino antiquo civili et canonico promulgatum legitur
Qui seminat metet ut habetur Esai 37 ibi. *In anno autem
tertio seminate et mettete et plantate vineas et commedite
fructum earum* non tamen cequitur (*sic*) quin dicta Animalia
plantis non utantur quia sunt irrationabilia et carentia
sensu neque ea posse dicernere quæ sunt usui hominum
destinata vel non certissimum est quia solo instinctu
nature ut supra dictum est vivunt non idcirco necesse
habent Agentes adversus dicta Animalia uti excommunicatione sed. . . . . peccata eorum universus populus
presertim quem hujusmodi flagella affligunt et prose-
quuntur et pœnitentiam agat exemplo Ninivitarum qui
ad solam vocem Jone prophete austeriter pœnitentiam
egerunt ad mittigandam et placandam iram Dei. Jon. 3.
veniat populus et imploret misericordiam Dei optimi et sic
maximi ut sua sancta gratia et per merita sanctissimæ
passionis excessum dictorum Animalium compessere et

refrenare dignetur et hoc modo dicta Animalia e vineis ejicient et non eo modo quo procedunt. Quibus universis consideratis evidentissime patet dicta Animalia e vitibus seu e vineis ejicienda non esse attento quod solo instinctu naturæ vivunt et ita per egregium Anthonium Fillioli eorumdem Brutorum legittimi actoris fieri instatur et ab ipso petitur ipsum monitorium requisitum in quantum concernit dicta Animalia revocari et annullari nec aliquo modo consentiendo quod dictum monitorium eis concedatur nec etiam aliqui visitationi vinearum ut est conclusum per Agentes in eorum supplicatione protestando de omni nullitate et hoc omni meliori modo via jure ac forma salvis aliis quibuscumque juribus ac deffentionibus competentibus aut competituris humiliter implorato benigno officio judicis.

PETRUS REMBAUDUS

MEMORIALE

Anno premisso et die duodecima mensis junii comparuerunt judicialiter coram nobis Vicario generali Maurianne prefato egregius Petremandus Bertrandi procurator dictorum Agentium petens alium terminum. Hinc et egregius Anthonius Fillioli procurator dictorum Animalium petiit viam precludi parti quidquiam ulterius deliberandi et producendi. Inde et nos Vicarius generalis Maurianne prefatus partibus premissis diem assignamus veneris proximam decimam nonam presentis mensis nisi etc. ad ibidem judicialiter coram nobis comparendum et tunc per dictum Bertrandi nomine quo suppra quid voluerit precise deliberare deliberandum. Datum Maurianne die et anno premissis.

MEMORIALE

Anno premisso et die veneris decima nona mensis junii preassignata comparuerunt judicialiter coram nobis Vicarium generalem Maurianne prefato egregius Petremandus Bertrandi procurator Sindicorum Sancti Julliani Agentium producens cedulam incohantem *Etiam si cuncta* et signatam *Franciscus Fay* dicens concludens et fieri requirens pro ut et quemadmodum in eadem cedula continetur.

Hinc et egregius Anthonius Fillioli procurator dictorum Animalium conventorum petiit copiam dicte cedulæ cum termino deliberandi et respondendi.

Inde et nos Vicarius generalis Maurianne prefatus copia prepetita concessa partibus premissis diem assignamus veneris proximam vigessimam sextam hujus mensis junii nisi etc. ad ibidem judicialiter coram nobis comparendum et tunc per dictum Fillioli nomine quo supra quid voluerit deliberare deliberandum. Datum Maurianne die et anno premissis.

MEMORIALE

Anno premisso et die sabatti vigesima septima mensis junii subrogata ob diem feriatum intervenientem comparuerunt judicialiter coram nobis Vicario generali prefato Catherinus Ameneti consindicus Sancti Julliani jurat venisse cum egregio Petremando Bertrandi ejus procuratore producens realiter cedulam signatam *Fay* dicens concludens prout in eadem cedula continetur. Hinc et egregius Fillioli procurator Animalium petens copiam cedule cum termino deliberandi. Inde et nos Vicarius

18

prefatus copia prepetita concessa partibus premissis diem
assignamus sabbati proximi quartam instantis mensi jullii
nisi etc. ad ibidem judicialiter coram nobis comprehen-
dum est tunc per dictum egregium Fillioli quid voluerit
deliberare deliberandum. Datum Maurianne die et anno
premissis.

COPIA CEDULÆ

Etiamsi cuncta ante hominem sint creata ex Genesi
non sequitur laxas habenas concessas fore immo contra ut
ibidem colligitur et apud D...... in 1. par. q. 26. ar. 1.
et psal. 8. Corin. 5. hominem fore creatum ac constitutum
ut cœteris creaturis dominaretur ac orbem terrarum in
æquitate et justitia disponeret. Non enim homo contem-
platione aliarum creaturarum habet esse sed contra. Nec
reperitur illam dominationem circa bruta animantia ac
eorum respectu suscipere limitationem verum in divinis
cavetur omne genuflecti in nomine Jesu.

Sed cum circa materiam majores nostri satis scripserint
in actis reassumptis et nihil novi adductum ex adverso
inveniatur frustra resumerentur. Unde inherendo re-
sponsis spectabilis domini Yppolyti de Collo et postquam
constat fore satisffactum ordinationi nihil est quod
impediri possit fines supplicatos adversus Animalia de
quorum conqueritur ad quod concluditur ac justitiam
ministrari omni meliori modo implorato benigno officio.

FRANC FAETI

MEMORIALE

Anno premisso et die quarta mensis jullii comparuerunt
judicialiter coram nobis Vicario generali Maurianne

prefato egregius Anthonius Fillioli procurator dictorum Animalium producens cedulam incohantem *Licet multis* signatam *Rembaudi* dicens et concludens prout in eadem cedula continetur hinc et egregius Petremandus Bertrandi procurator dictorum Agentium petit copiam cedule cum termino deliberandi. Inde et nos Vicarius generalis Maurianne prefatus copia prepetita concessa partibus premissis diem assignamus sabbati proximam undecimam presentis mensis jullii nisi etc. ad ibidem judicialiter coram nobis comparendum et tunc per dictum egregium Bertrandi nomine quo supra quid voluerit deliberare deliberandum. Datum Maurianne die et anno premissis.

MEMORIALE

Anno premisso at die quarta jullii comparuerunt coram nobis Vicario prefato egregius Petremandus Bertrandi procurator Agentium petit alium terminum. Hinc et egregius Anthonius Fillioli procurator Conventorum inheret cedulatis suis et fieri petitis super quibus petit justitiam sibi ministrari. Inde et nos Vicarius generalis Maurianne prefatus partibus premissis diem assignamus sabbati proximam decimam octavam presentis mensis jullii nisi etc. ad ibidem judicialiter coram nobis comparendum et tunc per dictum Bertrandi nomine quo supra quid voluerit deliberare deliberandum. Datum Maurianne die et anno premissis.

COPIA CEDULÆ

Licet multis in locis reperiatur hominem creatum fuisse ut cæteris Animalibus et creaturis dominaretur non

idcirco opus est ut Agentes adversus dicta Animalia
excommunicatione utantur sed via usitata et ordinaria
et præsertim ut dictum est quod dicta Animalia jus naturæ
sequantur quod quidem jus nusquam immitatum (*sic*) reperitur nam jus divinum et naturale pro eodem sumuntur.
Can. 1. dist. 1. at jus divinum mutari non potest quod
est in preceptis moralibus et naturalibus per consequens
nec jus naturale mutari potest nam jus naturale manat ab
honesto nempe ac ratione immortali et perpetua, at ratio
jubet ut dicta Animalia vivant potissimum hiis nempe
plantis que ad usum dictorum Animalium videntur creata
ut supra dictum est ergo Agentes nulla ratione debent
uti via excommunicationis. Igitur ne in causa ulterius
progrediatur potissimum cum cedula pro parte Sindicorum totius communitatis Sancti Julliani producta
signata *Fran: Faeti*. nullam penitus mereatur respon-
sionem obstante quod nihil novi in dicta cedula pro-
positum comperitur etiam quod contentis cedulæ parte
gregii (egregii) Anthonii Fillioli procuratorio nomine
dictorum Animalium producte mimime sit responsum
idcirco cum omnia que videbantur adducenda ex parte
dictorum Animalium adducta et proposita fuerunt ut
ample patet in dicta cedula superius producta signata : *P.
Rembaudus*. ad quam impugnatus semper relatio habeatur
non igitur alia ex parte dictorum Animalium adducenda
nec proponenda videntur presertim ut dictum est quod
ratio et equitas dicta Animalia non regat quapropter
egregius Anthonius Fillioli nemine dictorum Animalium
suppra relatorum suœ cedule et fieri recuisitis inhœrendo
concludit super eis jus dici et deffiniri et justiciam sibi
in hujusmodi causa adversam fieri et promulgari implorans
benignum officium omni melliori modo.

                                         P. Rembaudus

MEMORIALE

Anno premisso et die decima octava mensis jullii comparuerunt ⁸⁄₉ judicialiter coram nobis Vicario prefato egregius Petremandus Bertrandi procurator Agentium petens alium terminum. Hinc et egregius Fillioli procurator dictorum Animalium petit viam precludi parti quidquam ulterius articullandi et deducendi et inherendo suis cedulatis petit sibi justitiam ministrari. Inde et nos vicarius generalis Maurianne prefatus de consensu procuratorum dictarum partium ipsis partibus diem assignamus primam juridicam post messes ad ibidem coram nobis comparendum et tunc per dictum egregium Bertrandi nomine quo suppra quid voluerit precise deliberare deliberandum.

MEMORIALE

Anno premisso et die veneris vigesima quarta mensis juli comparuerunt judicialiter coram nobis Vicario generali Maurianne prefato egregius Petremandus Bertrandi procurator Sindicorum Agentium produxit testimoniales sumptas per communitatem Sancti Julliani congregatam coram visecastellano Maurianne continentes declarationem loci quem offerunt relaxare et assignare eisdem Animalibus pro eorum pabulo quathenus indigent ad formam earumdem testimonialium signatarum *Prunier* adversus quas petit adverso viam precludi quicquam opponendi et exipiendi et deffendendi quominus dicta Animalia devastantia non debeant arceri ambigi cogi et in virtute sancte Dei obedientiæ vineta loci predicti Sancti Julliani relinquere et in locum assignatum accedere et divertire ne deimpceps (deinceps) officiant eisdem vineis que sunt usui humano pernecessariæ et alias ulterius super cause exigentia provideri benignum officium R. D. V. implorando et ita intimari egregio Fillioli procuratori ex adverso.

Quiquidem egregius Fillioli procurator dictorum Animalium petiit copiam et communicationem dictarum testimonialium cum termino deliberandi et deffendendi.

Inde et nos Vicarius generalis Maurianne prefatus copia et communicatione prepetitis concessis partibus premissis diem assignamus primam juridicam post ferias messium proxime venturam ad ibidem judicialiter coram nobis comparendum et hinc per dictum egregium Fillioli nomine quo suppra quid voluerit deliberare deliberandum. Datum Maurianne die et anno premissis.

EXTRAICT DU REGESTRE DE LA CURIALLITE DE SAINCT JULLIEN

Du penultiesme jour du moys de juing mil cinq cent huictante sept.

Ont comparu pardevant Nous Jehan Jullien Depupet notaire ducal et Vichastellain pour son Altesse au lieu de Sainct Jullien et Montdenix honnestes Francoys et Catherin Aimenetz conscindicz dudict lieu maistres Jehan Modere Andre Guyons Pierre Depupet notaires ducaulx maistre Reymond Thabuys honnestes Claude Charvin Jehan Prunier Claude Fay Françys Humbert et Vuilland Duc conseilliers dudict lieu avec des manantz et habitantz dudit lieu les deux partyes les troys faisantz le tout tous assembles au son de la cloche au Parloir damon place publicque dudit lieu de Sainct Jullien au conseil general suyvant la publication d'icelluy faicte cejoudhuy mattin a lyssue de la parocchielie dudit lieu et au lieu ce fere accoustume par Guilliaume Morard metral dudict lieu ce a Nous rapportant disantz les susnommez scindicz comme au proces pas eulx au nom de ladicte communaulte intenre et poursuyvy contre les Animaulx brutes vulgairement appelez Amblevins pardevant le Seigneur Reverendissime Evesque et Prince de Maurianne ou son Official est requis et necessayre syvant le conseil a eulx donne par le sieur Fay leur advocat de ballier ausdictz Animaulx place et lieu de souffizante pasture hors les vigniables dudict lieu de Sainct Jullien et de celle qu'il y en puissent vivre pour eviter de manger ny gaster lesdictes vignes. A ceste cause ont tous les susnommes et aultres y assembles delibere leur offrir la place et lieu appelle la Grand Feisse ou elle se treuvera souffizante pour les pasturer et que le sieur advocat et procureur diceulx Animaux se veuillent contempter laquelle place est assize sur les fins dudict Sainct Jullien audessus du village de Claret jouxte la Combe descendant de Roche noyre passant par le Crosset du levant la Combe de Mugnier du couchant ladicte Roche noyre dessus la Roche commencant a la Gieclaz du dessoubz laquelle place sus coufinee centient de quarent a cinquante sesteries ou environ peuplee et garnye de plusieurs espresses de boes plantes et feuillages comme foulx allagniers cyrisiers chesnes planes et aultres arbres et buissons oultre lerbe et pasture qui y est en asses bonne quantité a laquelle les susnommes au nom de ladicte communaulte lon offre ny prendre chose que ce soyt moing permettre a leur sceu y es tre prins et emporte chose que soyt dans lesdictz confins soyt par gens ou bestes saufz toutteffoys que ou le passaige des personnes y seroyt neces-

sayre a quelque lieu ou endroit ou lon ne puisse passer
par ledict lieu sans fere aulcung prejudice a la pasture
desdicts Animaulx comme aussi dy pouvoir tirer mynes
de colleurs et aultres si alcune en y a dequoy lesdictz
Animaulx ne se peuvent servir pour vivre et par ce que
le lieu est une seure retraicte en temps de guerre ou
aultres troubles par ce quelle est garnye des fontaynes
qui aussi servira ausdictz Animaulx se reservent sy
pouvoir retirer au temps susdict et de necessite et de
leur passer contract de ladicte piece aux conditions sus-
dictes tel que sera requis et en bonne forme et vallable a
perpetuyte a tel sy que ou le Sieur Advocat et Procureur
desdicts Animaulx ne ce contenteroyent de ladite place
pour la substentation et vivre diceulx animaux visitation
prealablement faicte si elle y exchoict de leur en baillier
davantage allieurs.   Et de laquelle deliberation les
susnommes Scindics conselliers et aultres Nous ont
requis acte leur octroyer que leur avons concede audict
lieu du Parloir damont place publique dudict Sainct
Jullien en presence de Pierre Reymond de Montriond
Urban Geymen de Sainct Martin de la Porte et de
Janoct Poinct de la paroisse de Montdenix tesmoingtz
a ce requis et a ce dessus assistantz les an et jour que
dessus.

L. PRUMIER
curial

MEMORIALE CONTINUATIONIS

Anno premisso et die undecima mensis augusti comparuerunt im banco actorum judicialium episcopatus
Maurianne procuratores ambarum partium qui citra
prejudicium jurium ipsarum partium prorogaverunt et

continuaverunt assignationem datam ipsis partibus usque ad vigesimam presentis mensis augusti. Datum die et anno premissis.

ALIA CONTINUATIO

Anno premisso et die vigesima mensis augusti comparuerunt in eodem bancho egregius Petremandus Bertrandi et Anthonius Fillioli procuratores partium lictigantium quiquidem de consensu eorumdem et citra prejudicium jurium partium et actento transitu armigerorum prorogaverunt assignationem ad hodie cadentem usque ad diem jovis proximam vigesimam septimam hujus mensis Augusti. Datum Maurianne die et anno premissis.

MEMORIALE REASSOMPTIONIS

Anno premisso et die jovis vigesimam septimam augusti comparuerunt judicialiter coram nobis Vicario prefato procuratores ambarum partium quiquidem citra derogationem jurium ipsarum partium prorogaverunt et continuationem ad hodie cadentem usque ad diem jovis proximam tertiam instantis mensis septembris. Datum die et anno premissis.

MEMORIALE AD JUS

Anno premisso et die tertia mensis septembris comparuerunt judicialiter coram nobis Vicario generali Maurianne prefato egregius Anthonius Fillioli procurator Animalium brutorum qui visis testimonialibus productis parte dictorum Agentium continentibus assignationem loci quem obtulerunt relaxare et assignare dictis Animalibus pro eorum pabulo dicit eumdem locum non esse sufficientem nec idoneum pro pabulo dictorum Animalium cum sit locus sterilis et nullius redditus. Et ampliando omnia et quecumque agitata in presenti processu parte dictorum Animalium petit Agentes repelli cum expensis et jus sibi ministrari. Hinc et egregius Petremandus Bertrandi procurator Scindicorum Sancti Julliani Agentium dicit locum destinatum et oblatum esse idoneum plenum virgultis et parvis arboribus prout ex testimonialibus oblationis constat et latius constare quathenus opus sit offert inherens suis conclusionibus petit jus dici et ordinari ac pronunciari. Inde et nos Vicarius generalis Maurianne prefatus mandamus nobis remitti acta ad fines providendi prout juris assignando partes ad ordinandum. Datum in civitate Sancti Johannis Maurianne die et anno premissis.

ORDINATIO IN CAUSA SCINDICORUM SANCTI JULLIANI SUPPLICANTIUM EX UNA

contra Animalia bruta ad formam muscarum volantia coloris viridis Supplicata

Visis actis dictorum Agentium signanter primo memoriali tento in eadem causa sub die vigesima secunda mensis aprilis anni 1545 coram spectabili domino Francisco Bonivardi jurium doctori—cedula producta parte egregii Petri Falconis procuratoris dictorum Animalium incipiente *Ut appareat* etc. signata *Claudius Morellus*—tenore supplicationis porrecte parte dictorum Agentium—tenore monitorii abjecti desuper ipsa supplicatione sub die 25 aprilis anni predicti millesimi quingentesimi quadragesimi quinti signati *Daprilis*—ordinatione lata in eadem causa sub die duodecima mensis junii ejusdem anni—testimonialibus visitationis facte per egregium Matheum Daprili signatis *Daprili*—cedula producta nomine ipsorum Animalium incipiente *Visitatio* et signata *Claudius Morellus*—allia cedula producta parte dictorum Agentium incipiente *Etsi rationes* etc. signata *Petrus de Collo*—tenore ordinationis late in eadem causa sub die sabatti octava mensis maii anni 1546 signate *Michaelis*—memoriali reassumptionis tento sub die tresdecima mensis aprilis anni presentis 1587—ordinatione lata in eadem causa per reverendum dominum Franciscum de Crosa antecessorem nostrum sub die decima sexta mensis maii anni presentis—supplicatione porrecta parte dictorum Agentium signata *Franciscus Faeti*—litteris obtentis virtute dicte ordinationis sub die decima sexta dicti mensis—attestatione signata *Romanet* sub die 24 ejusdem mensis maii — cedula producta pro parte dictorum Animalium incipiente *Approbando* etc. signata *Petrus Rembaudus* — allia cedula producta parte Agentium signata *Franciscus Faeti* incipiente *Etiam si cuncta* etc.—allia cedula producta pro parte Animalium incipiente *Licet multis* etc. signata *Petrus Rembaudus*—memoriali tento sub die vicesima quarta mensis jullii proxime fluxi —testimonialibus signatis *Prunier* sumptis coram Vice-castellano Maurianne sub die penultima mensis junii anni presentis continentibus declarationem loci quem dicti Agentes obtulerunt relaxare pro pabulo dictorum Animalium — memoriale ad jus tento coram eodem domino Vicario antecessore nostro sub die tertia mensis septembris proxime fluxi—ceterisque videndis diligenter consideratis.

Nos·Vicarius generalis Maurianne subsignatus ante-
quam ad diffinitivam procedamus dicimus et ordinamus
in primis et ante omnia esse inquirendum super statu
loci oblati p. . . . .
quem locum. . . . . .
visitandum. . . . . .
mensem ut f. . . . .
et nobis rem. . . . . .
fuerit provid. . . . . .
Mermetus vis. . . . . .
generalis. . . . . .
in civitate S. . . . . .
die decima. . . . . .
anno domini. . . . . .
octuagesimo sep. . . . . .
Petremandi Bertr. . . . . .
dictorum Scind.. . . . . .
et egregii. . . . . .
dictorum Animal.
ordinationem. . . . . .
acceptandum. . . . . .
facit die et. . . . . .
   (pro visitatione III flor)

locus sigilli.

Solverunt Scindici Sancti Julliani incluso processu
Animalium sigillo ordinationum et pro copia que com-
petat in processu dictorum Animalium omnibus inclusis
XVI flor.

Item pro sportulis domini Vicarii III flor—20 decem-
bre 1587.

Published by Léon Ménebréa in the appendix to his
treatise : *De l'Origine, de la forme et de l'esprit des
jugements rendus au Moyen-âge contre les Animaux*,
Chambery, 1846.   Cf. *Mémoires de la Société Royale
Académique de Savoie*, Tome XII. pp. 524–57, where it
first appeared.

According to M. J. Desnoyers (*Recherches sur la
coutume d'exorciser et d'excommunier les insectes et autres
animaux nuisibles à l'agriculture*, p. 15), it is still the
custom, in Provence, Languedoc, le Bordelais, and other
provinces of France, for the peasants to ask the country
curates for prayers, sprinklings with holy water, consecrated boughs, and extraordinary processions, for the
purpose of expelling noxious insects from the vineyards
and warding off disease from the grapes and the silk-
worms.   These ceremonies are accompanied with adjurations and maledictions.   In Protestant lands official
days of fasting and prayer are supposed to produce the
same results.

The form of exorcism given by an Antwerp canon,
Maximilian d'Eynatten, in his *Manuale Exorcismorum*, is
as follows :—" Exorcizo et adjuro vos, pestiferi vermes,
per Deum patrem omnipotentem ✠, et per Jesum
Christum ✠ filium ejus Dominum nostrum, et Spiritum
Sanctum ✠ ab utroque procedentem, ut confestim re-
cedatis ab his campis, pratis, hortis, vineis, aquis, si Dei
providentia adhùc vitam vobis indulgeat, nec amplius
in eis habitetis, sed ad illa ac talia loca transeatis, ubi
nullis Dei servis nocere poteritis.   Vobis, si per maleficium diabolicum hic estis, pro parte divinae majestatis,
totius curiae coelestis, necnon ecclesiae hic adhùc
militantis, impero, ut deficiatis in vobisipsis, ac de-

crescatis, quatenus reliquiae de vobis nullae reperiantur, nisi ad gloriam Dei et ad usum et salutem humanum conducibiles. Quod praestare dignetur qui venturus est judicare viros et mortuos et saeculum per ignem, Resp.— Amen." *Thesaurus Exorcismorum, Coloniae,* 1626, p. 1204.

B

II[1]

DE L'EXCELLENCE DES MONITOIRES

PAR GASPARD BAILLY

Il ne favt pas mépriser les Monitoires, veu que c'est
vne chose grandement importante, portant auec soy le
glaiue, le plus dangereux dont nostre Mere sainte l'Eglise
se sert, qui est l'Excommunication, qui taille aussi bien
le bois sec que le verd, n'épargnant ny les viuans, ni les
morts; et ne frappe pas seulement les Creatures raison-
nables, mais s'attache aux irraisonnables, tels que sont
les animaux. Les exemples en sont fréquens, pour
preuue de cette verité. Car on a veu en plusieurs en-
droits qu'on a excommunié les bestioles et insectes, qui
apportoient du dommage aux fruits de la terre, et
obeïssans aux commandemens de l'Eglise se retiroient
dans le lieu ordonné par la sentence de l'Euesque qui
leur formoit leur procès. Au Siecle passé, il y auoit telle
quantité d'Anguilles dans le Lac de Geneue, qu'elles
gastoient tout le Lac : De sort que les Habitans de la
Ville et enuirons, recoururent à l'Euesque pour les Ex-

---

[1] The first part of this treatise, consisting of seventeen chapters,
discusses the different kinds of "monitoires" and their applications.
Only the second part, describing the legal procedure, is here
printed.

communier, ce qu'ayant esté fait, le Lac fut deliuré de ces animaux.

Du temps de Charles Duc de Bourgogne fils de Philippe le Bon, il y eut telle quantité de Sauterelles en Bresse, en Italie qu'elles mirent presque la famine dans tout le Mantoüan, si on n'y eût apporté du secours par l'Excommunication, et de ce nous parle Altiat dans ses Emblémes, sous l'intitulation *nihil reliqui.*

> *Scilicet hoc deerat post tot mala denique nostris,*
> *Locustæ vt raperent, quidquid inesset agris.*
> *Uidimus innumeras Euro Duce tendere turmas ;*
> *Qualia non Athilæ, Castrave Cersis erant.*
> *Hæ fœnum milium farra omnia consumpserunt ;*
> *Spes in Augusto est, stant nisi vota super.*

On raconte en la vie de S. Bernard, qu'il se leua vne si grande quantité de Mouches, d'vne Eglise qu'on auoit basti à Loudun, que par le myen du bruit qu'elles faisoient, elles empéchoient à ceux qui entroient de prier DIEV, ce que voyant le S. Personage il les Excommunia, de sorte qu'elles tomberent toutes mortes ayant couuert le paué de l'Eglise.

Nous lisons qu'en l'année 1541, il y eut vne telle quantité de Sauterelles en Lombardie, qui tomberent d'vne nuëé ; qu'ayant mangé les fruits de la terre, elles causerent la famine en ces lieux-la. Elles estoient longues d'vne doigt, grosse teste, le ventre remply de vilenie et ordure ; lesquelles estant mortes infecterent l'Air de si mauuaises odeurs, que les Courbeaux et autres animaux carnassiers ne les pouuoient supporter.

On dit aussi qu'en Pologne il y eut aussi telle quantité de ces animaux au commencement sans aisles, et apres ils en eurent quatre, qu'ils couuroient deux mille, et d'vne coudée d'auteur, et tellement épaisses qu'en volant elles leuoient la veüe de la clarté du Soleil, ces animaux firent un dégat non-pareil aux biens de la terre, et ne purent estre chassés par autre force ny industrie, que par la malediction Ecclesiastique.

Saint Augustin raconte au Liure de la Cité de Dieu, Chap. dernier, qu'en Afrique il y eut telle quantité de Sauterelles, et si prodigieuses, qu'ayans mangé tous les fruits, feüiles, et écorces des arbres iusques à la racine, elles s'éleuerent comme vne nuëe ; et tombées en la Mer, causerent vne peste si forte, qu'en vn seul Royaume il y morut huit cens mille Habitans.

Du temps de Lotaire troisième Empereur apres Charlemagne, il y eut dans la France des Sauterelles en nombre prodigieux, ayans six aisles auec deux dents plus dures que de pierre, qui couurirent toute la terre, comme de la neige, et gasterent tous les fruits, arbres, blé, et foins, et tels animaux ayans esté jettés à la Mer ; il s'ensuiuit vne telle corruption en l'Air, que la peste rauageât grande quantité de monde en ce pays là. Voilà quantité d'exemples quo nous font voir le dommage que nous apportent ces bestioles et insectes. Maintenant voyons comme on leur forme leur procés afin de s'en garantir par le moyen de la malédiction que leur donne l'Eglise.

Premièrement, sur la Requeste presentée par les Habitans du lieu qui souffrent le dommage, on fait informer sur le dégat que tels animaux ont fait, et estoient en danger de faire, laquelle information rapportée, le Juge Ecclesiastique donne vn Curateur à ses bestioles pour se présenter en jugement, par Procureur, et là deduire toutes leurs raisons, et se defendre contre les Habitans qui veulent leur faire quitter le lieu, où elles estoient, et les raisons veuës et considerées, d'vne part et d'autre il rend sa Sentence. Ce que vous verrez clairement par le moyen du plaidoyer suiuant.

19

Requeste des Habitans

Svpplie hvmblement N. Exposans comme riere le liieu de N. il y a quantité de Souris, Taupes, Sauterelles et autres animaux insectes, qui mangent les blés, vignes et autres fruits de la terre, et font vn tel dégat aux blés, et raisins qu'ils n'y laissent rien, d'où les pauures supplians souffrent notable prejudice, la prise pendante par racine estant consommée par ces animaux, ce qui causera vne famine insupportable.

Qui les fait recourir à la Bonté, Clemence et Misericorde de Dieu, à ce qu'il vous plaise faire en sorte que ces animaux ne gastent, et mangent les fruits de la terre qu'il a pleu à Dieu d'enuoyer pour l'entretient des hommes, afin que les supplians puissent vacquer, auec plus de deuotions au seruice Diuin, et sur ce il vous plaira pouruoir.

Plaidoyer des Habitans

Messievrs, ces pauures Habitans qui sont à genouy les larmes à l'œil, recourent à votre Iustice, comme firent autre-fois ceux des Isles Maiorque et Minorque, qui enuoyerent vers Aug. Cesar pour demander des Soldats, afin de les defendre, et exempter du rauage que les Lapins leur faisoient : vous aués des armes plus fortes que les Soldats de cette Empereur pour garantir les pauures supplians de la faim et necessité de laquelle ils sont menacés, par le rauage que font ces bestioles, qui n'épargnent ny blé, ny vignes ; rauage semblable à celuy que faisoit vn Sanglier, qui gasta toutes les Terres, Vignes, et Oliuiers du Royaume de Calidon, dont parle Homere dans le premier Liure de son Hiliade, ou de ce Renard qui fut enuoyé par Themis à Thebes, qui n'épargnoit ny les fruits de la terre, ny le bestail attaquant les Paysans mesmes. Vous sçauez assez les maux que raporte la faim, vous aués trop de douceur, et de Iustice pour les laisser engager dans cette misere qui contraint à s'abandonner à des choses illicites, et cruelles, *nec enim rationem patitur, nec vlla æequitate mitigatur : nec prece vlla flectitur esuriens populus* : Témoins les Meres dont il est parlé au quatrième des Roys, qui pendant la famine de Samarie, mangerent les enfans, l'une de l' autre. *Da filium tuum, vt comedamus hodie, et filium meum comedimus cras : Coximus ergo filium meum, et comedimus. Quid turpe non cogit fames, sed nihil turpe, nihilve, vetitum esuriens credit, sola enim cura est, vt qualicumque sorte iuuetur.* La mort qui vient par la famine est la plus cruelle entant qu'elle est pleine de langueurs, débilités et foiblesses de cœur, qui sont autant de nouuelles, et diuerses especes de mort.

> *Dura quidem miseris, mors est, mortalibus omnis,*
> *At perijsse fame, Res vna miserrima longè est.*

Et Auian Marcellin dit, *Mortis grauissimum genus, et vltimum malorum fame perire.* Ie crois que vous aurés compassion, de ce pauuve Peuple, si on vous le represente, par aduance en l'estat qu'il serait reduit si la faim l'accabloit.

> *Hirtus erat crinis, cana lumina, pallor in ore,*
> *Labia incana siti, scabri rubigine dentes.*
> *Dura cutis, per quam spectari viscera possunt.*
> *Ossa sub incuruis extabant arida lumbis ;*
> *Ventus erat, pro ventre locus.*

Les Gabaonistes, reuestus d'habits dechirés, et des visages affamés, auec de contenances toutes tristes, firent pitié et compassion au grand Capitaine Iousë, et en cét estar obtiendrent grace et misericorde.

Les Informations et visites qui ont esté faites par vos
commandements, vous instruisent suffisamment du dégat
que ces animaux ont fait. Ensuite dequoy on a fait les
formalités requises et necessaires, ne restant plus maintenant que d'adjuger les fins et conclusions prises par la
Requeste des demandeurs, qui sont ciuiles et raison-
nables, sur lesquelles il vois plaira de fairé reflection, et
à cét effet leur enioindre de quitter le lieu et se retirer
dans la place qui leur sera ordonnées en faisant les
execrations requises et necessaires, ordonnées par nostrc
Mere Sainte l'Eglise, à quoy les pauures demandeurs
concluent.

Plaidoyer pour les Insectes

Messievrs, dépuis que vous m'aués choisi pour la
defense ces pauures bestioles, il vois plaira que je
remontre leur droit, et fasse voir que les formalités, qu'on
a faites contre elles, sont nulles : m'étonnant fort de la
façon qu'on en vse, on donne des plaintes contre elles,
comme si elles auoient commis quelque crime, on fait
informer du dégat qu'on pretend qu'elles ayent fait, on les
fait assigner par-deuant le Juge pour respondre, et comme
on sçait qu'elles sont muettes, le Juge voulant suppleer à
ce defaut, leur donne vn Aduocat, pour representer en
Justice les raisons qu'elles ne peuuent deduire ; et
parceq; Messieurs, il vous a pleu de me donner la
liberté de parler pour les pauures animaux, je diray pour
leur defence en premier lieu.

Qve l'adiovrnement laxé contr'elles est nul comme laxé
contre des bestes, qui ne peuuent, ny doiuent se presenter
en jugement ; la raison est, que celuy qu'on appelle, doit
estre capable de raison, et doit agir librement, pour pouuoir
connoitre vn delict. Or est-il que les animaux estans

priués de cette lumiere qui a esté donnée au seul homme,
il faut conclurre par necessaire consequence, que telle
procedure est nulle ; cecy est tiré de la Loi premieree, *ff.
si quadrupes, pauper feciss. dicat ;* et voyci les mots. *Nec
enim potest animal, iniuriam fecisse, quod sensu caret.*

La seconde raison est, que l'on ne peut appeller personne en jugement sans cause ; car autrement celuy qui
fait adjourner quelqu'vn sans raison, il doit subir la peine
portée sous le tiltre des instituts *de pœn. tem. litig.* Mais
ces animaux ne sont obligés par aucune cause, ny en
aucune façon, *non tenentur enim ex contractu,* estans incapables de contracter, *neque ex quasi contractu, neque ex
stipulatione, neque ex pacto,* moins *ex delicto, seu quasi ;*
parce que comme il a esté dit cy-deuant, pour commettre
vn crime, il faut estre capable de raison, qui ne se rencon-
tre pas aux animaux, qui sont priués de son vsage.

De plus dans la Iustice, on ne doit rien faire qui ne
porte coup, la Iustice en cela imitant la Nature ; laquelle,
comme dit le Philosophe, ne fait rien mal à propos, *Deus
enim, et Natura nihil operantur frustra.* Je laisse à penser quest-ce qu'on pretend de faire ayant adjourné ces
bestioles, elles ne viendront pas respondre ; car elles sont
muettes, elles ne constitueront pas des Procureurs, pour
defendre leur cause, moins leur donneront des memoires,
pour deduire en jugement, leur raison : Car elles sont
priuées de raisonnement, en sorte que tel adjournement
ne pouuant auoir aucun effect, est nul. Si donc l'adjournement qui est la base de tous les actes judiciels est nul, le
reste comme en dependant, ne pourra subsister *cum enim
principalis causa non consistat, neque ea quœ consequuntur
locum habent.*

On dira peut-estre que si bien tels animaux, ne peuuent
constituer vn Procureur, pour la defense de leur droict,

et instruction de leur cause que le Juge de son office le
peut faire, et partant que le fait du Juge, est le fait de la
partie. A cela on respond qu'il est vray lors qu'il le fait
selon la disposition du droict, *In administratione suæ iuris-
dictionis*, mais non pas en ce cas, où la partie n'en pouuait
constituer, le Juge aussi, ne le peut faire, cecy est décidé
par la glose de la Loy 2 *ff. de administrat. res ad Civit.
pertinent*, et pour preuue de cette proposition faite à propos
L'axiaume qui dit *quod directè fieri prohibetur, per indirectum concedi non debet, cap. tuae de procuratoribus, gloss. c.
1. de consanguinibus, et affinibus.* Mais ce que je treuue plus
estrange, on pretend faire prononcer contre ces pauures
animaux vne Sentence d'Excommunication, d'Anathema
et malediction, et à quel sujet vser contre des bestioles
qui sont sans defense, du plus rigoureux glaiue que
l'Eglise aye en sa main, qui ne punit et ne châtie que les
Criminels ; ces animaux estans incapables de faire faute,
ni peché, parce que pour pecher il faut auoir la lumiere
de la raison laquelle dicernant le bien d'auec le mal, nous
monstre ce qu'il faut suiure, et ce qu'il faut fuir, et de plus
il faut auoir la liberté de prendre l'vn et laisser l'autre.

On vovdra peut-estre dire qu'elles ont manqué en ce
qu'elles ne se sont presentées ayant esté adjurnées, et
partant que la Contumace et defaut estant vn crime, on
peut faire rendre contre elles Sentence Contumaciale, à
cause de leur desobeïssance : Mais à cela on respond
qu'il ny a point de Contumace, ou il n'y a point d'adjournement, ou du moins qui soit valable *quia paria sunt
non esse citatum, vel non esse legitimè citatum, ita dd. com-
muniter Bartol., in l. ea quae C. quomodo*, etc.

De plus, si on prend garde à la définition de l'Excommunication, on verra qu'on ne peut prononcer telle Sentence
contre ces animaux : car l'Excommunication est dite *extra*

Ecclesiam positio, vel è qualibet communione, vel è quolibet legitimo actu separatio. Tellement que tels animaux ne peuuent estre dechassés de l'Eglise, n'y ayans jamais esté, d'autant qu'elle est pour les hommes qui ont l'ame raisonnable, non pas pour les brutes, qui ne sont doüées d'aucune raison, et l'Apostre S. Paul *ad Corinth.* 5 dit *quòd de iis quae foris sunt nihil ad nos quoad Excommunicationem, quia Excommunicare non possumus,* l'Excommunication *afficit animam non corpus, nisi per quandam consequentiam, cuius Medicina est,* cap. 1, *de sentent. Excomm. in* 6. C'est pourquoy l'ame de ces animaux, n'estant immortelle, elle ne peut estre touchée par telle Sentence, *quae vergit in dispendium aeternae salutis.*

L'autre raison est, *quòd facienti actum permissum non imputatur, id quod sequitur ex illo, licèt consecutiuum sit repugnans statui* suo cap. *de occidendis* 23 q. 5 cap. *sicut dignum extra de homicid.* Ces animaux font vn acte permis mesme par le droit Diuin. Car il est dit dans la Genese *fecit Deus bestias terrae iuxta species suas, iumenta, et omne reptile terrae in genere suo dixitque Deus, ecce dedi vobis, omnem herbam afferentem semen super terram, et vniuersa ligna, quae habent in semetipsis sementem generis sui, vt sint vobis in escam ; et cunctis animalibus terrae, omnique volucri coeli, vniuersis quae mouentur in terris, et in quibus est anima viuens ; vt habeat ad vescendum.* Que si les fruits de la terre ont esté faits pour les animaux et pour less hommes, il leur est permis d'en manger et prendre leur nourriture, aussi Cicéron dit au premier des Offices *principio generi omnium animantium est à natura attributum, vt se vitam, corpusque tueantur, quaeque ad vescendum necessaria sunt inquirant.* Par ces raison on voit qu'ils n'ont commis aucun delict, ayant fait ce qui leur est permis par le droit Diuin et de Nature, et par ainsi ils ne peuuent estre punis, ny maudis, *cum etiam creaturae intellettuali, et rationali delinquenti seu damnum afferenti, eo quòd secundum solitum facit; non est Angelo licitum maledicere, multo minùs erit licitum homini*, veu qu'on lit dans l'Epistre de S. Iude, *cum altercaretur Michaël cum Diabolo de corpore Moysis non fuit ausus maledicere* Cap. *Si igitur Michaël*, 23. *q*. 3. S. Thomas 2. 2. *q*. 76. dit que de donner des maledictions aux choses irraisonnables, estans Creatures de Dieu s'est peché de blasphemer et de les maudire, les considérans en eux mesmes, *est otiosum, et vanum, et per consequens illicitum*.

Que si toutes ces raisons ne vous touchent, peut-estre cette-cy vous féra donner les mains, et persuadera à vostre Esprit, qu'on ne peut donner aucune sentence d'Excommunication contre elles ny jetter aucun Anatheme. Car prononçant telle Sentence s'est s'en pendre à Dieu, qui par sa justice le enuoye pour punir les hommes et chastier leurs péchés, *immitamque in vos bestias agri quae consumant vos, et pecora vestra, et ad paucitatem cuncta redigant*, pouuant dire maintenant ce que Dieu a dit auant le Deluge *omnis Caro corrupit viam suam*. Et Ouide en ses Metamorphoses voyant que le vice auoit pris le haut bout, Triomphant, et faisant des conquestes par tout, au contraire la vertu estoit abaissée, exilée, et reduite en tel estat qu'elle ne treuuoit aucune demeure parmy les Hommes.

> *Protinus irrupit venæ prioris in œuum,*
> *Omne nefas, fugere pudor, verùmque fidésque,*
> *In quorum subiere locum, fraudésque, dolùsque.*
> *Insidiæque, et ars, et amor sceleratus habendi,*
> *Uiuitur ex rapto, non hospes ab hospite tutus,*
> *Non socer à genero, fratrum quoquè gratia rara est,*
> *Imminet exitio vir, conjugis, illa mariti*
> *Liuida terribiles miscent aconitæ nouercæ*
> *Filius ante diem, patrios inquirit in annos,*
> *Uita iacet pietas, et virgo cæde madentes.*
> *Ultima Cilestum, Terras Astrea reliquit.*

Par les quelles raisons on voit, que ces animaux sont en nous absolutoires, et doiuent estre mis hors de Cour et de Procès, à quoy on conclud.

Replique des Habitans

Le principal motif qu'on a rapporté pour la deffense de ces animaux, est qu'estans priués de l'vsage de la raison, ils ne sont sommis à aucunes Loix, ainsi que dit le Chapitre *cum mulier* 1. 5. q. l. la *l. congruit in fin.* et la Loix suiuante. *ff. de off. Praesid. sensu enim carens non subjicitur rigori Iuris Ciuilis.* Toutesfois, on fera voir que telles Loys ne peuuet militer au fait qui se présente maintenant à juger, car on ne dispute pas de la punition d'vn delict commis ; Mais on tasche d'empescher qu'ils n'en commettent par cy-après, et partant ce qui ne seroit loisible à vn crime commis, et permis afin d'empescher *ne crimen committatur.* Cecy ce preuue par la Loy *congruit* sus cité, où il est dit qu'on ne peut pas punir vn furieux et insensé du crime qu'il a commis pendant sa fureur, parce qu'il ne scait ce qu'il fait, toutesfois on le pourra renfermer et mettre dans des prisons, afin qu'il n'offence personne et pour faire voir combien cét Axiome est vray, ie me sers de l'authorité du Chapitre *omnis vtriusque sexus de poenitent. et remiss.* ou il est dit qu'on peut deceller ce qu'on a pris si on ne la pas executé, afin d'y rapporter du remede, cette proposition est confirmée par la glose *in cap. tua nos ext. de sponsal.* qui dit qui si quelqu'vn s'accuse d'auoir Fiancé une fille, par parolles de présent ; on pourra deceller ce qui a esté dit, afin que le Mariage se consume. La raison est, qu'ayant espousé telle fille, si on nie de l'auoir fait, et on refuse d'accomplir le Mariage, *Videtur esse delictum successiuum, et durare vsque illam acceperit, vt ergo tali delicto obuietur.* Il este loisible de publier ce

qu'on a pris secretement Estant vray par les raisons de-
duites qu'on a peu adjourner, tels animaux, et que l'adjournement est valable, d'autant qu'il est fait afin qu'ils
ne rapportent du dommage d'ores en auant, non pas pour
les chastier de celuy qu'ils ont fait. Il reste maintenant
de respondre à ce qu'on a aduancé à sçauoir que tels
animaux ne peuuent estre Excommuniés, Anathematisés,
maudis ny execrés ; à cela il semble que se serait doubter
de la puissance que Dieu a donné à l'Eglise, l'ayant fait
Maitresse de tout l'Vnivers, comme sa chere Espouse,
de qui on peut dire, auec le Psalmiste, *omnia subiecisti sub
pedibus ejus, oues, et boues et omnia quæ mouentur in aquis,*
et estant conduite par le S. Esprit, ne fait rien que sage-
ment, et s'il y a chose où elle doiue monstrer son pouuoir,
c'est à la Conservation du plus parfait ouurage de son
Espoux ; à sçauoir de l'Homme, qu'il a fait à son Image
et semblance, *faciamus hominem, ad imaginem, et simili-
tudinem nostram* et luy a donné le Gouuernement de
toutes les choses crées *crescite et multiplicamini et domina-
mini piscibus maris, volatilibus cœli, et omnibus animantibus
Cœli ;* Aussi Pline en son Liure premier de l'Histoire
naturelle dit *quod causâ hominis, videtur cuncta alia
genuisse natura.* Les Jurisconsultes sont d'accord, *quod
hominis gratia, omnes fructus à natura comparati sunt, l.
pecudum. ff. de vsur. et §. partus ancillarum. instit. de rer.
diuis.* et Ouide descriuant l'excellence de l'Homme parle
de la sorte,

*Pronaque, cum spectent animalia cætera terras
Os homini sublime dedit, cælumque tueri
Iussit, et erectos ad sidera tollere vultus.*

et vn autre Poëte,

*Nonne vides hominem, vt Celsos ad sidera vultus
Sustulerit Deus, ac sublimia finxerit ora.
Cum pecudes, volucrumque genus, formasque ferarum,
Segnem, atque obscœnam, passuri strauisset in aluum.*

Picus Mirandulanus, en vne de ses Oraison parlant de
la grandeur de l'Homme dit *hominem tantæ excellentiae,*
ac sublimitatis esse, vt in se omnia continere dicatur, vti
Deus, sed diuersimodè, Deus enim omnia in se continet, vti
omnium medium principium, homo verò, in se omnia con-
tinet, vti omnium medium, quo fit, vt in Deo sint omnia
meliore nota, quàm in seipsis, in homine inferiora nobiliori
sint conditione, superiora autem degenerent sicut aër, ignis,
aqua et terra per verissimam proprietatem naturæ suæ, in
crasso hoc, et terreno, hominis corpore, quo nos videmus, hinc
etenim nulla creata substantia seruire dedignatur, hinc
Terra, et Elementa, huic bruta præesto sunt, famulantur,
hinc militat cælum, hinc salutem bonumque procurant
Angelicæ mentes.

Et se seroit vne chose, si j'ose dire hors de raison, que
celuy pour qui la terre produit tous ces fruits, en fut
priué, et que de chétifs animaux, prissent leur norriture,
à l'exclusion de l'Homme pour qui ils sont destinés
de Dieu. C'est sur ce sujet qu'il dit *Increpabo pro te*
locustas dummodò posueris de fructibus tuis in horrea
mea.

Et pour responce à ce qu'escrit S. Thomas qu'il n'est
loisible de maudire tels animaux, si on les considere en
eux mesmes, on dit qu'en l'espece qu'on traitte, on ne
les considere pas, comme animaux simplement : mais
comme apportans du mal aux Hommes, mangeans et
détruisans les fruits qui seruent à son soutient, et
nourriture.

Mais à quoy, nous arrestons-nous depuis qu'on voit
par des exemples infinis que quantité de saints Person-
nages, ont Excommunié des animaux apportans du
dommage aux Hommes. Il suffira d'en rapporter vn pour
tout, qui nous est cogneu, et familier, que nous voyons

continuellement, à sçauoir dans la ville d'Aix, où S.
Hugon Euesque de Grenoble Excommuniat les serpens,
qui y estaient en quantité à cause des bains chauds de
souffre, et d'Alun, qui faisaient vn grand dommage aux
Habitans de ce lieu par leur piqueures.   De sorte que
maintenant si bien les Serpens piquent, quelqu'vn dans
le lieu, et confins : Telle piqueure ne fait aucun mal, le
venin de ces bestes estant arresté, par le moyen de telle
Excommunication, que si quelqu'vn est piqué hors de ce
lieu par les mesmes Serpens, la piqueure sera venimeuse
et mortelle ainsi qu'on a veu par plusieurs fois.   Ie
laisse à part quantité de passages de l'Escripture par
lesquels on voit que Dieu a donné des maledictions aux
choses inanimées, et Creatures sans raison, ainsi qu'on
pourra voir au *Leuitic. Ch.* 26. *et Deutheronome* 27.
Genes. 2. il maudit le Serpent *Maledictus es, inter omnia
animantia, et bestias Terræ.*

De dire, qu'excommuniant, Anathematisant tels
animaux, s'est s'en prendre à Dieu, qui les a enuoye
pour le chastiment des hommes.   A cela on respond
que ce n'est pas s'ens prendre à Dieu que de recourir à
l'Eglise, et la prier de diuertir, et chasser le mal, qu'il a
pleu à sa Diuine Majesté de nous enuoyer, à cause de
nos fautes et pechés ; au contraire c'est vn acte de
Religion que de recourir à elle, lors q'on voit que Dieu
leue sa main pour nous frapper.

Conclusion du Procureur Episcopal

Les defenses rapportées par l'Aduocat de ces animaux,
contre les Conclusions prises par les Habitans sont
considerables qui meritent qu'on les examine meure-
ment ; car il ne faut pas ietter le carreau d'Excommunication à la volée, et sans sujet, estant vn foudre qui est si

agissant, que s'il ne frappe celuy contre lequel on le jette, il embrase celuy qui le lance. Le discours de cét Aduocat est appuyé sur la règle de Droict, qui dit, *qui iussu iudicis aliquid facit, pœnam non meretur,* et vraye-ment c'est le Iuge des Iuges, qui ne laisse rien d'impuny, et qui distribue les peines à l'égal des offences, sans auoir égard à personne, de qui les jugemens nous sont incognus, *quàm abscondita iudicia Dei, inuestigabiles viæ ejus.* C'est vne Mer profonde d'ont on ne peut découurir le fonds. De dire pourquoy il n enuoyé ces animaux, qui mangent les fruits de la terre : Ce nous sont lettres closes ; peut estre veut-il punir ce Peuple, pour auoir fait la sourde oreille aux pauures qui demandoient à leurs portes, estant vn Arrest infaillible, que qui fait aux pauures la sourde oreille, attende de Dieu la pareille.

Ceux qui donnent l'aumosne sont toûjours sous la protection Diuine, aussi S. Gierosme dit *non memini me legisse mala morte mortuum, qui libenter opera charitatis exercuit, habet enim multos intercessores, et impossibile est, multorum preces non exaudiri,* et S. Ambrojse parlant de ceux qui donnent l'aumône aux pauures, *si non pauisti necasti, pascendò seruare poteras,* de mesmes la Loy *de lib. agnoscend.* repute pour homicide celuy qui denie, et refuse les alimens à ceux qui en ont besoin, et le Prophete Ezechiel, c. 18. parlant de la recompense, que Dieu a destinée à ceux qui font du bien aux pauures, *qui panem suum esurienti dederit et nudum operuerit vestimento, justus est, et vità viuet ;* Lesquelles paroles Eusèbe expliche de la sorte, *fregisti esurienti panem tuum, in Coelo vitae pane qui Christus est satiaberis, hic peregrinis domus tua patuit, in domo Angelorum, Ciuis efficieris tu hic trementia membra destijsti, illic liberaberis ab illo frigore, in quo erit fletus, et stridor dentium.*

C'est vn acte de Charité, que d'assister le pauures, *frange esurienti panem tuum et egenos, vagosque indue in domum tuam, cum videris nudum, operi eum, et carnem tuam ne despexeri,* dit Iosuë *c.* 38. aussi la récompense est asseurée, ainsi qu'escrit S. Mathieu cap. 25. *venite Benedicti patris mei, possidete paratum vobis regnum à constitutione mundi ; esuriui enim, et dedistis mihi manducare ; sitiui, et dedistis mihi bibere ; hospes eram et Collegistis me ; nudus eram, et operuistis me, amen dico vobis quod vni fecistis ex fratribus meis minimis, mihi fecistis.* C'est vne œuure de Misericorde d'auuoir compassion de son prochain, ainsi que dit S. Ambroise *lib.* 2. *off. cap.* 28. *hoc maximum Misericordiæ, vt compatiamur alienis calamitatibus necessitates aliorum, quantum possumus iuvemus, et plus interdum quàm possumus* l'Hospitalité est recommandée par S. Paul *hospitalitatem nolite obliuisci, per hanc enim placuerunt quidam, Angelis hospitio receptis,* et S. Augustin *disce Christiane sine discretione exhibere hospitalitatem, ne fortè cui domum clauseris, cui humanitatem negaueris ipse sit Christus.* L'ordinaire recompence qui suit l'aumosne est le centuple, *honora Dominum de tua substantia, et de primitiis omnium fructuorum tuorum de pauperibus, et implebuntur horrea tua saturitate et vino torcularia tua redundabunt.* Les abismes de la Diuinité ne s'épuisent jamais, pour donner, et le sage Salomon, *fœneratur Domino qui miseretur pauperi, et vicissitudinem suam reddet.* S. Paul aux Corinthiëns Chap. 2. parle de la sorte, *qui administrat semen seminanti, et panem ad manducandum præstabit, et multiplicabit semen suum.*

Seroit-ce point à cause des irreuerences qu'on commet aux Eglises pendant le service Diuin, ou sans aucun égard à la presence de Dieu, *conduntur stupra, tractantur lenocinia, adulteria meditantur, frequentiùs deniquè ; in ædituorum cellulis quòd in ipsis lupanaribus flagrans libido defungitur,* pour parler auec Tertullien ; car c'est là bien souuent où se donne le mot, où se prennent les assignations, où se lancent les meschantes œilliades, *Impudicus oculus, impudici cordis est nuncius,* dit S. Augustin. Sur tous les arbres et plantes, qui estaient en Ægypte, le péché était consacré à Harpocrates qui prenait soin du langage qu'on deuait tenir aux Dieux, parce que le fruit du peché ressemble au cœur, et la feuille à la langue, inferant de là que ceux qui allaient aux Temples, deuoient penser saintement honestement, et sombrement parler.

Numa Pompilius ne volut pas qu'on assistât au culte Diuin par maniere d'aquit : Mais qu'en quittant toutes choses, on y employat entièrement sa pensée, comme au principal acte de la Religion, et d'actions enuers les Dieux, ne voulant pas mesme pendant le Seruice, qu'on entendit parmy les Ruës aucun bruit, et lors que les Prestres faisoient le Sacrifices et ceremonies, il y auoit des Sergens qui crioent au Peuple que l'on se tue, laissant toute autre œuvre pour estre attentif au Culte.

Que si les Payens ont esté si exats en leur fausse Religion au Culte de leurs Idoles, et imaginaires Diuinités, nous qui sommes Chrestiens, et auons la conoissance du vray Dieu ; quel respect ne luy deuons-nous pas porter dans les Eglises, pendant le S. Sacrifice de la Messe et autres Offices Diuins.

Mais si bien Dieu est Iuste iusticier, qui ne laisse rien impuni toutesfois la Iustice ne tient pas si fort le haut bout, que la misericorde, n'y treuue place. Il est autant Misericordieux que Iuste, et s'il enuoit quelques aduersités aux pecheurs et les visite par quelque coup de fouët :

C'est pour les aduertir de faire penitence, par le moyen
de laquelle ils puissent détourner son courroux, et iuste
vengeance, et par ce moyen, ils se puissent reconcilier
auec luy, et obtenir ses graces, et pardon de leurs fautes
et pechés.

Nous voyons ces habitans la larme à l'œil, qui
demandent pardon d'vn cœur contrit de leurs fautes,
ayans horreur des crimes commis par le passé, et
employent l'assistance de l'Eglise pour les soulager en
leurs nécessités, et détourner le Carreau qui leur pend
sur la teste, estans menacés d'vne famine insuportable si
vous ne prenés leur droit, et cause en protection, et faire
déloger ces animaux, qui les menaçent d'vne ruine totale,
à quoy nous n'empeschons.

Concluans à cét effect, qu'il plaise de rendre vostre
Sentence d'execution contre ces animaux, afin que d'ores
en auant ils n'apportent du dommage aux fruits de
la terre enjoignans aux Habitans, les Penitences, et
Oraisons, à ce conuenables et accoustumées.

La Sentence du Iuge d'Eglise

In nomine Domini amen, visa supplicatione pro parte
habitantium loci, nobis officiali in iudicio facta, aduersus
Bronchos, seu Erucas, vel alia non dissimilia animalia
fructus vinearum eiusdem loci à certis annis, et adhuc
hoc praesenti anno, vt fide dignorum Testimonio, et quasi
publico Rumore asseritur, cum maximo incolarum loci,
et vicinorum locorum incommodo depopulantia, vt praedicta animalia per nos moneantur, et remediis Ecclesi-
asticis mediantibus compellantur, à territorio dicti loci
abire, visisque diligenter, inspectis causis praedictae
supplicationis, necnon pro parte, dictarum Erucarum, seu
animalium, per certos Conciliari s eosdem, per nos

deputatos, propositis et allegatis, audito etiam super praemissis promotore, ac visâ certâ informatione, et ordinatione nostra, per certum dictae Curiae, Notarium, de damno in vineis, iam dicti loci, per animalia illato. Quoniam, nisi eiusmodi damno, nisi diuina ope succurri posse existimatur attenta praedictorum habitantium, humili, ac frequenti, et importuna requisitione praesertim magnae pristinae vitae errata emendandi per eosdem habitantes, edicto spectaculo, solemniter supplicationum nuper ex nostra ordinatione, factarum prompta exhibitione, et sicut Misericordia Dei, peccatores ad se cum humilitate reuertentes non respuit, ita ipsius Ecclesia eisdem recurrentibus, auxilium seu etiam solatium qualecunque denegare non debet.

Non praedictus, in re quamquam noua, tam fortiter tamen efflagitata Maiorum vestigiis inhaerendo, pro tribunali, sedentes, ac Deum prae oculis habentes, in eius Misericordiâ, ac pietate confidentes, de peritorum consilio, nostram sententiam modo quae sequitur, in his scriptis ferimus.

In nomine, et virtute Dei, Omnipotentis, Patris, et Filij, et Spiritus sancti, Beatissimae Domini nostri Jesu Christi Genetricis Mariae, Authoritateque Beatorum Apostolorum, Petri et Pauli, necnon ea qua fungimur in hac parte, praedictos Bronchos, et Erucas, et animalia praedicta quocunque nomine censeantur, monemus in his scriptis, sub pœnis Maledictionis, ac Anathematisationis, vt infrà sex dies, à Monitione in vim sententiae huius, à vineis, et territoriis huius loci discedant, nullum vlterius ibidem, nec alibi documentum, praestitura, quod si infrà praedictos dies, iam dicta animalia, huic nostrae admonitioni non paruerint, cum effectu. Ipsis sex diebus elapsis, virtute et auctoritate praefatis, illa in his scriptis

20

Anathematizamus, et maledicimus, Ordinantes tamen, et
districtè praecipientes, praedictis habitantibus, cuius-
cumque gradûs, ordinis, aut conditionis existant, vt
faciliùs ab Omnipotente Deo, omnium bonorum largitore,
et malorum depulsore, tanti incommodi liberationem,
valeant promereri, quatenùs bonis operibus, ac deuotis
supplicationibus, iugiter attendentes, de caetero suas
decimas, sine fraude secundum loci approbatam con-
suetudinem persoluant, blasphemiis, et aliis peccatis,
praesertim publicis sedulò abstineant.

C

Allegation, replication, and judgment in the process against field-mice at Stelvio in 1519.

KLAG

Schwarz Mining hat sein Klag gesetzt wider die Lutmäuse in der Gestalt, dass diese schädliche Tiere ihnen grossen merklichen Schaden tun, so wurde auch erfolgen, wenn diese schädliche Tiere nit weggeschaft werden, dass sie ire Jarszinse der Grundherrschaft nit nur geben könnten und verursacht wurden hinweg zu ziehen, weil sie solcher Gestalten sich nit wüssten zu ernehren.

ANTWORT

Darauf Grienebner eingedingt, und diese Antwort geben und sein Procurey ins Recht gelegt : er hab diese wider die Tierlein verstanden ; es sey aber männiglich bewusst, dass sie allda in gewisser Gewöhr und Nutzen sitzen, darum aufzulegen sei——: Derentwegen er in Hoffnung stehe, man werde ihnen auf heutigen Tage die Nutz und Gewöhr mit keinem Urtel nehmen oder aberkennen. Im Fall aber ein Urtel erging, dass sie darum weichen müssten, so sey er doch in Hoffnung, dass ihnen ein anders Ort und Statt geben soll werden, uf dass sie sich erhalten mögen : es soll ihnen auch bei solchem Abzug ein frei sicher Geleit vor iren Feinden erteilt, es seyn Hund

Katzen oder andre ihre Feind : er sey auch in Hoffnung,
wenn aine schwanger wäre, dass derselben Ziel und Tag
geben werde, dass ir Frucht fürbringen und alsdann auch
damit abziehen möge.

URTEL

Auf Klag und Antwort, Red und Widerred, und uf
eingelegte Kundschaften und Alles was für Recht kommen,
ist mit Urtel und Recht erkennt, dass die schädlichen
Tierlein, so man nennt die Lutmäuse, denen von Stilfs
in Acker und Wiesmäder nach Laut der Klag in vierzehn
Tagen raumen sollen, da hinweg ziehen und zu ewigen
Zeiten dahin nimmer mehr kommen sollen ; wo aber ains
oder mehr der Tierlein schwanger wär, oder jugendhalber
nit hinkommen möchte, dieselben sollen der Zeit von
jedermann ain frey sicheres Geleit haben 14 Tage lang ;
aber die so ziehen mögen, sollen in 14 Tagen wandern.

Vide Hormayr's *Taschenbuch für die vaterländische
Geschichte.* Berlin, 1845, pp. 239–40.

D

Admonition, denunciation, and citation of the inger by the priest Bernhard Schmid in the name and by the authority of the Bishop of Lausanne in 1478.

Du vnvernünfftige/ vnvollkommne Creatur/ mit nammen Inger/ vnd nenne dich darumb vnvollkommen/ dann deines geschlechts ist nit geseyn in der Arch Noe/ in der Zeit der vergifftung vnd plag des Wassergusses. Nun hast du mit deinem anhang grossen schaden gethan im Erdtrich vnd auff dem Erdtrich ein mercklichen abbruch zeitlicher nahrung der Menschen vnd vnvernüfftigen thiere. Vnd von des nun/ sömlicher und dergleichen/ durch euch vnd euweren anhang nit mehr beshäch/ so hat mir mein gnädiger Herr vnd Bischoff zu Losann gebotten in seinem nammen/euch zeermannen/ zeweichen vnd abzestahn. Vnd also von seiner Gnaden gebotts wegen vnd auch in seinem nammen als obstaht/ vnd bey krafft der heiligen hochgelobten Dreyfaltigkeit/ vnd durch krafft vnd verdienen des Menschen–geschlechts Erlösers/' vnsers behalters Jesu Christi/ vnd bey krafft vnd gehorsamkeit der heiligen Kirchen gebieten vnd ermannen ich euch in 6. nächsten tagen zeweichen/ all vnd jegliche besonders/ auss allen Matten/ Ackeren/ Gärten/ Feldern/ Weiden/ Bäumen/ Krüteren/ vnd von allen örteren/ an denen wachsend vnd entspringend nahrungen der Menschen vnd der Thieren/vnd an die ort vnd stätt euch fügend/ dass ihr mit ewerem anhang nimmer kein schaden vollbringen mögen an den früchten vnd nahrungen der Menschen

vnd Thieren/ heimlich noch offentlich. Were aber sach/
dass ihr dieser ermannungen vnd gebott nit nachgiengend/
oder nachfolgeten/ vnd meinten vrsach haben/ das nit
zeerfüllen/ so ermannen ich euch alsvor/ vnd laden vnd
citieren euch bey krafft vnd gehorsamkeit der heiligen
Kirchen am 6. tag nach diser execution/ so es eins
schlecht/ nach mitten tag/ gen Wifflispurg/ euch zu
verantworten/ oder durch eweren Fürsprechen antwort zu
geben/ vor meinem gnädigen Herren von Losann/ oder
seinem Vicario vnd statthaltern/ vnd wird drauff mein
gnädiger Herr von Losann oder sein statthalter fürer/
nach ordnungen des rechten/ wider euch/ mit verflüchen
vnd beschweerungen/ handeln/ alss sich dann in solchem
gebürt/ nach form vnd gestalt des rechten.   Lieben
Kind/ ich begären von ewerem jeglichen zu bätten mit
andacht auff ewerem knyen 3 Paternoster vnd Ave Maria,
der hochen heiligen Dreyfaltigkeit zu lob vnd ehr anze-
rüffen/ vnd zebitten ihr gnad vnd hilff zesenden/ damit die
Inger vertriben werdind.

    Job. Heinrich Hottinger: *Historia ecclesiastica novi
testamenti* iv. pp. 317—321, on the authority of Schilling's
Chronica, the manuscript of which is in the Zurich
library.

E

Decree of Augustus, Duke of Saxony and Elector, commending the action of Parson Greysser in putting the sparrows under ban, issued at Dresden in 1559.

Von Gottes Gnaden Augustus, Herzog zu Sachsen und Kurfürst.—Lieber Getsener, welchergestalt und aus was Ursachen und christlichem Eifer, der würdige, Unser lieber andächtiger Hr. Daniel Greysser, Pfarrherr allhier in seiner nächst getanen Predigt, über die Sperlinge etwas heftig bewegt gewesen und dieselbe wegen ihres unaufhörlichen verdriesslichen grossen Geschreis und ärgerlichen Unkeuschheit, so sie unter der Predigt, zu Verhinterung Gottes Worts und christlicher Andact, zu tun und behegen pflegen, in den Bann getan, und männiglich preis gegeben, dessen wirst du dich als der damals ohne Zweifel aus Anregung des heiligen Geistes im Tempel zur Predigt gewesen, guter massen zu erinnern wissen.

Wiewohl Wir uns nun vorsehen, du werdest, auf gedachten Herrn Daniels Vermahnen und Bitten, so er an alle Zuhörer insgemein getan, ohne das allbereit auf Wege gedacht haben ; sintemal Wir diesen Bericht erlangt, dass du dem kleinen Gevögel vor andern durch mancherlei visirliche und listige Wege und Griffe nachzustellen, auch deine Nahrung unter andern damit zu suchen und dasselbe zu fahen pflegest,—dass ihnen ihrem Verdienst nach gelohnt werden möge nach weiland des Herrn Martini seligen Urtheil—ist demnach

unser gnädiges Begehren— zu eröffnen, wie und welchergestalt auch durch was Behändigkeit und Wege, du für
gut ansehest, dass die Sperlinge eher dann, wann sie
jungen, und sich durch ihre tägliche und unaufhörliche
Unkeuschheit unzählich vermehren, ohne sonderliche
Kosten aus der Kirche zum heiligen Kreuz gebracht, und
solche ärgerliche Vöglerei und hinterlicher Getzschirpe
und Geschrei im Hause Gottes, verkümmert werden
möge. . . . Das gereicht zur Beförderung guter Kirchen-
zucht und geschieht daran unsere gnädige Meinung.
Datum Dresden, den. 18. Februar 1559.—Unserm
Secretario und lieben getreuen Thomas Nebeln.

Vide Hormayr's *Taschenbuch, etc.*, 1845, pp. 227–8.

F

Chronological List of Excommunications and Prosecutions of Animals from the Ninth to the Nineteenth Century.[1]

Sources of Information	Dates	Animals	Places
Annales Ecclesiastici Francorum	824	Moles	Valley of Aosta
Muratori: Rer. Ital. Scriptores, iii	886	Locusts	Roman Campagna
Gaspard Bailly: Traité des Monitoires	9th cent.	Serpents	Aix-les-Bains
Sainte-Foix: Oeuvres, iv, p. 97, Mémoires de la Société Royale des Antiquaires de France, viii, p. 427	1120	Field-mice and Caterpillars	Laon
Théophile Raynaud: De Monitoriis in Opusc. nissc. ejus, xiv, p. 482. Mémoires, cit., viii, p. 415. Note, Vita S. Bernhardi, i, No. 58. Acta., SS. Aug. iv, p. 272	1121	Flies	Foigny near Laon
	1121	Horseflies	Mayence

[1] A few early instances of excommunication and malediction, our knowledge of which is derived chiefly from hagiologies and other legendary sources, are not included in the present list, such, for example, as the cursing and burning of storks at Avignon by St. Agricola in 666, and the expulsion of venomous reptiles from the island Reichenau in 728 by Saint Perminius.

Sources of Information	Dates	Animals	Places
Malleolus : De Ex-orcismis	1225	Eels	Lausanne
L'Abbé Leboeuf: Hist. de Paris, ix, p. 400. Mémoires, cit., viii, p. 427	1266	Pig	Fontenay-aux-Roses near Paris
Sainte-Foix : Oeu-vres Thémis, viii	1314	Bull	Moiey-le-Temple
„ „ „	1320	Cockchafers	Avignon
Carpentier to Du Cange, *vide* Homicida	1322		Not specified
„ „ „ Both cited by Von Amira, p. 552	1323		Abbeville
Zeitschrift für deutsche Kultur-geschichte, ii, p. 544 ; also Germania, iv, p. 383. Von Amira, p. 561	1338		Kaltern
Delisle : Etudes sur la condition de la classe agricole, p. 107. Von Amira, p. 552	1356	Pig	Caen

Sources of Information	Dates	Animals	Places
Carpentier to Du Cange. *Vide* homicida. Von Amira, p. 552	1378		Abbeville
Garnier: Revue des Sociétés Savantes, Dec. 1866, pp. 476, *sqq.* From the archives of Côte-d'Or	1379	Three sows and a pig. Rest of the two herds pardoned	Saint-Marcel les-Jussey
Charange: Dict. des Titres Originaux, ii, p. 72. *Also* statistique de Falaise, i, p. 63. Mémoires, cit., viii, p. 427	1386	Sow	Falaise
Auranton : Annuaire de la Côte-d'Or	1389	Horse	Dijon
Berriat - Saint- Prix in Mémoires, cit., viii, p. 427. From MSS. in la Bibliothèque du Roi	1394	Pig	Mortaing
Malleolus : De Exorcismis, Tract. ii, Mémoires, cit., viii, p. 411	14th cent.	Spanish flies	Mayence

Sources of Information	Dates	Animals	Places
MS. of Judge Hérisson, published by Lejeune in Mémoires, cit., viii, p. 433 ; *also* Loriol : La France Eure et Loire, p. 108	1403	Sow	Meulan
Auranton : Annuaire de la Côte-d'Or	1404	Pig	Rouvre
MS. Bibliothèque du Roi Mémoires, cit., viii, p. 427	1405	Ox	Gisors
MS. Bibliothèque du Roi Mémoires, cit., viii, p. 428	1408	Pig	Pont-de-l'Arche
Louandre: Histoire d'Abbeville	1414	,,	Abbeville
,, ,, ,,	1418	,,	,,
Auranton : Annuaire de la Côte-d'Or	1419	,,	Labergement-le-Duc
,, ,, ,,	1420	,,	Brochon
,, ,, ,,	1435	,,	Trochères
Malleolus : De Exorcismis, Mémoires, cit., viii, p. 423	1451	Rats and Bloodsuckers	Berne

Sources of Information	Dates	Animals	Places
Garnier: Revue des Sociétés Savantes, iv, p. 476 *sqq.* Dec. 1866	1452	Sixteen cows and one goat	Rouvre
Gui-Pape: Decisiones Thémis, i, p. 196	1456	Pig	Bourgogne
Mémoires, cit., viii, pp. 441–445. From Archives of Monjeu and Dependencies	1457	Sow	Savigny-sur-Etang, Bourgogne
Desnoyers : Recherches, etc.	1460–1	Weevils	Dijon
A. Duboys: Justice et Bourreau à Amiens	1463	Two pigs	Amiens
Sauval: Histoire de Paris, iii, p. 387. Mémoires, cit., viii, p. 428	1466	Sow	Corbeil
A Duboys: Histoire de Paris	1470	Mare	Amiens
Promenades pittoresques dans l'Evêché de Bâle. Journal du Départment du Nord, Nov. 1, 1813. Mémoires, cit., viii, p. 428. Johann Gross: Kleine Baseler Chronik.	1474	Cock	Bâle

Sources of Information	Dates	Animals	Places
Schilling: Chronica (Zurich MS.), Hottinger: Hist. Eccles. Pars iv, pp. 317–321	1478	Inger (sort of weevil)	Berne
Ruchat: Hist. Eccles. du Pays de Vaud	1479[1]	Inger	,,
Hist. de Nismes. Mémoires, cit., viii, p. 428.	1479	Rats and Moles	Nîmes
Louandre: Hist. d'Abbeville	1479	Pig	Abbeville
Chasseneus: Consilia von Amira, p. 561	1481	Caterpillars	Macon
Victor Hugo: Nôtre Dame de Paris	1482	Goat	Paris
Chasseneus: Consilia. Mémoires, cit., viii, p. 416	1487	Snails	Macon
,, ,, ,,	1488	,,	Autun
,, ,, ,,	1488	Weevils	Beaujeu
Louandre: Hist. d'Abbeville	1490	Pig	Abbeville

[1] This case is probably identical with and an adjournment of that of 1478.

Sources of Information	Dates	Animals	Places
Annuaire de l'Aisne 1812, p. 88. Mémoires, cit., viii, p. 428, 446	1494	Pig	Clermont-les-Moncornet near Laon
Saint-Edme : Dict. de la Penalité, sub verb. Animaux	1497	Sow	Charonne
Voyage Littéraire de deux Bénédictins (Durand et Martenne), 1717, ii, p. 166–7	1499	Bull	Beauvais
Archives de l'Abbaye de Josaphat. Mémoires, cit., viii, p. 434–5	1499	Pig	Sèves near Chartres
Mémoires, cit., viii, p. 434	15th cent.	Sow	Dunois
Malleolus : De Exorcismis	,,	Caterpillars	Coire
,, ,, ,,	,,	Worms	Constance
,, ,, ,,	,,	Beetles	Coire
Louandre : L'Épopée des Animaux	1500	Flies	Mayence
Chasseneus : Consilia.	1500	Snails	Lyon

Sources of Information	Dates	Animals	Places
Chasseneus: Consilia	1500–1530	Vermin (Rats, etc.)	Autun
Mémoires et Documents, publ. par la Soc. de la Suisse Romande, vii, No. 97, pp. 675–677	1509	Vermin	Lausanne
Annuaire de la Côte-d'Or	1510	Pig	Dijon
Annuaire de la Côte-d'Or. Mémoires, cit., viii, p. 447	1512	,,	Arcenaux
Mathieu: Hist. des Évêques de Langres, p, 188	1512–13	Rats and Insects	Langres
Groslée: Ephémérides, 1811, ii, p. 153, 168. Cf. Théophile Raynaud: Opusc, 1665, p. 482. Mémoires, cit., viii, p. 413, 418, 424	1516 (1506 according to some authorities)	Weevils	Troyes in Champagne
Habasque: Not. hist. sur le Litoral des Côtes-du-Nord, p. 89	1516	Locusts	Tréguier
Scheible: Das Kloster, xii, pp. 946–48	1519	Field-mice	Glurns (Stelvio)

Sources of Information	Dates	Animals	Places
Saint-Edme : Dict. de la Penalité. *Cf.* Chasseneus	1522[1]	Rats	Autun
Vernet in Thémis ou Bibliothèque des Jurisconsulte, viii	1525	Dog	Parliament of Toulouse
Papon and Boesius: Decisiones. *Cf.* Thémis, viii	1528	Not specified	Parliament of Bordeaux
,, ,, ,,	1528	,,	,, ,,
Ménebréa : Jugements rendus contre les Animaux, p. 505. From Grenier : Documents relatifs à l'hist. du pays de Vaud.	1536	Weevils	Lutry (on Lake Leman)
Lerouge : Registre secret manuscrit	1540	Bitch	Meaux
Annuaire de la Côte-d'Or	1540	Pig	Dijon
Lerouge : Registre secret manuscrit	1541	She-Ass	Loudun
Bailly : Traité des Monitoires, ii	1541	Grasshoppers	Lombardy

[1] Identical with the sentences covering the period of 1500–1530.

21

Sources of Information	Dates	Animals	Places
Malleolus : De Exorcismis	1541	Vermin (worms, rats, bloodsuckers)	Lausanne
Berriat-Saint-Prix in Thémis, i, p. 196	1543	Snails and Locusts	Grenoble
Ménebréa : Jugements rendus contre les Animaux, pp. 544, 545, 556. De Actis Scindicorum com. St. Jul., etc.	1545 and 1546	Weevils	St. Jean de Maurienne
Dulaure : Hist. de Paris, iii, p. 28, Registres manuscrits de la Tournelle. *Cf.* Mémoires, cit., viii, p. 429	1546	Cow	Parliament of Paris
Lerouge : Registre secret manuscrit	1550	,,	,, ,,
,, ,, ,,	1551	Goat	Ile de Rhé
,, ,, ,,	1554	Sheep (ewe)	Beaugé
Aldrovande : De Insectis, 1602, lib. vii, 724. Mémoires, cit. viii, p. 429	1554	Bloodsuckers	Lausanne

Sources of Information	Dates	Animals	Places
Desnoyer, cited in Revue des questions historiques, v, p. 278. Von Armira, p. 567	1554	Insects	Langres
Lerouge : Registre secret manuscrit	1556	She-Ass	Sens
Lecoq : Hist. de la Ville de Saint-Quintin, p. 143. Sorel : Procès contre des animaux, etc., p. 9	1557	Pig	Saint-Quintin
Lerouge : Registre secret manuscrit	1560	She-Ass	Loigny near Châteaudun
,, ,, ,,	1561	Cow	Augoudessus in Picardy
Lessona : I Nemici del Vino. Regist. Epir. Par. for May 8	1562	Weevils	Argenteuil
Ranchin on Gui. Pape Quaest., 74. Thémis, i, p. 196. Mémoires, cit., viii, p. 429	1565	Mule	Montpellier
Papon : Decisiones. Thémis, viii	1565	Not specified	Parliament of Toulouse
Louandre : L'Epopée des Animaux	1566	She-Ass	Parliament of Paris

Sources of Information	Dates	Animals	Places
MSS. of Bibliothèque Nationale of Paris	1567	Sow	Senlis
Lionnois : Hist. de Nancy, 1811, ii, p. 374	1572	Pig	Moyen-Montier, near Nancy
Lersner : Chronica, 1706, p. 552	1574	,,	Frankfort-on-the-Main
Brillon : Decisiones Thémis, viii	1575	She-Ass	Parliament of Paris
Haus-Chronik von Schweinfurt, in Zeitschrift für deutsche Kulturgeschichte, i, 156	1576	Pig	Schweinfurt
Cannaert : Bydragen tot de Kennis van het oude strafrecht in Vlandern, 1835, p. vii	1578	Pig (?)	Ghent
Derheims : Hist. de Saint-Omer, p. 327	1585	Pig	Saint-Omer
Chorier : Hist. du Dauphiné. *Cf.* Thémis, i, p. 196	,,	Locusts	Valence

Sources of Information	Dates	Animals	Places
Ménebréa : Jugements rendus contre les animaux, etc., pp. 546, 549	1587	Weevils	St. Jean-de-Maurienne
Fornery and Laincel	1596	Dolphins	Marseilles
Théophile Raynaud : De Monitoriis, p. 482. Mémoires, cit., viii, p. 429	16th cent. (first half)	Weevils and Grasshoppers	Cotentin
Chasseneus : Consilia. Mémoires, cit., viii, p. 415	,,	Snails	Lyons
,, ,, ,,	,,	Weevils	Mâcon
,, ,, ,,	,,	Pig	Dijon
Louandre : L'Épopée des Animaux	,,	Dog	Scotland
Duboys : Hist. du Droit Crim. de la France	16th cent. second half	Weevils	Angers
Azpilcueta Martinus Doctor Navarrus : Consilia seu Responsa, 1602, ii, p. 812. Mémoires, cit., viii, p. 419. Théoph. Raynaud, cit., p. 482	,,	Rats	Spain

Sources of Information	Dates	Animals	Places
Francesco Vivio: Decisiones, No. 68. Cited by D'Addosio: Bestie Delinq., p. 125	16th cent. second half	Divers animals	Aquila in Italy
Archives of Obwalden	,,	Gadflies	Aargau
Leonardo Vairo: De Fascino. *Cf.* D'Addosio, cit., p. 115.	,,	Locusts	Naples
Sardagna: L'uomo e le Bestie. Cited by D'Addosio	,,	Horse	Portugal
Mornacius to Du Cange, *s.v.* Homicida	1600		Beauvais
Lerouge: Registre secret manuscrit	,,	Cow	Thouars
,, ,, ,,	,,	,,	Abbeville
Lessona: I Nemici del Vino, 1890, p. 141	,,	Weevils	Vercelli
Papon: Decisiones. Thémis, viii. Lerouge: Reg. secret manuscrit	1601	Dog	Brie
Lerouge: Registre secret manuscrit	,,	Mare	Provins

Sources of Information	Dates	Animals	Places
Papon : Recueil d'Arrets	1601	Not specified	Parliament of Paris
Charma : Leçons de Philosophie	1604	Ass	Parliament or Paris
Guerra : Diurnali	,,	,,	Naples
Lerouge : Registre secret manuscrit	,,	Mare	Joinville
,,　,,　,,	1606	Sheep	Riom
,,　,,　,,	,,	Cow	Château-renaud
,,　,,　,,	,,	Mare	Coiffy near Langres
Lejeune: Mémoires, cit., viii, p. 418	,,	Bitch	Chartres
Lerouge : Registre secret manuscrit	1607	Mare	Boursant near d'Epernay
,,　,,　,,	1609	,,	Montmorency
,,　,,　,,	,,	,,	Niederrad
Voltaire : Siècle de Louis XIV, ch. i. Louandre : Rev. des deux Mondes, 1854, i, p. 334	,,	Cow	Parliament of Paris

Sources of Information	Dates	Animals	Places
Lerouge: Registre secret manuscrit	1610	Horse	Paris
,, ,, ,,	1611	Goat	Laval
,, ,, ,,	,,	Cow	St. Fergeux near Rethel
,, ,, ,,	1613	Sow	Montoiron near Chatelleraut
,, ,, ,,	1614	She-Ass	Le Mans
Desnoyers: Recherches, etc., p. 13	1616	Rats and insects	Langres
Anzeige für Kunde der deutschen Vorzeit, 1880, col. 102	1621	Cow	Machern near Leipsic
Lerouge: Registre secret manuscrit	1621	Mare	La Rochelle
,, ,, ,,	1622	,,	Montpensier
,, ,, ,,	1623	She-Ass	Bessay near Moulins
,, ,, ,,	1624	Mule	Chefboutonne (Poitou)
Döpler: Theat. pen., ii, p. 574	1631	Mares and Cows	Greifenberg

Sources of Information	Dates	Animals	Places
Marchisio Michele: Gatte ed. insetti noc- ivi, 1834, p. 63 *sqq.*	1633	Weevils	Strambino (Ivrea)
Lerouge: Registre secret manuscrit	,,	Mare	Bellac
Carpentier to Du Cange, *s. v.* Homicida	1641	Pig	Viroflay
Lerouge: Registre secret manuscrit	1647	Mare	Parliament of Paris
,, ,, ,,	1650	,,	Fresnay near Chartres
Crollolanza: Storia del Contado di Chia- venna, p. 455 *sqq.*	1659	Caterpillars	Chiavenna
Perrero: Gazzetta Litteraria di Torino, Feb. 24, 1883	1661	Weevils	Turin
Cotton Mather: Magnalia Christi Americana, Book vi. London, 1702	1662	Cow, two Heifers, three Sheep, and two Sows	New Haven, Conn.
Lerouge: Registre secret manuscrit	1666	Mare	Tours
,, ,, ,,	,,	,,	St. P. Lemon- tiers

Sources of Information	Dates	Animals	Places
Lerouge : Registre secret manuscrit	1667	She-Ass	Vaudes near Bar-sur-Seine
,, ,, ,,	1668	Mare	Angers
Annales scientifiques de l'Auvergne, Vol. vii, p. 391	1670	Locusts	Clermont
Döpler : Theatrum pen., ii, p. 5	1676	Mare and Cow	Silesia
Lerouge : Registre secret manuscrit	1678	,,	Beaugé
Perrero : Gaz. Litter. di Torius, Feb. 24, 1883	,,	Weevils	Turin
Brillon : Decisiones, i, p. 914. Mémoires, cit., viii, p. 431. Boniface: Traité des matières criminelles, 1785, p. 31	1679	Mare	Parliament d'Aix
Chorier : Hist. du Dauphiné. Thémis, viii	Before 1680	Worms	Constance and Coire
Lerouge : Registre secret manuscrit	1680	Mare	Fourches nea Provins

Sources of Information	Dates	Animals	Places
Heinrich Roch: Schlesische Chronik, p. 342. Döpler: Theat. pen., ii, p. 573 *sqq.*	1681	Mare	Wünschelburg in Silesia
,, ,, ,,	1684	Mare	Ottendorf
,, ,, ,,	1685	,,	Striga
Dulaure: Description des principaux lieux de la France, 1789, v, p. 493 *sqq.* Mémoires, cit., viii, p. 412	1690	Locusts	Pont-de-Château in Auvergne
Lerouge: Registre secret manuscrit	1692	Mare	Moulins
La Hontan: Voyages, Let. xi, p. 79. Mémoires, cit., viii. p. 431	End of 17th cent.	Turtle-doves	Canada
Meiners: Vergleichung des ältern u, neuern Russlands, p. 291. *Cf.* Amira, p. 573	,,	He-Goat, banished to Siberia	Russia
Registres de la Paroise de Grignon	1710	Rats	Grignon

Sources of Information	Dates	Animals	Places
Sorel: Procès contre des animaux, etc., p. 23	1710	Vermin	Autun
Rinds Herreds Krönike and other sources given by Amira, p. 565	1711	,,	Als in Jutland
Agnel : Curiosités judiciaires et historiques du moyen-âge, p. 46. *Cf.* Manoel Bernardes : Nova Floresta ou Sylva de varios apophthegmas, etc. 5 tom. Lisboá, 1706–47	1713	Termites	Piedade no Maranhão in Brazil
MSS. of Bibliothèque Nationale of Paris, No. 10,970. D'Addosio : Best. Del., p. 107	1726	Not specified	Paris
Ménebréa : Jugements contre les animaux, p. 508	1731	Insects	Thonon
La Tradition, 1888, p. 363 *sqq.* Amira, p. 564	1733	Vermin	Buranton

Sources of Information	Dates	Animals	Places
Rousseaud de Lacombe: Traité des matières crim. D'Addosio: Best. Del., p. 107	1741	Cow	Poitou
Ant. de Saint-Gervais: Hist. des Animaux	1750	She-Ass	Vanvres
A Report of the Case of Farmer Carter's Dog. Amira, p. 559	1771	Dog	Chichester, England
Comparon: Hist. du Tribunal Révolutionnaire de Paris. Cf. Sorel, op. cit., p. 16	1793	,,	Paris
Filangieri: Scienza della Legislazione	18th cent.	Dogs	Italy
Det. Kong. Danske Landhusholdnings-Selskabs Skrifter. Ny Saml. ii, 1, 22. Amira, p. 565.	1805–6	Vermin	Lyö in Denmark
Desnoyers: Recherches, etc., p. 15	1826	Locusts	Clermont-Ferrand

Sources of Information	Dates	Animals	Places
Gazette des Tribunaux, Jan. 23, 1845	1845	Dog	Paris
,, ,, ,,	1864	Pig	Pleternica in Slavonia
Krauss, quoted by Amira, p. 573	1866	Locusts	Pozega in Slavonia
,, ,, ,,	,,	Grass-hoppers	Vidovici in Slavonia
Desnoyer : Recherches, etc., p. 15	19th cent.	Locusts	Catalonia
Allg. deutsche Strafrechts-zeitung, 1861, No. 2. Also Pertile : Gli animali in giudizio	,,	Cock	Leeds in England
Cretella : Gli Animali sotto processo in Fanfulla 1891, No. 65. Cf. Amira, p. 569	,,	Wolf	Calabria
New York Herald and Echo de Paris, May 4, 1906[1]	1906	Dog	Délémont in Switzerland

[1] In this latest record of such prosecutions a man named Marger was killed and robbed by Scherrer and his son, with the fierce and effective co-operation of their dog. The three murderers were tried and the two men sentenced to lifelong imprisonment, but the dog, as the chief culprit, without whose complicity the crime could not have been committed, was condemned to death.

G

Receipt dated Jan. 9, 1386, in which the hangman of Falaise acknowledges to have been paid by the Viscount of Falaise ten sous and ten deniers tournois for the execution of an infanticidal sow, and also ten sous tournois for a new glove.

Quittance originale du 9, janvier 1386, passée devant Guiot de Montfort, tabellion à Falaise, et donnée par le bourreau de cette ville de la somme de *dix sols et dix deniers tournois* pour sa peine et salaire d'avoir trainé, puis pendu à la justice de Falaise une truie de l'age de 3 ans ou environ, qui avoit mangé le visage de l'enfant de Jonnet le Maux, qui était au bers et avoit trois mois et environ, tellement que ledit enfant en mourut, et de *dix sols tournois pour un gant neuf* quand le bourreau fit la dite execution ; cette quittance est donné á Regnaud Rigault, vicomte de Falaise ; le bourreau y declare qu'il se tient pour bien content des dites sommes, et qu'il en tient quitte le roy et ledit vicomte.

Charange : *Dictionnaire des Titres Originaux.* Paris, 1764. Tome II. p. 72. Also *Statistique de Falaise,* 1827. Tome I. p. 63.

H

Receipt, dated Sept. 24, 1394, in which Jehan Micton, hangman, acknowledges that he received the sum of fifty sous tournois from Thomas de Juvigney, viscount of Mortaing, for having hanged a pig which had killed and murdered a child in the parish of Roumaygne.

A tous ceulx qui ces lettres verront ou orront, Jehan Lours, garde du scel des obligacions de la vicomté de Mortaing, salut, Sachent tous que par devant Bynet de l'Espiney, clerc tabellion juré ou siege dudit lieu de Mortaing, fut present mestre Jehan Micton, pendart,[1] en la viconté d'Avrenches, qui recognut et confessa avoir eu et repceu de homme sage et pourveu Thomas de Juvigney, viconte dudit lieu de Mortaing, c'est assavoir la somme de cinquante souls tournois pour sa paine et salaire d'estre venue d'Avrenches jusques à Mortaing, pour faire acomplir et pendre à la justice dudit lieu de Mortaing, un porc, lequel avait tué et meurdis un enfant en la paroisse de Roumaygne, en ladite viconté de Mortaing. Pour lequel fait ycelui porc fut condanney à estre trayné et pendu, par Jehan Pettit, lieutenant du bailli de Co . . . . rin, es assises dudit lieu de Mortaing, de laquelle somme dessus dicte le dit pendart se tint pour bien paié, et en quita le roy nostre sire, ledit

---

[1] In modern French *pendard* means hang-dog. M. Lejeune states that he can recall no other instance of its use as synonymous with bourreau or hangman. Perhaps a facetious clerk may have deemed it applicable to a person whose office was in the present case that of a hang-pig.

viconte et tous aultres. En tesmoing de ce, nous avons
sellé ces lettres dudit scel, sauf tout autre droit. C'en
fut fait l'an de grace mil trois cens quatre-vings et
quatorze, le XXIIIIe jour de septembre. Signé
J. LOURS. (Countersigned) BINET.

[Extract from the manuscripts of the *Bibliothèque
du Roi*. Vide *Mémoires, ibid*. pp. 439--40.]

22

I

Attestation of Symon de Baudemont, lieutenant of the bailiff of Mantes and Meullant, made by order of the said bailiff and the King's proctor, on March 15, 1403, and certifying to the expenses incurred in executing a sow that had devoured a small child.

A tous ceuls qui ces lettres verront : Symon de Baudemont, lieutenant à Meullant, de noble homme Mons. Jehan, seigneur de Maintenon, chevalier chambellan du Roy, notre sire, et son bailli de Mante et dudit lieu de Meullant : Salut. Savoir faisons, que pour faire et accomplir la justice d'une truye qui avait devoré un petit enffant, a convenu faire necessairement les frais, commissions et dépens ci-après déclarés, c'est à savoir : Pour dépense faite pour elle dedans le geole, six sols parisis.

Item, au maître des hautes-oeuvres, qui vint de Paris à Meullant faire ladite exécution par le commandement et ordonnance de nostre dit maistre le bailli et du procureur du roi, cinquante-quatre sols parisis.

Item, pour la voiture qui la mena à la justice, six sols parisis.

Item, pour cordes à la lier et hâler, deux sols huit deniers parisis.

Item, pour gans, deux deniers parisis.

Lesquelles parties font en somme toute soixante neuf sols huit deniers parisis ; et tout ce que dessus est dit nous certifions être vray par ces présentes scellées de notre scel, et à greigneur confirmation et approbation de ce y avons fait mettre le scel de la châtellenie dudit lieu de Meullant, le XVᵉ de mars l'an 1403. Signé de Baudemont, avec paraffe, et au dessous est le sceau de la châtellenie de Meullant.

[Extract from the manuscripts of M. Hérisson, judge of the civil court of Chartres, communicated by M. Lejeune to the *Mémoires de la Société Royale des Antiquaires de France.* Tome viii, pp. 433–4.]

J

Receipt, dated Oct. 16, 1408, and signed by Toustain Pincheon, jailer of the royal prisons in the town of Pont de Larche, acknowledging the payment of nineteen sous and six deniers tournois for food furnished to sundry men and to one pig kept in the said prisons on charge of crime.

Pardevant Jean Gaulvant, tabellion juré pour le roy nostre sire en la viconté du Pont de Larche, fut présent Toustain Pincheon, geolier des prisons du roy notre sire en la ville du Pont de Larche, lequel cognut avoir eu et recue du roy nostre dit sire, par la main de honnorable homme et saige Jehan Monnet, viconte dudit lieu du Pont de Larche, la somme de 19 sous six deniers tournois qui deus lui estoient, c'est assavoir 9 sous six deniers tournois pour avoir trouvé (livré) le pain du roi aux prisonniers debtenus, en cas de crime, es dites prisons. (Here the names of these prisoners are given.) *Item* à ung porc admené es dictes prisons, le 21ᵉ jour de juing 1408 inclus, jusques au 17ᵉ jour de juillet après en suivant exclut que icellui porc fu pendu par les gares à un des posts de la justice du Vaudereuil, à quoy il avoit esté condempné pour ledit cas par monsieur le bailly de Rouen et les conseuls, es assises du Pont de Larche, par lui tenues le 13ᵉ jour dudict mois de juillet, psource que icellui porc avoit muldry et tué ung pettit enfant, auquel temps il a xxiiii jours, valent audit pris de 2 deniers tournois par jour, 4 sols 2 deniers, et pour avoir trouvé et baillé la corde qu'il esconvint à lier icelui porc qu'il reschapast de ladite prison où il avait esté mis, x deniers tournois. Du 16 Octobre 1408.

[Derived from manuscripts of the *Bibliothèque du Roi*, *Vide* Mémoires, cit., pp. 428 and 440-1.]

K

Letters patent, by which Philip the Bold, Duke of Burgundy, on Sept. 12, 1379, granted the petition of the friar Humbert de Poutiers, prior of the town of Saint-Marcel-lez-Jussey, and pardoned two herds of swine which had been condemned to suffer the extreme penalty of the law as accomplices in an infanticide committed by three sows.

Phelippe, filz du Roi de France, duc de Bourgoingue, au bailli de noz terres au conté de Bourgoingue, salut.

Oye la supplication de frère Humbert de Poutiers, prieur de la prieurté de la ville de Saint-Marcel-lez-Jussey, contenant que comme le Ve jour de ce présent mois de septembre, Perrinot, fils Jehan Muet, dit *le Hochebet*, pourchier commun de ladite ville, gardant les pors des habitans d'icelle ville ou finaige d'icelle, et au cry de l'un d'iceulx pors, trois truyes estans entre lesdits pors ayent couru sus audit Perrenot, l'ayent abattu et mis par terre entre eulx, ainsi comme par Jehan Benoit de Norry qu'il gardoit les pourceaulx dudit suppliant, et par le père dudit Perrenot a esté trouvé blessier à mort par lesdites truyes, et si comme icelle Perrenot la confessè en la présence de son dit père e dudit Jehan Benoit, et assez tost après il soit eu mort. Et pour ce que ledit suppliant auquel appartient la justice de ladite ville ne fust repris de negligeance son maire arresta tous lesdits porcs pour en faire raison et justice en la manière qu'il appartient, et encore les détient prissonniers tant ceux de ladite ville comme partie de ceulx dudit suppliant, pour ce que dit ledit Jehan Benoit ils furent trouvez ensemble avec lesdites truyes, quand ledit Perrenot fut ainsi blessié. Et ledit prieur nous ait supplié que il nous plaise consentir que en faisant justice de trois ou quatres desdits porcs le demeurant soit delivré. Nous inclinans à sa requeste, avons de gràce especiale ouctroyé et consenty, et par ces présentes ouctroyons et consentons que en faisant justice et execution desdites trois truyes et de l'ung des pourceaulx dudit prieur, que le demeurant desdits pourceaulx soit mis à delivre, nonobstant qu'ils aient esté à la mort dudit pourchier. Si vous mandons que de notre presente gràce vous faictes et laissiez joyr et user ledit prieur et autres qu' il appartiendra, sans les empescher au gràce.

Donné à Montbar, le XIIe jour de septembre de l'an de grâce mil CCC LXX IX. Ainsi signé. Par monseigneur le duc : *J. Potier.*

[Published by M. Garnier in the *Revue des Sociétés Savantes,* Dec. 1866, pp. 476 *sqq.*, from the archives of Côte-d'Or and reprinted by D'Addosio in *Bestie Delinquenti*, pp. 277–8.]

L

Sentence pronounced by the Mayor of Loens de Chartres on the twelfth of September, 1606, condemning Guillaume Guyart to be hanged and burned together with a bitch. Extract from the records of the clerk's office of Loing under the date of Sept. 12, 1606.

Entre le procureur de messieurs[1] demandeur et accusateur au principal et requérant le proffit et adjudication de troys deffaulx et du quart d'abondant, d'une part, et Guillaume Guyard, accusé, deffendeur et défaillant, d'autre part.

Veu le procès criminel, charges et informations, décret de prise de corps, adjournement à troys briefs jours, les dicts trois deffaulx, le dict quart d'habondant, le recollement des dicts témoings et *recognaissance faicte par les dicts témoings de la chienne dont est question,* les conclusions dudict procureur, tout veu et eu sur ce conseil, nous disant que lesdicts troys deffaulx et quart d'habondant ont esté bien donnés pris et obtenus contre ledict Guyard accusé, attainct et convaincu. . . . .

Pour réparation et punition duquel crime condempnons ledict Guyard estre pendu et estranglé à une potence qui, pour cest effet, sera dressée aux lices du Marché aux Chevaux de ceste ville de Chartres, au lieu et endroict où

---

[1] Under this term are included the dean, canons, and chapter of the Cathedral of Chartres.

les dict sieurs ont tout droit de justice. Et auparavant ladicte exécution de mort, que ladicte chienne sera assommée par l'exécuteur de la haute justice audict lieu, et seront les corps morts, tant dudict Guyard que de la dicte chienne brûlés et mis en cendres, si le dict Guyard peut estre pris et apprehendé en sa personne, sy non pour le regard du dict Guyard, sera la sentence exécuté par effigie en un tableau qui sera mis et attaché à ladicte potence, et déclarons tous et chascuns ses biens acquis et confisqués à qui il appartiendra, sur cieux préalablement pris la somme de cent cinquante livres d'amende que nous avons adjugées auxdicts sieurs, sur laquelle somme seront pris les fraicts de justice. Prononcé et exécuté par effigie, pour le regard du dict Guyard les jour et an cy dessus. Signé *Guyot.*

[A true copy of the original extract extant in the office of M. Hérisson, judge of the civil court of Chartres, made by M. Lejeune and communicated to the Société Royale des Antiquaires de France. *Vide* Mémoires of this Society, cit., pp. 436–7.]

M

Sentence pronounced by the judge of Savigny on Jan. 1457, condemning to death an infanticidal sow. Also the sentence of confiscation pronounced nearly a month later on the six pigs of the said sow for complicity in her crime.

Jours tenus au lieu de Savigny, près des foussés du Chastelet de dit Savigny, par noble homme Nicolas Quarroillon, ecuier, juge dudit lieu de Savigny, et ce le 10ᵉ jour du moys de janvier 1457, présens maistre Philebert Quarret, Nicolas Grant-Guillaume, Pierre Bome, Pierre Chailloux, Germain des Muliers, André Gaudriot, Jehan Bricard, Guillaume Gabrin, Philebert Hogier, et plusieurs autres tesmoins à ce appellés et requis, l'an et jour dessus dit.

Huguemin Martin, procureur de noble damoiselle Katherine de Barnault, dame dudit Savigny, demandeur à l'encontre de Jehan Bailly, alias Valot dudit Savigny, et promoteur des causes d'office dudit lieu de Savigny, demandeur à l'encontre de Jehan Bailly, alias Valot dudit Savigny *deffendeur*, à l'encontre duquel par la voix et organ de honorable homme et saige Mr. Benoit Milot d'Ostun, licencié en loys et bachelier en décret, conseïllier de monseigneur le duc de Bourgoingne, a été dit et proposé que le mardi avant Noel dernier passé, *une truye*, et six coichons ses suignens, que sont présentement prisonniers de ladite dame, comme ce qu'ils été prins en

flagrant délit, ont commis et perpetré mesmement ladicte
truye murtre et homicide en la personne de Jehan
Martin en aige de cinq ans, fils de Jehan Martin dudit
Savigny, pour la faulte et culpe dudit Jehan Bailly, alias
Valot, requerant ledit procureur et promoteur desdites
causes d'office de ladite justice de madite dame, que
ledit défendeur répondit es chouses dessus dites, desquelles
apparaissoit à souffisance, et lequel par nous a esté sommé
et requis ce il vouloit avoher ladite truhie et ses
suignens, sur le cas avant dit, et sur ledit cas luy a esté
faicte sommacion par nous juge avant dit, pour la
première, deuxiéme et tierce fois, que s'il vouloit rien
dire pourquoi justice ne s'en deust faire l'on estoit tout
prest de les oïr en tout ce qu'il vouldrait dire touchant
la pugnycion et exécution de justice que se doit faire de
ladite truhie ; veu ledit cas, lequel deffendeur a dit et
respondu qui'l ne vouloit rien dire pour le present et pour
ce ait esté procédé en la manière qui s'ensuit ; c'est
assavoir que pour la partie dudit demandeur, avons esté
requis instamment de dire droit en ceste cause, en la
présence dudit défendeur présent et non contredisant,
pourquoy nous juge, avant dit, savoir faisons à tous que
nous avons procédé et donné nostre sentence deffinitive
en la manière que s'ensuit ; c'est assavoir que veu le cas
lequel est tel comme a esté proposé pour la partie dudit
demandeur, et duquel appert à souffisance tant par
tesmoing que autrement dehuëment hue. *Aussi conseil
avec saiges et practiciens*, et aussi considéré en ce cas
l'usance et coustume du païs de Bourgoingne, aïant
Dieu devant nos yeulx, nous disons et pronunçons
par notre dite sentence, déclairons la tryue de Jehan
Martin, de Savigny, estre confisquée à la justice de Madame
de Savigny, pour estre mise à justice et au dernier

supplice, et estre pendus par les pieds derriers à ung arbre esproné en la justice de Madame de Savigny, considéré que la justice de madite dame n'est mie présentement elevée, et icelle truye prendre mort audit arbre esproné, et ansi le disons et prononçons par notre dicte sentence et à droit et au regard des coichons de ladite truye pour ce qui n'appert aucunement que iceuls coichons ayent mangiés dudit Jehan Martin, combien que aient estés trovés ensanglantés, l'on remet *la caüse d'iceulx coichons* aux tres jours, et avec ce l'on est content de les rendre et bailler audit *Jehan Bailly*, en baillant caucion de les rendre s'il est trové qu'il aient mangiers dudit Jehan Martin, en païant les poutures, et fait l'on savoir à tous, sous peine de l'amende et de 100 sols tournois qu'ils le dieut et déclairent dedans les autres jours, de laquelle nostre dicte sentence, après la prononciation d'icelle, ledit procureur de ladite dame de Savigny et promoteur des causes d'office par la voix dudit maistre Benoist Milot, advocat de ladite dame ; et aussi ledit procureur a requis et demandé acte de nostre dicte court à lui estre faicte, laquelle luy avons ouctroyé, et avec ce instrument, je, Huguenin de Montgachot, clerc, notaire publicque de la court de monseigneur le duc de Bourguoigne, en la présence des tesmoings ci-dessus nommés, je lui ai ouctroyé, ce fait l'an et jour dessus dit et présens les dessus tesmoings. *Ita est.* Ainsi signe, Mongachot, avec paraphe, et de suite est écrit :

Item, en oultre, nous juge dessus nommé, savoir faisons que incontinent après nostre dicte sentence ainsi donnée par nous les an et jour, et en la présence des temoings que dessus, avons sommé et requis ledit Jehan Bailli, se il vouloit avoher lesdits coichons, et

se il vouloit bailler caucion pour avoir recréance
d'iceulx; lequel a dit et répondu qui ne les avohait
aucunement, et qui ni demandait rien en iceulx
coichons; et qui s'en rapportoit à ce que en ferions;
pourquoy sont demeurez à la dicte justice et seignorie
dudit Savigny, de laquelle chouse ledit Huguenin
Martin, procureur et promoteur des causes d'offices,
nous en a demandé acte de court, lequel lui nous
avons ouctroyé et ouctroyons par ces présentes, et
avec ce ledict procureur de ladicte dame, à moy
notaire subescript, m'en demanda instrument, lequel
je luy ait ouctroyé en la presénce desdits tesmoings
cy-dessus nommés.

Item, en après, nous Nicolas Quaroillon, juge avant
dit, savoir faisons à tous que incontinent après les
chouses dessus dictes, avons faict delivrer réalement et
de fait ladicte truye à maistre Etienne Poinceau,
maistre de la haute justice, demeurant à Châlons-sur-
Saône, pour icelle mettre à exécucion selon la forme
et teneur de nostre dicte sentence, laquelle délivrance
d'icelle trühie faicte par nous comme dit est, incontinent
ledit maistre Estienne a mené sur une chairette ladicte
truye à ung chaigne esproné, estant en la justice de ladite
dame Savigny, et en icelluy chaigne esproné, icelluy
maistre Estienne a pendu ladite truye par les piez
derriers; en mectant à exécution deue nostre dicte
sentence, selon la forme et teneur de laquelle délivrance
et exécution d'icelle truye, ledit Huguenin Martin, procureur de ladicte dame de Savigny nous a demandé acte
de nostre dicte court à lui estre faicte et donnée, laquelle
luy avons ouctroyée, et avec ce à moi, notaire subscript,
m'a demandé instrument ledit procureur à luy estre
donnée, je luy ai ouctroyé en la présence des temoings

cy-dessus nommez, ce fait les au et jour dessus ditz.
Ainsi signé Mongachot, avec paraphe.

Nearly a month later, on "the Friday after the Feast of
the Purification of Our Lady the Virgin" (which occurred
on Feb. 2.), "the six little porklets or sucklings" were
brought to trial. The following is the *procès verbal.*

Jours tenus au lieu de Savigny, sur la chaussée de
l'Estang dudit Savigny, par noble homme Nicolas
Quarroillon, escuier, juge dudit lieu de Savigny, pour
noble damoiselle Katherine de Barnault, dame dudit
Savigny, et ce le vendredy après la feste de la Purification
Notre Dame Vierge, présens Guillaume Martin, Guiot de
Layer, Jehan Martin, Pierre Tiroux et Jehan Bailly,
tesmoings, etc.
Veue les sommacions et réquisitions faicte par nous
juge de noble damoiselle Katherine de Barnault, dame
de Savigny, à Jehan Bailly alias Valot de advohé on
repudié les coichons de la truye nouvellement mise
à exécution par justice à raison du murtre commis et
perpetré par la dicte truye en la personne de Jehan
Martin, lequel Jehan Bailli a esté remis de advoher
lesdites coichons et de baillier caucion d'iceulx coichons
rendre, s'il estoit trouvé qu'ils feussions culpables du
délict avant dict commis par ladicte truye et de payer les
poutures, comme appert par acte de nostre dicte court,
et autres instrumens souffisans ; pourquoi le tout veu en
conseil avec saiges, déclairons et pronuncons par nostre
sentence deffinitive, et à droit : iceulx coichons compéter
et appartenir comme biens vaccans à ladite dame de
Savigny et les luy adjugeons comme raison, l'usence et
la coustume de païs le vueilt. De laquelle nostre dicte

sentence, ledit procureur de ladite dame en a demandé acte, de nostre dicte court a luy estre donnée et ouctroyée. Avec ce en a demandé instrument à moy notaire subscript, lequel il luy a ouctroyé en la présence des dessus nommés. Signé Mongachot avec paraphe.

[Extract from the archives of Monjeu and Dependencies, belonging to M. Lepelletier de Saint-Fargeau. (Savigny-sur-Etang, boëte 25e, liasse 1, 2, & 3, etc.) *Vide* Mémoires, cit., pp. 441–5.]

N

Sentence pronounced April 18, 1499, in a criminal prosecution instituted before the Bailiff of the Abbey of Josaphat, in the Commune of Sèves, near Chartres, against a pig condemned to be hanged for having killed an infant. In this case the owners of the pig were fined eighteen francs for negligence, because the child was their fosterling.

Le lundi 18 *avril* 1499.

Veu le procès criminel faict par-devant nous à la requeste du procureur de messieurs le religieux, abbé et convent de Iosaphat, à l'encontre de Iehan Delalande et sa femme, prisonniers èsprisons de céans, pour raison de la mort advenue à la personne d'une jeune enfant, nommée Gilon, âgée de un an et demi ou environ ; laquelle enfant avoit eté baillée à nourrice par sa mère : ledict meurtre advenu et commis par un pourceau de l'aage de trois mois ou environ, aulxdits Delalande et sa femme appartenant ; les confessions desdicts Delalande et sa femme ; les informations par nous et le greffier de ladite jurisdiction faictes à la requête dudict procureur ; le tout veu et en sur ce conseil aulx saiges, *ledit Jehan Delalande et sa femme, avons condampnés et condampnons en l'amende envers de justice de dix-huit franz*, qu'il a convenus pour ce faire, tel que de raison, et à tenir prison jusqu'à plein payement et satisfaction d'iceulx à tout le moins qu'ils avoient baillé bonne et seure caution d'iceulx.

Et en tant que touche le dict pourceau, pour les causes

contenues et établies audict procès, *nous les avons con-
dampné et condampnons à être pendu et executé par justice,*
en la jurisdiction des mes dicts seigneurs, par notre
sentence définitive, *et à droit.*

Donnè sous la contre scel aux causes dudict baillage,
les an et jour que susdicts. *Signé* C. Briseg avec
paraphe.

[The complete record of this trial contains the minutest
details of the proceedings, ending with the execution of
the pig, and was taken from the archives of the Abbey
Josaphat at the time of the Revolution by M. B.,
Secretary-general of the department. Since then it has
disappeared; but this copy of the original, made at that
time, is declared by M. Lejeune to be perfectly exact.
Vide Mémoires, cit., pp. 434–5.]

O

Sentence pronounced June 14, 1494, by the grand mayor of the church and monastery of St. Martin de Laon, condemning a pig to be hanged and strangled for infanticide committed on the fee-farm of Clermont-lez-Montcornet.

A tous ceulx qui ces présentes lettres verront ou orront, Jehan Lavoisier licentie ez loix, et grand mayeur de l'église et monastère de monsieur St. Martin de Laon, ordre de Prémontré, et les echevins de ce même lieu; comme il nous eust été apporté et affirmé par le procureur-fiscal ou syndic des religieux, abbé et convent de Saint-Martin de Laon, qu'en la cense de Clermont-lez-Mont-cornet, appartenant en toute justice haulte, moyenne et basse auxdits relligieux, ung jeune pourceaulx eust éstranglé et *défacié* ung jeune enfant estant au berceau, fils de Jehan Lenfant, vachier de ladite cense de Clermont, et de Gillon sa femme, nous advertissant et nous requér-ant à cette cause, que sur ledit cas voulussions procéder, comme justice at raison le désiroit et requerroit; et que depuis, afin de savoir et cognoitre la vérité dudit cas, eussion ouï et examiné par serment, Gillon, femme dudit Lenfant, Jehan Benjamin, et Jehan Daudancourt, censiers de ladite cense, lesquels nous eussent dit et affirmé par leur serment et conscience, que le lendemain de Pasques dernier passé ledict Lenfant estant en la garde de ses bestes, ladicte Gillon sa femme desjettoit de ladicte cense, pour aller au village de Dizy......, ayant délaissé

en sa maison ledict petit enfant........ Elle le renchargea
à une sienne fille, âgée de neuf ans........ pendant et
durant lequel temps ladite fille s'en alla jouer autour
de ladite cense, et laissé ledit enfant couché en son
berceau ; et ledit temps durant, ledit pourceaulz entra
dedans ladite maison....... et défigura et mangea le
visage et gorge dudit enfant....... Tôt après ledit
enfant, au moyen des morsures et dévisagement que lui
fit ledit pourceaulz, de ce siecle trépassa : savoir faisons
...... Nous, en detestation et horreur dudit cas, et
afin d'exemplaire et gardé justice, avons dit, jugé, sen-
tencié, prenoncé et appointé, que ledit pourceaulz *estant
detenu prisonnier* et enferme en ladite abbaye, sera par le
maistre des hautes-oeuvres, pendu et estranglé, en une
fourche de bois, auprès et joignant des fourchee patibu-
laires et haultes justices desdits relligieux, estant auprès
de leur cense d'Avin....... En temoing de ce nous
avons scellé ces presentes de notre scel.

Ce fut fait le quatorzième jour de juing, l'an 1494, et
scellé en cire rouge ; et sur le dos est écrit :

Sentence pour ung pourceaulz executé par justice,
admené en la cense de Clermont, et étranglé en une
fourche les gibez d'Avin.

[M. Boileau de Maulaville, in *L'Annuaire de l'Aisne*
1812, p. 88. *Vide* Mémoires, cit., pp. 428 and 446-7.]

P

Sentence pronounced, March 27, 1567, by the royal notary and proctor of the bailiwick and bench of the court of judicatory of Senlis, condemning a sow with a black snout to be hanged for her cruelty and ferocity in murdering a girl of four months, and forbidding the inhabitants of the said seignioralty to let such beasts run at large on penalty of an arbitrary fine.

A tous ceulx qui ces présentes lettres verront, Jehan Lobry, notaire royal et procureur au bailliage et siège présidial de Senlis, bailly et garde et seigneurie de Saint-Nicolas d'Acy, les le dit Senlis, pour M.M. les religieux, prieur et coivent du dict lieu, salut ; savoir faisons :

Veu le procès extraordinairement fait à la requête du Procureur de la seigneurie du dict Saint-Nicolas, pour raison de la mort advenue à une jeune fille âgée de quatre mois ou environ, enfant de Lyénor Darmeige et Magdeleine Mahieu sa femme, demeurant au dict Saint-Nicolas, trouvée avoir esté mangée et devorée en la tete, main senestre et au dessus de la mamelle dextre par une truye ayant le museau noire, appartenant à Louis Mahieu, frère de la dite femme et son proche voisin ;

Le procès verbal de la visitation du dict enfant en la presence de son parrain et de sa marraine qui l'ont recogneu ;

Les informations faites pour raison du dit cas, interro-gatoires des dits Louis Mahieu et sa femme, avec la

visitation faicte de la dicte truye à l'instant du dit cas
advenu et tout consideré en conseil, il a été conclu et
advisé par justice que POUR LA CRUAUTÉ ET FEROCITÉ
COMMISE PAR LA DITE TRUYE, elle sera exterminée par
mort et pour ce faire sera pendue par l'executeur de la
haulte justice en ung arbre estant dedans les fins et
mottes de la dicte justice sur le grande chemin rendant
de Saint-Firman au dit Senlis, en faisant deffenses à tous
habitans et sujet des terres et seigneurie du dit Saint-
Nicolas de ne plus laisser échapper telle et semblables
bestes sans bonne et seure garde, sous peine d'amende
arbitraire et de pugnition corporelle s'ily échoit, sauf et
sans préjudice à faire droit sur les conclusions prinses
par le dit Procureur à l'encontre des dits Mahieu et sa
femme ainsi que de raison, au témoin de quoy nous
avon scellé les présentes du scel de la dicte justice.

Ce fu faist le jeudi 27ᵉ jour de Mars 1557 et exécuté
ledit jour par l'executeur de la haulte justice du dit
Senlis.

[Dom. Grenier, *Manuscrits de la Bibliothèque Nationale
de Paris*, tome xx. p. 87. Quoted by D'Addosio, who,
however, confounds the prosecution of 1567 with that
of 1499.]

Q

Sentence of death upon a bull, May 16, 1499, by the bailiff of the Abbey of Beaupré, for furiously killing Lucas Dupont, a young man of fourteen or fifteen years of age.

A tous ceux qui ces presentes lettres verront, Jean Sondar, Lieutenant du Bailly du temporel de l'église & abbaye nôtre Dame de Beauprés de l'ordre de Cisteaux, pour venerables & discretes personnes & mes tres-honorez seigneurs, messeigneurs les religieux abbé & convent de ladite abbaye, salut. Comme à la requeste du procureur de mesdits seigneurs, & par leur justice temporelle qu'ils ont en leur terre & seigneurie du Caurroy eût été nagaires prins & mis en la main d'icelle leur justice ung thorreau de poil rouge, appartenant à Jean Boullet censier & fermier de mesdits seigneurs, demeurant en leur maison & cense dudit Caurroy, lequel thorreau étant aux champs & sur le territoiiere d'icelle église, auroit par furiosité occis & mis à mort un joine fils, nommé Lucas Dupont, de l'âge de quatorze à quinze ans, ou environ, serviteur dudit censier, lequel il avoit mis à la garde de ces bestes à corne, entre les-quelles estoit ledit thorreau. Duquel thorreau ledit procureur de mesdits seigneurs requeroit la justice estre faite, & qu'il fut executé jusqu'à mort inclusive-ment par la justice de mesdits seigneurs pour occasion de icelui crimme de omicide & de la detestation d'iceluy.

Sur quoy enqueste & information eussent été faites de
la forme & maniere iceluy homicide, par laquelle ledit
procureur nous eust requis sur ce luy estre fait droit.
Savoir faisons que veu laditte enqueste & information &
sur tout en conseil & advis, nous par nostre sentence &
jugement, avons dies & jugié, que pour raison de l'omicide, dont dessus est touchié, fait par ledit thorreau en
la personne d'iceluy Lucas, & pour la detestation du
crime d'iceluy homicide, ledit thorreau nommé confisqué
à mesdits seigneurs sera executé jusques à mort inclusive-
ment par leurdite justice, & pendu à une fourche ou
potence es mettes de leurdite terre & seigneurie dudit
Caurroy, aupres du lieu ou solloit estre assise la justice.
Et ad ce le avons condamné & condamnons.   En
tesmoing de ce avons mis nostre scel à ces lettres qui
furent faites & pronunchiés audit lieu du Caurroy en la
presence de Guillaume Gave du Mottin, Jehan Custien
l'aisné, Jehan Henry, Jehan Boullet, hommes & sub-
jets de mesdits seigneurs, Jehan Charles, & Clement le
Carpentier, & plusieurs autres les seizieme jour de May
l'an mil quatre cens quatre-vingt-dix-neuf.   Ainsi signé,
Ileugles, ad ce commis.

[The original records of this trial for homicide are in
the archives of the Abbey of Beaupré.   Vide *Voyage
Littéraire de deux Religieux Benedictins de la Congrega-
tion de St. Maur.* Seconde Partie, pp. 166–7. Paris,
1717. The Benedictins were Dom. Edmond Martene
and Dom. Ursin Durand.]

R

Scene from Racine's comedy *Les Plaideurs*, in which a dog is tried and condemned to the galleys for stealing a capon.

After the accused had been found guilty, his counsel brings in the puppies and thus appeals to the compassion of the court:

> "Venez, famille desolée;
> Venez, pauvres enfants qu'on veut rendre orphelins;
> Venez faire parler vos esprits enfantins.
> Oui, messieurs, vous voyez ici notre misère;
> Nous sommes orphelins, rendez-nous notre père,
> Notre père par qui nous fûmes engendrés,
> Notre père qui nous . . . .

DAUDIN.

Tirez, tirez, tirez.

L'INTIME.

Notre père, messieurs . . . .

DAUDIN.

> Tirez donc, Quels vacarmes!
> Ils ont pissé partout.

L'INTIME.

> Monsieur, voyez nos larmes.

DAUDIN.

> Ouf! je me sens dejà pris de compassion.
> Ce que c'est qu' à propos toucher la passion!
> Je suis bien empêché. La vérité me presse;
> Le crime est avéré, lui-même il le confesse.
> Mais, s'il est condamné, l'embarras est égal;
> Voilà bien des enfants réduits à l'hopital."

Les Plaideurs, Act III, sc. 3.

S

Record of the decision of the Law Faculty of the University of Leipsic condemning a cow to death for having killed a woman at Machern near Leipsic, July 20, 1621.

Ao 1621 den 20 July ist Hanss Fritzchen weib Catharina alhier zu Machern wohnende von Ihrer eigen Mietkuhe,[1] da sie gleich hochleibss schwanger gang, auff Ihren Eigenen hofe zu Tode gestossen worden. Vber welch vnerhörten Fall der Juncker Friederich von Lindenau, als Erbsass diesess ortes, in der Jurisstischen Facultet zu Leipzig sich darüber dess Rechtes belernet: Welche am Ende dess Vrtelss diese wort also aussgesprochen: So wird die Kuhe, als abschewlich thier, an Einen abgelegenen öden ort billig geführet, daselbst Erschlagen oder Erschossen, vnnd vnabgedecht begraben. Christoph Hain domalss zu Selstad wohnend hat sie hinder der Schäfferey Erschlagen vnd begraben, welchess geschehen den 5. Augusti auff den Abend, nach Eintreibung dess Hirtenss zwischen 8 vnd 9 vhren.

[Extract from the parish-register of Machern, near Leipsic, printed in *Anzeiger für Kunde der deutschen Vorzeit.* No. 4, April 1880, col. 102.]

---

[1] *Mietkuhe,* a cow pastured or wintered for pay.

BIBLIOGRAPHY

ABELE VON LILIENBERG, MATTHIAS: Metamorphosis Telae Judiciariae, Das ist: Seltsame Gerichts-Händel, etc.; 8th ed., Nürnberg, 1712. 1st ed., 1667. The funny incidents narrated in this work are cited as "queer judicial procedures" in Joh. Weidneri Apophthegmata, Part III., No. 69. Abele was evidently a great humorist, and must have been a jolly member of the "Hochlöbl. Fruchtbringende Gesellschaft," to which he belonged.

ADDOSIO, CARLO D': Bestie Delinquenti. Napoli, 1892.

AGNEL, EMILE: Curiosités judiciaires et historiques du Moyen-Âge. Paris, 1858. Only Part I. published.

AMIRA, KARL VON: Thierstrafen und Thierprocesse. Innsbruck, 1891. Printed originally in Mittheilungen des Instituts für Oestterreichische Geschichtsforschung, xii., pp. 546–601.

ANGELIS, FRANCISCO GIUSEPPE DE: De Delictis et Poenis. Opera Omnia. Vol. i., p. 76. Napoli, 1783.

Anzeiger für Kunde der deutschen Vorzeit, xxvii. April, No. 4, p. 102. Nürnberg, 1880.

AQUINAS, THOMAS. See THOMAS.

ARBOIS DE JUBAINVILLE, H. D': Les excommunications d'animaux. Art. in Revue des Questions Historiques, v., pp. 275–280. Paris, 1868.

AYRAULT, PIERRE: Des Procez faicts au cadaver, aux cendres, à la mémoire, aux bestes brutes, aux choses inanimées et aux contumax. Angers, small 4to, 1591. This work is opposed to such prosecutions, and is reprinted as an appendix to the same author's L'Ordre,

Formalité, et Instruction Judiciaire, etc. Paris, 1598, 1604, 1610. Lyon, 1642. For an account of Pierre Ayrault *see* Eloge de Pierre Ayrault prononcé devant le cour royale d'Angers, à l'audience solonnelle de rentrée le 6 novembre, 1844, pas M. Félix Belloc, avocat-général.

AZPILCUETA, MARTIN : Opera. 3 vols., fol. Lyon, 1589 ; 6 vols. 4to, Ven., 1601, 2 ; 5 vols., Col., 1616. In his Consiliorum, lib. v. De Senten. Excom. Consil. 52, he criticises the views of Chassenée. The author is commonly known as Dr. Navarre.

BAER, A. : Der Verbrecher in anthropologischer Beziehung. Leipzig, 1893.

BAILLY, GASPARD : Discours des Sorciers.

——Traité des Monitoires, avec un plaidoyer contre les Insects. Lyon, 1668.

This work contains a full account of the method of procedure in the penal prosecution of animals.

BEAUMANOIR, PHILIPPE DE : Les Coutumes de Beauvoisis. Paris, 1690. New edition by Le Comte Beugnot. 1842.

BENEDICTUS, GUILIELMUS : Tractatus Criminalis. Lugduni. 1562.

BENEDIKT, M. : Anatomische Studien in Verbrecher Gehirnen. Wien, 1879. Translated into English. New York, 1881.

BERRIAT-SAINT-PRIX : Rapport et Recherches sur le Procès et Jugemens relatives aux Animaux. In Mémoires de la Société Royale des Antiquaires de France. Tome viii., pp., 403–450. Paris, 1827.

BISCHOFF, THEODOR L. W. : Das Hirngewicht des Menschen. Eine Studie. Bonn, 1880.

BOERIUS : Decisiones aureae Parlamenti Burdegalensis. Dec. 316. Nos. 3, 4, 6. Lyon, 1620.

BONIFACE, H : Recueil d'Arrêts notables. Liv. iv.

—— Traité des Matières Criminelles, p. 31. Paris, 1785.

BOUCHEL, LAURENT : La Bibliothèque ou Thresor du Droict Francois. Art. Bestail. Paris, 1615. New and enlarged edition, 3 tom., Paris, 1671.

BOUGEANT, PÈRE G. H. : Amusement Philosophique sur le Language des Bestes. Paris, 1739. Published anonymously, but written by the Jesuit Père Bougeant.

BOUTHORS, A. : Coutumes locales . . . d'Amiens, I., pp. 354 358. 1845.

BREGENZER, IGNAZ : Thier-Ethik. Darstellung der sittlichen und rechtlichen Beziehungen zwischen Mensch und Thier. Bamberg, 1894.

BRILLON, P. J. : Dictionnaire des Arrêts. Art. Bétail. Paris, 1711.

BRUNNER, H. : Über absichtslose Missethaten im altdeutschen Strafrechte. Sitzungsberichte der Berliner Akademie, xxxv., 1890, pp. 834–839.

BUCHNER, AUGUST : Miscellanea Curiosa. 1686.

CANNAERT : Bydragen tot de kennis van het oude Strafrecht in Vlanderen. 3rd. ed., Gent, 1835.

CARPZOV, BENEDICT : Practica Nova Rerum Criminalium. Wittenberg, 1635. See especially Cap. De Crimine Parricidii.

CHASSENÉE, BARTHOLOMEW : Consilium Primum, quod tractatus jure dici potest propter multiplicem et reconditam doctrinam, ubi luculenter et accurate tractatur quaestio illa : De excommunicatione animalium insectorum. 1531 ; 1511 ; 1588.

(Chassenée was afterwards first president of the Parlement de Provence, a position corresponding to chief justice.)

CHORIER, NICOLAS : Histoire générale de Dauphiné. 2 tom. (II. p. 712). Valence, 1778.

—— La Jurisprudence du Jurisconsult Guy Pape dans ces Decisions. Avec plusieurs remarkes importantes par McN. C., etc. Liv. iv. Sect. 8, Art. 14. 1769.

CLARUS, JULIUS : Opera Omnia. Sive practica civilis atque criminalis, etc. [Geneva], 1637.

CROLLANZA : Storia del Contado di Chiavenna, pp. 445–899.

DAMHOUDER, JODOCUS : Rerum Criminalium Praxis. Antwerp, 1562.

DESNOYERS, J. : Recherches sur la coutume d'exorciser et d'excommunier les insectes et autres animaux nuisibles à l'agriculture. Paris, 1853.

Originally published in Bulletin du comité historique des monuments écrits de l'histoire de la France.

DESSAIX, A. : L'excommunication des Glaciers. Revue des Traditions Populaires. Vol. v. 1890.

DÖPLERI, JACOBI : Theatrum Poenarum, Suppliciorum et Executionum Criminalium, oder Schau-Platz derer Leibes- und Lebens-Straffen, etc. Sondershausen, Anno MDCXCIII.

DULAURE, J. H. : Histoire physique, civile et morale de Paris. 7th ed. III. p. 298 ; 308. Paris, 1856.

DUMÉRIL, H. : Les Animaux et les Lois, pp. 6–13. Paris, 1880.

DURET, JEAN : Traicté des Peines et Amendes tant pour les Matières criminelles que civiles. Lyon, 1573 ; 1603 ; 1610.

EVEILLON, JACQUES : Traité des Excommunications et Monitoires. Chap. 39, vol. ii., pp. 436–449. Rouen, 1712.

FERRI, ENRICO : I Nuovi Orizzonti del Diritto e della Procedura penale.

—— Das Verbrechen in seiner Abhängigkeit von dem jährlichen Temperaturweschsel. Berlin, 1882.

FEVRET, CHARLES : Traité de l'Abus. Lib. vii., ch. 2. No. 38.

FLESCH, M. : Untersuchungen über Verbrecher-Gehirne. Würzburg, 1882.

FRANCK, Wilhelm : Geschichte der Ehemaligen Reichsstadt Oppenheim am Rhein. Darmstadt, 1859.

FRIEDMANN, F. : Verbrechen im Roman und auf der Bühne. Berlin, 1890.

FRIEDRICH, GEORG : Die Krankheit des Willens vom Standpunkt der Psychologie aus betrachtet. München, 1885.

GALTON, F. : Inquiries into Human Faculty in its Development. London, 1883.

GAROFALO, R. : La Criminologie. Paris, 1888.

GIERKE, O. : Humor im deutschen Recht. 2 aufl. 1886, pp. 23-25, 61.

GIURIATI, DOMENICO : Gli Errori Giudiziari, Diagnosi e Rimedi. Milano, 1893. (See especially chapter iv.)

GRENUS, THEODORE BARON DE : Documents relatifs à l'Histoire du Pays de Vaud. p. 160.

GRIMM, JACOB : Deutsche Rechtsalterthümer. 2 aufl. Göttingen, 1844.

GROSLÉE : Ephémerides. Tom ii., pp. 153-168. Ed. 1811.

Guidonis Papae Decisiones. q. 238.

HEFFTER, AUG. WILH. : Athenäische Gerichtsverfassung. Köln, 1822.

HOTTINGER, JOH. HEINRICH : Historia Ecclesiastica

Bibliography 367

Novi Testamenti. Seculum xv., pars quarta, pp. 317-21. Tigvri (Zurich), 1667.

JETS: Over het oude Strafregt in Belgie. p. 89. Brussels, 1826.

LACASSAGNE, A. : De la Criminalité chez les Animaux. Revue Scientifique. January 14, 1882. *Cf.* Kosmos, Zeitschrift für Entwicklungslehre, 1882. pp. 264-67.

LA HONTAN, BARON DE : Voyages. Lettre xi., p. 79. Treats of Excommunication of Turtle-Doves in Canada.

LALANNE, L. : Curiosités des Traditions. Paris, 1847. pp. 429-436.

LAVANDERIUS, PETRUS : Tractatus de Doctoribus. Pars I., quaest. 18.

LEBEUF, L'ABBÉ : Histoire de Paris, i. ix., 400.

LEBRUN, PIERRE : Histoire Critique des Pratiques Superstitieuses. Rouen, 1702.

Le Conservateur Suisse. Vol. iv., p. 43. Lausanne, 1814.

LIONNOIS: Histoire de Nancy, ii., 373. 1811.

LERSNER : Der Stadt Frankfurt Chronica, i. pp. 551, 552. Proceedings against Animals in 1552 and 1574.

LESSONA, C. : Giurisprudenza Animalesca. Gazzetta Litteraria, Turin 1887, Nos. 46 and 48.

LITCHENBERG, G. C. : Vermischte Schriften, iv., pp. 477-81. Göttingen, 1802.

LOMBROSO, C. : Il Delitto negli Animali. Archivio di Psichiatria. Vol. ii. Torino, 1881.

—— L' Uomo Delinquente. 2 vols. Torino, 1889.

—— Il Delitto politico, e le Revoluzioni in Rapporto al Diritto, etc. Torino, 1890.

——L' Uomo di Genio. Torino, 1888.

——Der Verbrecher in anthropologischer, ärztlicher,

und juristischer Beziehung. Deutsche Bearbeitung von M. O. Fränkel. Hamburg, 1887.

LOUANDRE, CHARLES: Les Animaux dans la Jurisprudence. Revue des Deux Mondes 1854. Tome v., pp. 331-36.

MALLEOLUS, FELIX: Tractatus de Exorcismis.

MANGIN, ARTHUR : L'Homme et la Bête. Paris, 1872.

MANOEL, BERNARDES : Nova Floresta ou Sylva de varios Apothegmas, e ditos sentencios espirituaes e moraes. 5 tome. Lisboa, 1706—1747.

MARCHISIO, MICHELE : Gatte o Insetti Nocivi, pp. 63 *sqq.* Turin, 1834.

MAUDSLEY, HENRY : Physiology and Pathology of Mind. London, 1868.

Mémoires de la Société des Antiquaires de Normandie. 2ᵉ série, vol. ix. (vol. xix. de la collection). Paris, 1851.

MÉNABRÉA, LEON : De l'Origine de la Forme et de l'Esprit des Jugements rendus au Moyen-Âge contre les Animaux. Chambery, 1846. Reprint in book form of a paper originally published in Mémoires de la Société Royale Académique de Savoie. Tome xii., 1846.

MIRAUT : Histoire de Sardaigne.

NEWELL, WILLIAM WELLS : Conjuring Rats. The Journal of American Folk Lore (January—March, 1892).

NOORDEWIER, M. J.: Nederduitsche Regtsoudheden. Utrecht, 1853.

NORK, F. : Article in Scheible's Das Kloster weltlich und geistlich, etc. Vol. xii., pp. 942-949. Stuttgart, 1849.

OPZOOMER, C. W. : Di Dieren voor den Rechter. Volksalmanak van het jaar 1862.

ORANO, G. : La Criminalità nelle sue relazioni col clima. Roma, 1882.

ORTOLI, FR. : Les Procès d'Animaux au moyen-âge. La Tradition. Paris, 1888. pp. 77-82. Based on Vernet in Thémis viii.

OSENBRÜGGEN, EDUARD : Studien zur deutschen und Schweizerischen Rechtsgeschichte. Schaffhausen, 1868. (vii. Die Personificirung der Thiere, pp. 139-149.)

PAPON : Recueil d'Arrêts notables des Cours Souveraines de France. Liv. xxii., Titre 7.

PEIGNOT, GABRIEL : Essai chronologique sur les mœurs, etc. les plus remarquables dans la Bourgogne, p. 68. Dijon, 1827.

PERTILE, ANTONIO : Gli Animali in Giudizio. Atti del Reale Instituto Veneto. Tomo iv., serie vi. Venezia, 1886.

PIERQUIN : Traité de la Folie des Animaux et de ses Rapports avec celle de l'Homme et les Legislations actuelles. Paris, 1839.

PORTO, V.: La Scuola criminale positiva et il progetto de nuovo codice. Verona, 1884.

PROAL, LOUIS : Le Crime et la Peine. Paris, 1892.
This work is opposed to the theories of Lombroso and the new school of criminal anthropologists, but states their views fully and clearly.

QUINONES, JUAN DE : Tratado de Langostas. Madrid, 1620. A treatise on exorcisms of locusts, weevils, rats, mice, and birds.

RAYNAUD, THEOPHILE : De Monitoriis, etc. (Part II. c. 12, No. 6) in his Opusc. Misc. 1665. Tom. xiv., p. 482.
The author criticises Chassenée.

RICCIUS, ALOYSIUS : Resolutiones (408).

24

ROCH, HEINRICH : Böhmische, Schlesische und Lausitzische Chroniken.

ROCHE-FLAVIN, DE LA : Arrêts notables du Parlement de Toulouse. Liv. iii. Titre 2.

ROCHER, LE PÈRE : Gloire de l'Abbaye et Vallée de la Novalaise.

ROSARIUS, HIEROLYMUS : Quod Animalia Bruta Ratione Utantur melius Homine. Amstel., 1654.

ROUSSEAU DE LACOMBE : Traité des Matières Criminelles. Part I, ch. 2, sect. 1, distinct. 8.

RUCHAT, ABRAHAM : Abrégé de l'Histoire Ecclésiastique du Pays de Vaud.

SAINT-FOIX : Oeuvres.   1778, iv., 97.

SAUVAL : Histoire de Paris.   Vol. iii., p. 387.

SCHLÄGER : Wiener Skizzen aus dem Mittelalter.

SCHMID, REINHOLD : Gesetze der Angelsachsen.   2nd ed. Leipzig, 1858.

SEIFART, K. : Hingerichtete Thiere und Gespenster. Zeitschrift für deutsche Kulturgeschichte, 1856, pp. 424—30.

SLOET : Die Dieren in het Germaansche Volksgeloof en Volksgebruik.   's-Gravenhage, 1887.

SOREL, ALBERT : Procès contre des Animaux et Insectes suivis au Moyen-âge dans la Picardie et le Valois. Compiegne, 1877.

STARK, HERMANN : Griechische Antiquitäten.   Vol. i., 487.

TESTRUP, KR. S. : Rinds Herreds Kronika (Samlinger til jydsk Historic og Topografi. ˙Vol. ii., pp. 62—64) 1711.

THEMIS JURISCONSULTI : Tome i., pp. 178—181 ; Tome viii., part 2, pp. 45 *sqq*.

THIERS : Des superstitions.   Vol. i., 48a.

THOMAS AQUINAS: Summa Theologiæ. Vol. ii., pars. lxxvi., art. 2.

THONISSEN, J. : Études sur l'Histoire du Droit Criminel. Vol. ii., pp. 198 *sqq.* Bruxelles, 1869.

—— Le Droit pénal de la République Athénienne, pp. 256, 412 *sqq.* 1875.

TOBLER, G. : Thierprocesse in der Schweiz. Bern, 1893.

TORNING, CHRISTIANUS J. : De Peccatis et Poenis Brutorum. A dissertation on graduating at the University of Upsala in Sweden. May 25, 1725.

VAN HAAFTEN : Die Dieren als misdadigers voor den Rechter. Eigen Haard, 1884.

VAIRO, LEONARDO : De Fascino libri tres, etc. Venet. 1599.

VERNET : Lettre . . . sur les Procès faits aux Animaux. Thémis, vol. viii. B., pp. 45—61.

VIVIO, FRANCESCO : Decisiones. No. 68. 1610.

DE WINDE : Byzonderheden uit de Geschiedeniss van het strafregt in de Nederlanden. Middelburg, 1827.

ZEROLA, THOMAS : Praxis Episcopalis. Sub verbo Superstitio. Venet. 1599.

INDEX

ABBOTT, Rev. Lyman, regards bad impulses as suggestions of evil spirits, 76

Achan, his severe punishment by Joshua, 180

Addosio, Carlo d', his *Bestie Delinquenti* cited, 1, 4; his list of animal prosecutions, 135; on pigs as a public nuisance in Italy, 159

Æschines, cited, 172

Æschylus, his *Choephoroi* cited, 174

Ahuramazda, 57, 61, 82, 176

Alard, Jean, burned alive as a Sodomite for coition with a Jewess, 153

Altiat, his poem quoted, 93

Amira, Prof. Karl von, his *Thierstrafen und Thierprocesse* cited, 1–3, 137

Anathemas, only effective when formally complete, as with all incantations and excommunications, 4, 36; citations from the Bible in proof of their power, 25; render an orchard barren and expel eels and blood-suckers from Lake Leman, 27; turn white bread black to punish heresy, 28; fatal to swallows and flies, which disturb religious services, 28, 29; sold by the Pope, 30; hurled against noxious vermin, 37; made more effective by the prompt payment of tithes, 37; differ from excommunications, 51–54; superseded in Protestantism by prayer and fasting and in science by Paris green, 53

Animals, prosecuted by civil and ecclesiastical courts, 2; office of the Church in repressing articulate and rodent, 3, 5; as satellites of Satan or agents of God, 5, 6, 52–57, 67; personification of, 10, 11; their competency as witnesses, 11; origin of their judicial prosecution, 12; as born criminals, 14; tendency of modern penology to efface the distinction between men and, 14, 193; instances of their criminal prosecution, 16, 18, 21, 37–50, 93–124, 134–157, 160–163; methods of procedure against, 31; whether legally laity or clergy, 32; punitive and

373

preventive prosecution of, 33; their consciousness of right and wrong, 35, 247; false conception of the purpose of their prosecution, 40; can be anathematized, but not excommunicated, 51; items of expense in prosecuting, 49, 138, 140–143; not mere machines, 66; in folk-lore, 84; worship of, 85; imperfect lists of prosecuted, 135–137; burned and buried alive, 138; put to the rack to extort confession, 139; confiscation of valuable, 164, 189; unclean flesh of executed, 169; imputed criminality of, 177; criminals as ferocious, 212; mental and moral qualities of men and, 234; six categories of their criminal offences, 235; the safety of society the supreme law in the judicial punishment of men and, 247–252

Anatolus, his "Geoponics," 133

Angel, Emile, cited, 124

Anglo-Saxon law, its retributive character, 168; its cruel doctrine of accessories, 178; on tainted swords, 187

Angrô-mainyush, 57, 59, 61, 82

Anthony, St., patron of pigs, 158

Anthropologists, criminal researches of, 211, 215

Aquinas. *See* Thomas

Arcadius, his atrocious edict, 179

Ashes, modern and mediæval use of vermifugal, 53

Augustine, St., cited, 94, 106

Aura corrumpens in houses and stalls, 8

Aurelian, Father, on diabolical possession, 75

Avesta, on exorcisms, 36; on good and evil creations, 57; on mad dogs, 176

Ayrault, Pierre, his protest against animal prosecutions, 109

Azpilcueta, Martin. *See* Dr. Navarre.

BAAL-ZEBUB (Beelzebub), fly-god, 84; his preference for black beasts, 165

Bailly, Gaspard, his *Traité des Monitoires* cited, 52, 92–108

"Basilisk-egg," 10

Basilius, St., his insect-expelling girdle, 136

Basilovitch, Ivan, his conception of retributive justice, 183

Bassos, Kassianos, prefers rat-bane to adjuration, 132

Beasts, sweet and stenchy, 55

Bees, tainted honey of homicidal, 9

Bell, banished to Siberia by the Russian Government, 175

Benedikt, Prof., on the brain-formation of criminals 212

Bernard, Claude, his idea of the physiologist, 245

Bernard, St., kills flies by cursing them, 28

Bernardes, Manoel, his *Nova Floresta*, 124

Berriat-Saint-Prix, his valuable researches, 2, 17, 20 ; list of prosecuted animals, 135-137

Bichat, his defective cranium, 217

Bischofberger, Dr. Theobald, his curious theory of the effects of unexpiated crime on persons and property, 6-8 ; his recent brochure in defence of exorcisms, 73

Bischoff, Prof., his hobby refuted by the weight of his own brain, 218

Blackstone, on deodands, 186, 189, 192

Blood-letting, as a panacea in law and medicine, 194

" Blue Laws," an advance in penal legislation, 209

Bodelschwingh, his *bacillus infernalis*, 91

Boehme, Jacob, his definition of magic, 127

Boër, Nicolaus, on cohabitation with a Jewess as sodomy, 153

Bogos, homicidal beasts executed by the, 155

Bonnivard, François, presides as judge in a trial of vermin, 38

Borromeo, Carlo, his cruelty in punishing heresy, 208

Bougeant, Père, his *Amuse-ment Philosophique* cited, 66-69 ; 80-86, 88-90, 92

Bracton, 167 ; on deodands, 186

Brain, its size not always a measure of mental capacity, 217-219

Browne, Dr. William Hand, cited, 187

Buggery, instances of this "nameless crime," 147-153 ; she-ass acquitted and man condemned to death for, 150 ; in the Carolina punished with death by fire, 151 ; in the Mosaic law, 152 ; sexual intercourse with a Jewess regarded as, 153

Bull, executed for murder, 161

Calvin, his conception of God, 59

Canute, King, 178

Carolina, the, its severe penalties, 182

Carpzov, Benedict, on sodomy, 151

Cattle, bewitched by bad air, 8

Cervantes, 167

Character, factors in the formation of, 219 ; responsibility for, 239, 243

Charcot, Dr., on the curative power of faith, 80, 225

Chassenée, Bartholomew, his *Consilia*, 2, 21-23 ; distinguished as a defender of prosecuted rats, 18 ; equal rights of rats and Waldenses recognized by,

20; his erudition, 24; his absurd deductions, 26; regards animals as laity in the eye of the law, 32
Chinese, recent beheading of idols for murder, 174
Church, the, its treatment of noxious insects as incarnations of Satan and as agents of God, 3-6; capital punishment never inflicted by, 31; its power to stay the ravages of vermin unquestioned, 50
Cicero, cited, 22, 101; his approval of atrocious penalties, 178
Cock, burned at the stake for laying eggs, 10, 11, 162; nature and origin of its supposed eggs, 163-5
Cockatrice, 12, 163
Coleridge, his definition of madman, 228
Corpses, prosecuted and executed, 110, 198, 199; cannot inherit, 110
"Corruption of blood," in theology and law, 181
Courcelle-Seneuil, his view of prisons, 212
Cows, executed for homicide, 169
Cranks, execution of, 249-251
Cretella, 17
Cretins, their brains not always abnormal, 219; sentenced to death, 251
Criminality, examples of imputed, 177-185; ancient and mediæval conceptions of, 200; punished for the

safety of society, 211, 248; compared to vitriol, 212; supposed physical indices of, 213-217; casual and constitutional, 214-223; ativism the source of, 212, 215; the result of hypnotism, 223-225; due to many uncontrollable conditions, 230; motives underlying animal, 235; animals conscious of, 247; contagiousness of, 252, 256
Crollanza, his record of the prosecution of caterpillars, 122
Crosiers, vermifugal efficacy of, 30
Cybele, invoked against vermin, 133

DAMHOUDER, Jacobus, picture of animal crimes in his Rerum Criminalium Praxis, 16; citations from this work, 109, 146; regards sexual intercourse with Jews, Turks, and Saracens as sodomy, 153
Dasturs, Parsi, Zarathushtra's teachings degraded by the, 59
Demosthenes, cited, 172
Deodands, nature of, 186-190, 192; abolished in England under Queen Victoria, 192
Devils, their damage to landed property, 7; multiplied by the spread of Christianity, 13, 80; destined to eternal torments after the Last Judgment, 68-70; incarnate in every babe, 70;

maladies produced by, 72 ; modern inventions the devices of, 229

Didymos, his "Geoponics," 133

Dimitri, Prince, bell banished to Siberia for rejoicing over his assassination, 175

Dogs, trial and execution of mad, 176 ; crucified in Rome for imputed crime, 177

Döpler, Jacob, on sodomy, 152 ; on Lex talionis, 182 ; on vampires, 197

Dove, symbol of the Holy Ghost, 57

Draco (Drakôn), his law punishing weapons, 172

Dreyfus, his prosecution instigated by a sensational novel, 253–255

Ducol, Pierre, prosecutor of weevils, 38

Dumas, his Count of Monte Christo cited, 240

Duret, Jean, his Treatise on Pains and Penalties, 108

ECCLESIASTICAL tribunal, an, rejects the Mosaic law and discusses crime from a psychiatrical point of view, 170

Eldrad, St., expels serpents, 50

Electricity, execution by, 210

Elk, as demon, 90

Erechtheus, punishment of deadly weapons, 172

Erinnys, appeasing the, 174

Escheat, in Scotch law, 189

Eusebius, describes hell as very cold, 105

Eustace, St., 56

Evolution, dogma of original sin supplanted by the doctrine of, 232

Excommunications, pronounced against insects by the Church, 3 ; sold at Rome, 30 ; properly speaking, animals not subject to, 51, 100 ; comical survivals of, 128. See Anathemas

Exorcisms, their efficiency recognized by Heidelberg professors, 27 ; applied as plasters, 72 ; superseded by conjurations among Protestants, 125 ; by Mohammedans, 137

FALCON, Pierre, defender of weevils, 38

Felo de se, a sort of treason, 190. See Suicide

Feuchtersleben, Baron Von, records cases of morbid imitation, 253

Field-mice, conjuration of, 133

Flesh of executed animals tainted, 169

Flies as demons, 28, 86

Florian, St., the protector of houses from fire, 136

Fly-flaps, papal, 29

Formosus, Pope, his corpse tried and condemned for usurpation, 198

Foscolo, Ugo, his cranium that of an idiot, 218

Fox, diabolical nature of the 56

Frederic the Great, his penal reforms, 207
Fricker, Thüring, doctor of laws, chancellor and prosecutor of inger, 116

GADFLIES, episcopal rescript against, 124
Galton, on heredity, 239
Gambetta, his small and abnormal brain, 217
Geese, sacred, rewarded at Rome for the vigilance of their foremothers, 177
Genius, to madness close allied, 228
Görres, recent case of conjuration recorded by, 125
Gratiolet, on the brain of the "Hottentot Venus," 218
Greeks, ancient, ascribed pestilence to the miasma of unexpiated murder, 9, 174
Gregory of Tours, on bronze dormice and serpents as talismans, 132
Greysser, Daniel, the efficiency of bans not supernatural, 128
Gross, his mis-statement concerning the cock of Bâle, 162
Guiteau, deterrent effect of his execution, 250

HARPOKRATION, Valerius, cited, 172
Harrison, Miss, cited, 187
Hart, symbolism of the, 56
Hawks, dead, as protectors of hens, 252

Hemmerlein, Felix. See Malleolus
Hens, crowing, 10
Heredity, its predetermining influence as viewed by theologians and scientists, 232
Heymanns, Mynheer, on responsibility for character, 243
Hierarchies, their failure in civil government, 249
Honorius, his atrocious edict, 179
Horses, condemned to death for homicide, 162
Hubert, St., 56
Hugon, St., expels venom from serpents by excommunication, 103
Hunters among savages, their superstitious fear of killing wild animals, 174
Hypnotism, its causal relation to crime, 223–226 ; as the basis of the witchcraft delusion, 225

IDOLS, decapitation of, 174
Inger, prosecuted and put under ban, 113–115 ; not in Noah's Ark, 120
Insanity, degrees of, 200–203 ; in Italian and German law, 204–206 ; difficulty of defining, 226–228 ; in English law, 246 ; moral, 250 ; as a shelter for crime, 256
Insects, prosecution of, 37, 41–49 ; incarnations of demons, 86
Italy, palliation of crime in, 203, 204

JEANNERET, Marie, her toxicomania, 240-246
Jews, in Christian legislation on a par with beasts, 152, 165
John the Lamb, his curse fatal to fish, 28
Jonson, Ben, cited, 130
Jordan, Father, casts out devils with Lourdes water in 1887, 74
Jörgensen, cited, 17
Joshua, his penal cruelty, 180

KING Mode, his discourse with Queen Reason, 55
Kirchenheim, Prof. Von, urges reform of our penal codes, 219
Koran, the, on the punishment of beasts, 171
Kukis, destroy homicidal trees, 171

LAAS, his definition of judicial punishment, 238
Lacassagne, his six categories of crime, 235
Langevin, Pierre Gilles, fresco of the execution of a sow described by, 141
Lapeyronie, his dissertation proving that cocks never lay eggs, 163
Le Bon, on hereditary criminality, 223
Leipsic, decision of the Law Faculty concerning a homicidal cow, 169
Leo XIII., his exorcism of Satan and apostate angels, 73

Letang, Louis, causal relation of his novel to the Dreyfus affair, 254
Lex talionis, striking applications of this oldest form of penal justice, 167 ; inflicts horrible mutilations, 182
Lilienberg, Mathias Abele Von, his record of a dog sentenced to prison, 175
Liszt, Prof. Von, on retributive and preventive penalties, 237
Locusts, expelled by exorcisms and aspergeoires, 3, 64 ; dispersed and destroyed by excommunication, 22, 93, 94 ; prosecution of, 95-108, 136
Lohbauer, Pater Franz Xaver, ascribes nervous disease to diabolical possession, 71
Lombroso, on animals as born criminals, 14 ; opposed to trial by jury, 185 ; regards tattooing, dark thick hair and thin beards, as signs of criminality, 213 ; on ativism as the source of crime, 215 ; innate criminality not eradicated by education, 223 ; compares the capital punishment of cretins and cranks to that of animals, 251
Lucifer, writhes under the water of Lourdes, 74
Lycia, punished by imputation, 180

MAJOLUS, cited, 86
Maledictions. See Anathemas

Malleolus, Felix, his theory of exorcisms endorsed by Heidelberg professors, 27 ; records a prosecution of Spanish flies, 110; his formula for banning serpents, 121

Mangin, Arthur, cited, 16, 139

Manicheans, their doctrine of good and evil, 60

Manouvrier, Dr., likens Gambetta's skull to that of a savage, 217

Mantegazza, Prof., his "tormentatore," 245

Manu, Institutes of, 168

Marro, on metaphors as facts, 216

Mather, Cotton, records the execution of a pious Sodomite and eight beasts, 148

Ménebréa, M. L., 2, 17 ; his theory untenable, 40

Mephistopheles, the lord of rodents and vermin, 85

Mithridates, experiments with poisons, 244

Moles, prosecution of, 111–113

Monks, as landed proprietors in France, 158

Monomania, frequency of, 227

Morel, Claude, defender of weevils, 38

Mornacius, his record of mad dogs sentenced to death, 176

Morselli, Prof., on the causes of suicide, 229

Mosaic law, the, rejected by an ecclesiastical court, 170 ; barbarity of, 167, 180

Murder, miasma of, 9, 174 ; weapons tainted by, 187–190

Mutilations, in accordance with the Lex talionis, 176, 182

Mythology, monstrosities and metamorphoses of classical, 64 ; in modern life, 228

NAQUET, regards criminals as no more culpable than poisons, 212.

Narrenkötterlein, dog sentenced to a, 175

Nature, imperfection of, 61

Navarre, Dr., regards fish as cacodemons, 90

Nebuchadnezzar, a satanic metamorphosis, 63

Nikôn, his statue punished for manslaughter committed in self-defence, 172

Noah, God's covenant with him required the capital punishment of beasts, 168

Novels, morbific influence of sensational, 253

Numa Pompilius, quoted, 106 ; his law for protecting boundary stones, 183

ORIGEN, believed in the ultimate redemption of Satan, 68

Osenbrüggen, Eduard, his theory of the personification of animals, 10, 17

Ovid, quoted, 101, 103

Oxen, executed, 168; punished although innocent, 183

PACHACUTEZ, barbarous code of this Peruvian Justinian, 179

Papal See, trial and punishment of corpses by the, 198

Pape, Guy, cited, 108

Paracelsus, on the magnetic power of the will, 126

Pardoning power, exercise of the, 248

Parsis, their Dasturs, 59; co-workers of Ahuramazda, 61, 82; no doctrine of atonement, 63

Pasteur, exterminates noxious microbes, 62

Patriotism as a perverter of justice, 185

Pausanias cited, 172

Penology, man and beast in modern, 14, 193; mediæval and modern, 15, 200, 206–210; in Italy and Germany, 203–206; brutality of mediæval, 206–209; moral and penal responsibility, 210; still inchoate, 15, 219–223, 257; deterrent aims of, 211, 248, 249; law of the survival of the fittest in, 221–223; punitive and preventive, 237; its relation to psycho-pathology, 248

Pereira Gomez, forerunner of Descartes, 66

Perjury, retaliative punishment of, 182

Perrodet, Jean, defender of inger, 118

Phlebotomy. See Bloodletting

Pico di Mirandola, quoted, 103

Piety, market value of, 7

Pigs. See Swine

Pirminius, St., his anathema of venomous reptiles, 29

Plato, his theory of creation, 59; on homicidal animals, 173; on retributive and preventive punishment, 237

Pliny, quoted, 103

Pollux, Julius, quoted, 172

Potter, a pious Sodomite executed, 148

Predestination in theology and science, 232–234

Prussia, barbarous punishments, 180; opposed to reform, 205

Prytaneion (Prytaneum), condemned inanimate objects for crime, 172; but not corpses, 199

Pufendorf, Samuel, on contagiousness in crime, 256

Puritans, their penal enactments, 209

Pythagoras, his doctrine of transmigration, 87

QUEEN Reason, her discourse on animals in reply to King Mode, 56–58

RACINE, his caricature of beast trials in Les Plaideurs, 166, 361

Ram, banished to Siberia, 175

Randolph, his allusion to rhyming rats, 130

Rats, prosecution of, 18–21, 136; friendly letters of advice to, 129; Irish custom of rhyming, 130

Raven, an imp of Satan, 57

Renaud d'Alleins, on equal rights of Waldenses and rats, 20

Responsibility, moral and penal, 210

Reusch, Prof. Dr. Fr. Heinrich, denounces bishops as promoters of superstition, 14

Ro-ro-ro-ro, an anti-semitic devil cast out in 1842, 73

Rosarius, Hierolymus, describes the exposure of crucified lions and gibbeted wolves as a warning to their kind, 251; regards animals as often more rational than men, 252

SATAN, his earthly sovereignty, 60, 70; the doctrine of his final redemption, 68

Schilling, on the prosecution of inger, 113, 120

Schläger, cited, 176

Schleswig, its punishment of homicidal timber, 187

Schmid, Bernard, his sermon on the devastations by inger, 113–115

Scholasticism, quiddities of, 33

Schopenhauer, his theory of the will, 127; man's responsibility for character alone, 239, 243

Schwabenspiegel, barbarity of this old German code, 178

Schwarz Mining, prosecutor of moles, 112

Schweinfurter Sauhenker, origin of the term, 147

Serpents, destroyed by St. Eldrad, 51; freed from poison by St. Hugon, 103

Shakespeare, alludes to "be-rhymed" rats, 130; and a wolf on the gallows, 157

Silius Italicus, quoted, 103

Simon, Max, on the morbid spirit of imitation, 253

Sociology, its influence on criminal jurisprudence, 238

Socrates, on self-perfection, 234

Sodomy. See Buggery

Soldan, cited, 17

Sparrows, put under ban by a Protestant parson, 128

Stephen VI., Pope, adjures locusts, 65; prosecutes the corpse of his predecessor, 198; strangled in prison, 199

Suicide, punishment of the wife and children of a, 190; condemned as a crime and also recognized as a right, 191, 192; due to manifold influences, 229

Superstition, fostered by bishops and Jesuits, 14

Swallows, anathematized for chattering in church, 28

Swine, execution of, 16, 140–

145, 149, 153–157, 161, 169 ; as stenchy beasts peculiarly attractive to devils, 56, 165 ; Gadarene, 69, 91, 165

Swords, tainted, 187

TAINE, his definition of man, 214

Tarde, defines the mob as a mad beast, 236

Tatian, his fellow-citizens punished for his offences, 180

Tattooing, not peculiar to criminals, 213

Termites, prosecuted by Franciscans in Brazil and praised by their defender as more industrious than the friars, 123

Tertullian, quoted, 106

Theognis, his bust punished for murder, 172

Thomas à Becket, his bones burned by Henry VIII., 198

Thomas Aquinas, regarded animals only as diabolical incarnations, 53–55, 88, 101, 103

Thurneysser, his bottled scorpions and elk feared as demons, 90

Tithes, importance of the prompt payment of, 37, 94, 107

Tobler, G., on animal prosecutions in Switzerland, 1, 170

Treason, barbarously punished by Roman, Prussian, and Judaic law, 179-181

Trench, Richard Chevenix, his justification of the cursing of the fig-tree, 25

Treufels, Richard, his belief in the exorcism at Wemding in 1891, 75

Tribunals, proper office of criminal, 211, 232, 248

Tritheim, on Satan's invisible apparition, 166

Tschech, executed, and his innocent daughter exiled for his crime, 179

Türler, records the rejection of the Mosaic law by the ecclesiastical court of Berne, 170

VAMPIRES, superstitions concerning, 195–198

Vendetta, in semi-civilized communities, 178

Venidad, quoted, 63

Ventilation, "bewitched kine" the result of bad, 8

Vermin. See Insects

Virgil, quoted, 26

WEEVILS, prosecuted for damage to vineyards, 38–49

Wemding, recent case of diabolical possession in, 75

Were - wolves, incarnate ghosts, 195 ; decree for their extermination, 198

Werther, Goethe's, sentimentalism and suicidism produced by, 253

Winterstetter, Georg, his rescript concerning gadflies, 125

Witches in Judaic and mediæval law, on a par with animals, 145 ; rendered harmless by burning, 196

Worms, Council of, its decree concerning tainted honey, 9

ZARATHUSHTRA (Zoroaster), his ethics and its workings, 57-59

Zoöpsychology, in its relation to anthropopsychology and criminology, 237

Zupetta, on partial vitiation of mind, 201

Richard Clay & Sons, Limited, London and Bungay.

Lightning Source UK Ltd.
Milton Keynes UK
21 June 2010

155897UK00003B/104/P